INTEGRATIVE
PROBLEM-CENTERED
THERAPY

INTEGRATIVE PROBLEM-CENTERED THERAPY

A Synthesis of Family, Individual, and Biological Therapies

WILLIAM M. PINSOF, PH.D.

BasicBooks
A Division of HarperCollins*Publishers*

Library of Congress Cataloging-in-Publication Data
Pinsof, William M.
    Integrative problem-centered therapy : a synthesis of family, individual, and
biological therapies / William M. Pinsof.
        p.   cm.
    Includes bibliographical references and index.
    ISBN 0-465-03328-8
    1. Problem-solving therapy.   2. Eclectic psychotherapy.   3. Psychiatry—
Differential therapeutics.   I. Title.
RC489.P68P54   1995   95-36800
616.89'14—dc20   CIP

95 96 97 98 ❖/HC 9 8 7 6 5 4 3 2 1

To Suzan,
My partner in heart and mind.

Contents

Introduction

C ONTEMPORARY PSYCHOTHERAPISTS face two major challenges. The first is to use effectively the various psychotherapeutic methods that have emerged within the last half of the twentieth century. The second, spurred on by the implementation of managed care, is to practice psychotherapy within time and financial constraints. The first constitutes the challenge of effective integration; the second, the challenge of cost-effectiveness.

This book presents a framework for the cost-effective integration of the major psychotherapies that have dominated the field at the end of the twentieth century. This framework, termed *integrative problem-centered therapy*, draws on recent advances within family therapy, individual psychotherapy, and biobehavioral medicine. It organizes these macro approaches, as well as specific approaches within each of them, with maximal efficiency. Although not essentially a time-limited therapy, problem-centered therapy can be used within a time-limited framework to provide effective episodes of care.

Viewing psychotherapy as human problem solving, the first chapter presents the core problem-centered concept: that voluntary psychotherapy rests on an informal contract in which the patient system hires the therapist system to help solve certain problems. These presenting problems define the starting point, ultimate reference points, and major outcome criteria for therapy. Each presenting problem has a unique problem-maintenance structure embodying constraints that block the patient system from solving the problem. These constraints derive from six metaframeworks: social organization; biology; meaning, with special reference to culture and gender; transgenerational processes; object relations; and self structure. The problem-maintenance structure, not the presenting problem or disorder, determines the psychotherapeutic requirements of each case. This point challenges conventional efforts to match treatments to disorders.

Chapter 2 delineates the problem-centered modalities and orientations. Problem-centered therapy integrates family–community, couple, and individual modalities with six orientations: behavioral, biobehavioral–psychopharmacological, experiential, family of origin, psychodynamic, and self psychological. These six orientations address constraints from the six metaframeworks. This chapter also presents underlying theory and the core principle of application, which specifies the sequence in which the modalities and orientations should be used to solve presenting problems. This principle derives from two linked propositions: (1) It is impossible to know the problem-maintenance structure in advance and, therefore, (2) the orientations and modalities should be applied in the most clinically appropriate and cost-effective sequence.

The relationship theory of problem-centered therapy emerges in Chapter 3. Using an integrative systems model of the therapeutic alliance, this chapter specifies the nature, role, and progressive unfolding of the alliance over the course of therapy. Maintaining and developing the therapeutic alliance is a primary task of the problem-centered therapist. When maintaining the alliance conflicts with the principle of application, maintaining the alliance takes priority unless it fundamentally compromises the therapy. This chapter also describes the tearing and repairing of the alliance as well as strategies for strengthening it.

Chapter 4 presents the assessment and intervention premises of problem-centered therapy. It defines assessment and intervention as inseparable processes that co-occur from the first phone call to the last goodbye. The assessment–intervention process is driven by a clinical experimental method that sequentially tests increasingly refined hypotheses about the problem-maintenance structure. This chapter delineates the health, problem-maintenance, cost-effectiveness, and interpersonal premises that guide assessment and intervention. Finally, therapy is defined as an educational enterprise in which the therapist empowers patients by teaching them more effective problem-solving rules and mechanisms.

Chapter 5 specifies who should be directly involved in the four different phases of therapy with five distinct types of patient systems. The four basic phases are the initial phase, which goes up to and includes the first session; the early sessions—approximately sessions 2 through 5; the middle sessions; and termination. The five types of patient systems are nuclear families presenting with a child as the identified patient; binuclear (divorced or divorced and remarried) families with a child as the identified patient; couples presenting with relationship problems; noncohabiting adults seeking individual therapy; and cohabiting adults seeking individual therapy. Most psychotherapy cases fall within one of these categories. The chapter presents guidelines for deciding which members to involve from each of the five systems in each of the four phases of therapy. This chapter also presents principles and strategies for conducting "guest sessions" with family-of-origin members or adult children.

Chapter 6 expands the idea of the presenting problem into the problem cycle, which consists of a problem sequence that includes the presenting problem and an alternative adaptive sequence in which the problem begins to emerge but is dealt with adaptively by key patients. This chapter links the problem cycle to the problem-maintenance structure and lays out steps for identifying the various components of the problem cycle. These steps include the identification of presenting problems, attempted solutions, the biological system, the emotional system, the cognitive system, and alternative adaptive solutions.

Chapter 7 describes how therapy actively and directly modifies the problem cycle. It specifies how the therapist helps key patients identify an adaptive solution to their presenting problem; establishes consensus with key patients about the suitability of the adaptive solution; teaches key patients to implement the adaptive solution; and, finally, evaluates, with key patients, the impact of the adaptive solution on the problem cycle. This chapter demonstrates how the problem-centered therapist gets clarity, consensus, and movement with the patient system about what needs to happen to resolve the presenting problem. It establishes the directionality of the therapy.

Chapter 8 describes the process of problem-centered therapy when the patient system is blocked: when it cannot do what needs to be done to implement the adaptive solution. Specifically, it describes how the therapist applies each of the orientations to modify potential constraints within each of the metaframework levels of the problem-maintenance structure. It illustrates how the therapist works through the problem-maintenance structure to ameliorate the relevant constraints that block problem solving and also shows how the therapist makes transitions from one orientation to another without disrupting the alliance.

The last chapter, the epilogue, targets two concluding issues. The first is the creation of a personal, authentic integration for each problem-centered therapist. It addresses how a therapist can find his or her own voice within the problem-centered framework. The second issue is the creation of a personal and responsible psychotherapy for every patient system over that system's life cycle. The chapter concludes by addressing how to craft, within or outside of managed care, a maximally effective, maximally efficient, minimally expensive, and ultimately humane psychotherapy.

Each chapter contains numerous examples to illustrate key concepts. In the last half of the book, transcripts are used to illustrate the process of problem-centered therapy. All of the examples cited in the book are fictitious, as are the transcripts. Although they derive from my clinical experience as a therapist, consultant, and supervisor over the last 25 years, none of the examples or transcripts directly reflects any case with which I have had the privilege to be involved.

I hope this book helps therapists work more efficiently, more effectively, and more humanely. The problem-centered model has been driven by failure as well as the quest to create a more effective psychotherapy. Each failure of mine, my colleagues, and my students helped to expand and improve the problem-centered model. When something I have tried with a case has not worked, I strive to understand why and look for what might be tried next. Each next step is informed by the feedback from prior steps and, in this way, the problem-centered model has grown. This book presents the status of problem-centered therapy today. I trust that its continued growth will make its subsequent formulations more efficient, effective, and humane.

Acknowledgments

MANY PEOPLE CONTRIBUTED to this book. Problem-centered therapy is the product of my intellectual development as a clinical family psychologist; my experience as a psychotherapist, psychotherapy consultant, and teacher; and my experience as a patient in many of the forms of therapy addressed in this model.

The problem-centered model and many of its premises, particularly its emphasis on problem solving, health, and resourcefulness, derive from the work of Nathan Epstein, M.D., and his colleagues in the Department of Psychiatry at the McMaster University Medical School in Hamilton, Ontario, during the 1970s. It is my hope that Nate's vision, integrity, and vitality permeate the problem-centered model. My primary supervisor at McMaster, Dorothy Horn, M.S.W., taught me how to be a problem-centered therapist. Her warmth, humanity, insight, and clinical skill, along with her friendship and respect, took the abstractions in my head and moved them into heart and soul. Finally, I will be forever grateful to Sol Levin, M.D., for giving me the opportunity to be a clinical fellow at McMaster from 1973 to 1975 and for giving me the confidence to trust and respect myself as a therapist.

At York University in 1970, Bob Mark, Ph.D., my first mentor and subsequently a lifelong friend, opened the doors of perception to family therapy. Laura Rice, Ph.D., taught me about psychotherapy research and, more fundamentally, about how to see and hear the process of therapy. Les Greenberg, Ph.D., my fellow student and friend, brought his intellectual rigor and clinical sensitivity to our many discussions over the years about therapy, research, and life. Our "twinship" helped develop my taste for what constitutes good psychotherapy.

During my almost 20 years at the Family Institute and Northwestern University, my work has been touched by many people. Many students and colleagues contributed to the development of problem-centered therapy. The contributions of Sherry Tucker, Ph.D., Jay Lebow, Ph.D., Don Catherall, Ph.D., and Ana Estrada, Ph.D., have been particularly important and encouraging. More recently, Cheryl Rampage, Ph.D., has patiently pried open the doors of gender perception for me. Over the last 5 years, Douglas Breunlin, L.C.S.W., has become my partner in integration. His broad, clear, and sustained thinking, coupled with his clinical creativity and sensitivity, informs the model and every page of this book. I am indebted to him for reading the entire first draft of this book and offering his helpful and generous criticism. My secretary, Royce Warren, skillfully protected me from intrusions as I wrote this book and showed great patience during the final phases of pulling it together. Dan Jefkin's help with the book figures was invaluable.

Two therapists over the years have had an enormous impact on my personal development and the growth of problem-centered therapy. Jack Graller, M.D., taught me how to be a couple therapist and how to conduct family-of-origin guest sessions from the inside. His directness, coupled with his knowledge of and respect for psychoanalysis, simultaneously expanded my horizons and emboldened me to "go for it." Meyer (Mike) Gunther, M.D., has taught me about my self and psychoanalysis, particularly self psychology, from the inside. His compassionate efforts to destroy my structures of meaning have softened and added depth and nuance to me and the problem-centered model.

Since we met as junior colleagues at the Family Institute and Northwestern in 1975, Jean Goldsmith, Ph.D., has been my friend and clinical partner. We are two peas that fell out of the same clinical pod. I feel blessed to have someone in my professional and personal life with whom I can so easily share my intellectual and clinical thinking and experience. Jean was the only person besides Doug to read the entire first draft of this book. Her criticisms have made it much better.

My wife, Suzan, and our daughters, Laura and Caitlin, have shown enormous patience and tolerance as I have "stolen" the time to write this book. They have also taught me what I know about being a husband and father, and their love has sustained me through the darker moments in the journey. Suzan has been a wonderful and true partner as the ideas in this book have resonated through our implicit and explicit conversations over the years.

Finally, the faith and patience of Jo Ann Miller and Stephen Francoeur at Basic Books have been extraordinary. In 1987 I told Jo Ann that I did not want a contract because I did not want to go through the process of repeatedly reporting that the book was still not done. The good news is that she persisted and a contract was signed. Undoubtedly, without that contract, the book would still be undone. The bad news is that I probably hold the record for reporting the most times that the book was still not done. I am very grateful to Jo Ann and Stephen for their friendly pressure to finish.

INTEGRATIVE
PROBLEM-CENTERED
THERAPY

CHAPTER 1

The Problem-Centered Approach, the Patient System, and the Problem-Maintenance Structure

THERAPY AS HUMAN PROBLEM SOLVING

PSYCHOTHERAPY IS human problem solving. People seek psychotherapy when psychological, psychosocial, or biopsychosocial problems interfere significantly with their capacity to function and enjoy life. Most people first attempt to solve their problems themselves and turn to therapy only when their efforts have failed. The problem-centered therapist teaches people more effective rules and mechanisms for solving their problems.

Patients' versions of their problems constitute the *presenting problems*. Presenting problems range from the mundane to the existential. Typically, patients present more than one problem, and if there are multiple patients, as in family therapy, there usually are different versions of the presenting problem as well as multiple presenting problems.

Presenting problems usually change over the course of therapy. Some may be resolved or improve to the point that they no longer present a sufficient burden to warrant treatment. Others may be defined out of existence or accepted as inevitable aspects of life. Problems evolve. Regardless, there is always at least one presenting problem, and it is whatever the patients are seeking help for at any particular moment in therapy.

THE LINK TO THE PRESENTING PROBLEM

In problem-centered therapy, the therapist is constantly concerned with the presenting problem. The presenting problem is the starting point, ongoing concern, and primary outcome criterion for problem-centered therapy. It provides the common ground on which the therapeutic contract develops and is the primary basis for the alliance between the therapist and the patient.

That the presenting problem serves as an ongoing concern throughout therapy does not mean that the therapist can address only the presenting problem. Other, nonpresenting problems can be addressed if they are or may be linked to the presenting problem. The therapist steps outside of the problem-centered framework when therapy focuses on problems that are not actually or potentially linked to the set of problems the patients present for treatment.

In a family-therapy session, a female therapist talks to the mother of a 6-year-old "hyperactive" boy, the identified patient, about her relationship with *her* mother when she was 6. The mother describes how her mother would frequently beat her with a belt for minor rule infractions. With tears, she recounts a particularly painful incident in which her mother hit her until she feared for her life.

This episode may or may not be problem-centered, depending on whether the therapist links the discussion of the mother–mother relationship to the problem for which the mother and father seek help: their son's alleged hyperactivity. After the session, when asked why she pursued the mother–mother relationship when the presenting problem was the child's difficulties, the therapist might answer that it was because the mother's difficulty in setting limits may derive from a negative identification with her abusive mother; in that case, the intervention is problem-centered. On the other hand, if the therapist responds that the mother–mother relationship seemed to be an important issue but cannot link it to the mother's problems with her son, the intervention is not problem-centered.

The presenting problem also constitutes the minimal outcome criterion for evaluating the therapy. The bottom-line question at the conclusion of treatment is, "Was the presenting problem resolved to the patients' satisfaction?" If the answer is no, treatment was not successful. However, the presenting problem is not the only criterion for evaluating therapy. Treatment evaluation must target other aspects of the patients' lives and the lives of people close to them. Focusing solely on the presenting problem can result in unbalanced and shortsighted conclusions that obscure crucial elements of the patients' lives. For instance, the fact that an alcoholic has stopped drinking but is now substantially depressed is at best a mixed outcome. The presenting problem must be included and heavily weighted within the outcome battery, but it should never constitute the sole evaluative criterion. Treatment evaluation requires multiple perspectives, variables, and measures.

PROBLEM- VERSUS VALUE-CENTERED PSYCHOTHERAPY

The alternative to problem-centered therapy, value-centered therapy, is organized not around presenting problems but around a definition of health, normality, or ideal functioning. Most psychotherapies are problem- or value-centered or some combination of both. Humanistic, experiential, and psychoanalytic therapies are value-centered: They attempt to move patients closer to a state of ideal functioning. In humanistic treatment, the goal is a self-actualized person, whereas in analysis the goal is a more integrated, aware, and cohesive person. Structural family therapy (Fishman, 1993; Minuchin, 1974), a value-centered treatment, moves families closer to the structural ideal of clear, distinct, yet adaptively flexible interpersonal boundaries. Bowen's (1978) family therapy creates higher levels of differentiation of self within individual and family systems. In addition to integrative problem-centered therapy, the behavioral therapies and the strategic (Haley, 1976; Watzlawick, Weakland, & Fisch, 1974), functional (Alexander & Parsons, 1982), and solution-focused (de Shazer, 1988) family therapies are problem-centered.

The link between the presenting problem and the therapist's intervention is like a rubber band that can be stretched but never broken. The link may or may not be explicit with patients, but it must exist within the mind of the therapist. Once the link is severed, treatment ceases to be problem-centered.

THE PATIENT SYSTEM

Problem-centered therapy integrates biological, individual, and family psychotherapies. A basic problem with this type of integrative therapy is determining what or who constitutes the system that contains the presenting problem. Who or what is the patient? Is it the individual, the nuclear family, the network, or something else? Problem-centered therapy treats the *patient system*, which *contains all of the human systems that are or may be involved in the maintenance or resolution of the presenting problem*. These systems may be biological, psychological, social, or any combination of these. The patient-system concept permits the therapist to address the relevant biopsychosocial reality without locking exclusively or irrevocably on to any particular systemic level. It facilitates examination of the entire complex of constraints that prevent problem resolution.

Every patient system is ineluctably linked to and defined by a particular presenting problem. *Every problem has its own, unique patient system.* Whether a subsystem (biological, psychological, or social) affects the maintenance or resolution, or both, of a presenting problem constitutes the operational criterion for including it within the patient system.

The patient-system concept is a pragmatic clinical tool. It defines the systems that are or may be involved in the maintenance of the presenting problem or its resolution. Factors that determined the problem initially may not be relevant. Etiological factors that created the problem but no longer maintain it are not included in the patient system. The patient system is concerned with etiologic factors that are or may still be active in maintaining the presenting problem.

Tim, age 45, feels moderately depressed after losing his job as a middle-level executive in a large, financially troubled corporation. He feels inadequate, unfairly treated, and resentful. To compensate for his lost income, his wife, Irene, has increased her work as a real-estate broker from 3 to 5 days a week. She resents having to work more and being less available to their four children. She has withdrawn from Tim, and their relationship has cooled. Sullen and worried, the children have pulled back from Tim as he has become more depressed.

Clearly, Tim and Irene constitute the two central subsystems within the patient system. Their children, as well as Tim's former employer, also constitute parts of the system. However, Tim's father, who died when Tim was 35, is not part of the patient system. Tim's father criticized him harshly and seldom acknowledged his achievements. Tim suffered a mild, unlabeled depression during much of his childhood and adolescence that was linked in part to his father's lack of support. It could be argued that the "first cause" of Tim's depression was paternal rejection. In regard to this depressive episode, however, his father's attitudes and behavior toward Tim may not be significant determinants. Even if Tim's father were alive today, without more evidence it would not be clear that he was part of the patient system.

The patient system can never be exactly defined. Its external boundary is always and appropriately vague. For instance, with a school-refusing or school-phobic boy, the patient system would include at least the child, his parents, his siblings, and his teachers and fellow students. Certain school administrators and support personnel may also be part of the system, not necessarily because they are part of the problem, but because of the role they may play in its resolution. Without knowing more about the family system, it is impossible to exclude grandparents and other extended family members from the patient system. The family doctor and other societal helpers may also be part of the system.

The patient system contains all of the human systems that *are* or *may be* involved in the maintenance or resolution of the presenting problem. The "are" refers to those systems for which the therapist possesses relatively direct evidence that supports their involvement. The "may be" refers to those systems about which the therapist has various hypotheses but no direct evidence to confirm their involvement.

It is generally better to err on the side of inclusion. If persons or systems may be involved but there is no clear evidence to confirm the suspicion, the therapist is better off including them in the patient system and thereby defining them as a potential target of understanding and intervention. For instance, if the therapist suspects that one of the members of a couple in marital therapy is engaged in an extramarital affair, the therapist should include that third party in the patient system. This does not mean that the therapist will discuss this decision with the couple, only that the "lover" goes on the therapist's map of the therapeutic terrain.

Seldom if ever is an entire patient system directly involved in therapy. As Figure 1.1 illustrates, the patient system can be divided into direct and indirect systems (Pinsof, 1989). The *direct system* consists of subsystems of the patient system that are directly involved in treatment at any particular time; the *indirect system* contains systems within the patient system that are not directly involved in treatment at any particular time. The wavy line in the middle of Figure 1.1 indicates that the boundary between direct and indirect subsystems is fluid. People move in and out of the direct system. The arrows reflect the ongoing mutual-influence process between direct and indirect systems.

The value of the direct–indirect system distinction is that therapists tend to forget about members of the patient system who are not directly involved in treatment. They forget about the power of grandparents, school personnel, and the family doctor when working with a school-phobic boy and his family. They forget about the role of the husband and children in facilitating a mother's continued appropriate use of antidepressants. The indirect-system concept forces therapists to remember the basic map of the terrain they are traversing, even though they may be in a small valley at a particular moment.

Additionally, the direct–indirect distinction also moves psychotherapy away from simplistic modality thinking toward an integrative and generic

Figure 1.1
The Structure of the Patient System

Patient System

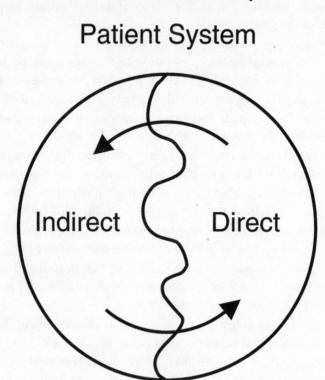

base theory. The direct–indirect distinction places all modalities of psychotherapy within the same basic framework. Individual, couple, and family therapy differ only in the point at which they draw the boundary between direct and indirect systems, not necessarily in their basic understanding of the patient system. From this perspective, family, couple, and individual therapy become three different theories about interventions into the same terrain.

The patient-system concept is at least as concerned with the resources that can be drawn on to resolve the presenting problem as it is with the determinants of the problem. Most patient systems involve members or subsystems that have nothing to do with maintaining the presenting problem but play a facilitative role in solving the problem. Frequently, the patients may not have accessed certain resource persons in the search for solutions before seeking therapy. For instance, if Tim's father were alive and more mellow, he might be a valuable resource in helping Tim weather the storm of his job loss and depression. The patient-system concept helps the therapist and the patient to access unused resource people within the patient system. These people can be crucial determinants of the therapeutic process. The patient-system concept focuses the therapist on the healthy aspects of the patient's world as much as if not more than on its pathological components.

THE PROBLEM-MAINTENANCE STRUCTURE

The critical question for the problem-centered therapist is, What prevents the patient system from solving the presenting problem? The generic answer to this question is the problem-maintenance structure. *The problem-maintenance structure embodies the constraints that prevent resolution of the presenting problem.* It covers all of the members of the patient system, including their actions, biology, cognitions, emotions, object relations, and self structures. The members of the patient system who play central roles in the problem-maintenance structures are referred to as *key patients*. The key patients are not limited to members of the direct system. Frequently, members of the indirect patient system play critical roles in the problem-maintenance structure.

Every presenting problem has its own, unique problem-maintenance structure. Problem-maintenance structures can be conceptualized as existing within a problem space that contains all of the potential factors that might make up any specific problem-maintenance structure. Seldom does any specific structure completely fill the problem-maintenance space, which means that seldom, if ever, does a problem-maintenance structure include every conceivable constraint. Similarly, seldom does a problem-maintenance structure include all of the members of the patient system. Logically, the members of the patient system who will be part of the solution but are not part of the problem do not fit within the problem-maintenance structure.

A generic model of the problem-maintenance space is presented in Figure 1.2. It organizes most if not all possible constraints on six levels. The wider any particular problem-maintenance structure is, the more constraints it includes from any particular level. The deeper the structure, the more levels it includes.

The model of the problem-maintenance space presented in Figure 1.2 has been influenced by the work of Breunlin, Schwartz, and Mac Kune-Karrer as presented in their book *Metaframeworks: Transcending the Models of Family Therapy* (1992). Problem-centered therapy borrows two concepts from the metaframeworks model: constraint and metaframework. Drawing on Bateson's (1972) concept of negative explanation, Breunlin et al. (1992) wrote: "The theory of constraints simply states that people do what they do or think what they think because they are prevented (that is, constrained) from

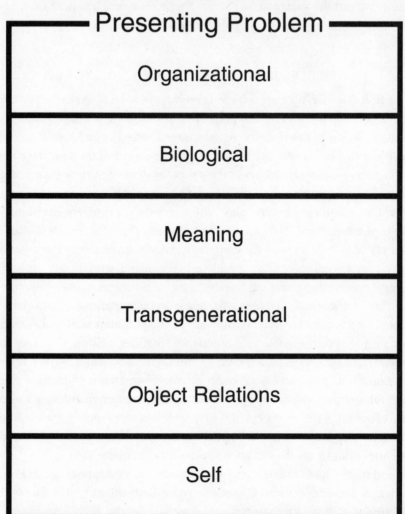

Figure 1.2
The Problem-Maintenance Space

Presenting Problem

Organizational
Biological
Meaning
Transgenerational
Object Relations
Self

doing or thinking something else" (1992, p. 36). A *constraint* is a factor in the problem-maintenance structure that prevents the patient system from solving the problem. The problem-maintenance structure can be thought of as a "web of constraints." "Constraints can exist at any level of a human system" (1992, p. 37).

A *metaframework* "classifies a domain of ideas and organizes it into metap-atterns" (Breunlin et al., 1992, p. 44). Within problem-centered therapy, a meta-framework organizes other frameworks or theories that pertain to a particular domain of human activity. Each level within the problem-maintenance structure can be thought of as a metaframework that incorporates other frameworks and metaframeworks that fit within a particular level of the structure by virtue of targeting a similar domain of human activity.

The first three levels and metaframeworks deal primarily with contemporary constraints for which an in-depth historical understanding is not necessary. Level 1 addresses the metaframework of *organization*—how the patient system organizes and conducts itself in regard to the presenting problem. The second level targets *biology*—how the patient system operates as a biological and physical system in regard to the presenting problem. The third level addresses *meaning*—how the patient system thinks and feels in regard to the problem and its potential solutions. Meaning subdivides into two specific metaframeworks—*culture* and *gender*—which organize cognition and emotion. Typically, the meaning metaframework begins to move into the historical domain, because so many of the meaning constraints have historical determinants.

The last three levels and metaframeworks within the problem-maintenance structure explicitly target historical constraints; these derive from the histories of the key patients and their families of origin. These constraints cannot be adequately addressed without an in-depth understanding of these histories. The fourth level, the *transgenerational* metaframework, targets issues and processes that derive from the families of origin of the key patients. The next two metaframeworks do not focus so much on the history of the families of origin of the key patients as on constraints that derive from the individual histories of the key patients in their families of origin. The fifth level deals with an *object relations* metaframework—the way in which the psychodynamic parts of key members are organized intrapsychically and interpersonally in regard to the presenting problem. The sixth and last level addresses a *self* metaframework—the way in which the collective self system and the individual self structures of the key patients interact with the presenting problem.

ALTERNATIVE SCENARIOS

Identical presenting problems can have different problem-maintenance structures. Two distinct patient systems—the Christmans and the Butlers—illustrate constraints on each of the six levels of the problem-maintenance structure. The description of each of these systems on each level represents a set of hypotheses about their problem-maintenance structures. For each system, the hypotheses presented on each level presume for purposes of illustration that the constraints on the level being described and on the higher levels are part of the problem-maintenance structure but that constraints on the lower levels, yet to be described, are not. In other words, what is presented in the following sections is a series of six problem-maintenance scenarios, each of which includes its predecessors. Each successive scenario presents a larger problem-maintenance structure than the one before and includes more vertical constraints.

Level 1: Organizational Constraints

The top level of the problem-maintenance structure addresses how the patient system works and, in particular, how it organizes itself in regard to the presenting problem. *Organization* targets boundaries—the rules that determine how members of the patient system relate to each other. This is the domain of action and behavior. It deals with the structure and process of the patient system. Organization encompasses balance, harmony, and leadership (Breunlin et al., 1992).

Balance refers to influence, access to resources, and level of responsibility. A patient system is balanced when each member or subsystem has the influence, access to resources, and responsibility appropriate to its needs and its level in the system. Generally, people at the same level in the system should have roughly equivalent influence, access, and responsibility. *Harmony* deals with the extent to which system members "cooperate, are willing to sacrifice some of their individual interests for the greater good, care about one another and feel valued by the larger system, and have clear boundaries that allow a balance between belonging and separateness" (Breunlin et al., 1992, p. 136). When systems are unbalanced, when one member has too much influence, access to resources, or responsibility, other members do not have enough. Such systems have unclear or inappropriate boundaries, or both, and are disharmonious and polarized. Different members take extreme and opposite positions that interfere with effective problem solving.

To have balance and harmony, a system must have leadership. Leaders have the responsibility and ability to mediate and adjudicate conflicts; allocate resources, responsibilities, and influence; enforce rules and discipline; encourage growth; represent members' as well as the whole system's interests in regard to other systems; and coordinate planning for the system's future (Breunlin et al., 1992, p. 138). Poor leadership constrains balance and harmony, and imbalance and disharmony constrain effective leadership.

Problem-centered therapy addresses systemic organization insofar as it constrains the patient system's ability to solve the presenting problem. Joanne and Stewart Christman, a Caucasian couple with a strong German-Catholic heritage, presented with the chief complaint of marital conflict.

They had experienced increasing conflict since their youngest child left for college, 8 months earlier. Joanne complained that Stewart wanted to control everything. She had accepted this situation while their three children were growing up, but now, in her early 50s, she was no longer willing to put up with his excessive control. In the first few sessions, she bitterly complained that for many years he insisted that she sign their joint tax return without being allowed to examine it. He also handled all of their money and gave Joanne an allowance that had not changed appreciably for the last 10 years, even though his income as a corporate attorney had increased substantially.

The problem-maintenance hypotheses on this level assert that the Christmans' disharmony derives from an extreme imbalance within their marriage and family life. Stewart has had much more influence, responsibility, and access to resources than Joanne, whose current attempts to rebalance their system have resulted in a marital war. Joanne is overflowing with anger about their past arrangement, and Stewart has reacted by polarizing even further—he has become more rigid and controlling. They are talking about separating, and Stewart has even consulted informally with a partner in his law firm who specializes in divorce and matrimonial law.

Initially, their therapist began teaching the Christmans communication and problem-solving skills. They needed to stop screaming and start listening to each other. They had never developed the ability to work together or to negotiate. These early attempts to diminish conflict and improve communication were not successful. It soon became clear that Joanne and Stewart needed more than communication and problem-solving skills. Their disharmony derived in part from their lack of communication and conflict-resolution skills but more significantly from the lack of balance in their relationship. To be successful, the therapy would have to help the Christmans to rebalance their relationship.

Loretta Butler, a 34-year-old African-American widow, presented for therapy with her obese 11-year-old daughter, Akisha, as the identified patient. Akisha had recently gotten into a physical fight at school with another girl and had been suspended for a day. During the first session, Loretta made it very clear that Akisha was not the only problem. She complained that Akisha and her two older sisters, Eileen, 14, and Betty, 16, constantly fought with each other and would not cooperate. This problem was not only described, it was also enacted. About three-quarters of the way through the session, Eileen criticized Akisha for acting like a "fat baby," at which point Akisha got up and physically assaulted her. Betty jumped in to calm the conflict, but she soon became embroiled with Eileen, who asserted that the fight was not her business and she should stay out of it.

While her girls were fighting, Loretta sat disconsolately. She told them to stop, but they ignored her entreaties. Betty tried to make peace, but her efforts were compromised by her tendency to side with Akisha and by Eileen's refusal to acknowledge her as a legitimate leader. As the girls fought, the therapist felt pulled into their conflict and ended up breaking up the fight. This role suction viscerally reflected the leadership vacuum in the family.

In terms of organizational hypotheses, the Butlers' primary problem is lack of leadership. Loretta, who works full-time as a nurse in a community hospital, has not been able to provide the leadership necessary to facilitate her girls' development. Since her husband's death 7 years ago, she has felt she has to be everything for her daughters and has been reluctant to empower Betty as a sibling leader. She feels helpless with her girls and does not know what to do.

To solve the Butlers' presenting problems on this level, Loretta needs to become a more effective parental leader. She needs to resolve conflicts among her daughters; protect them, particularly Akisha, from sibling taunting; set appropriate limits on all the daughters; and provide more nurturance. Additionally, it would help if she could establish a leadership hierarchy among the girls that would rebalance responsibility. Currently, all responsibility falls on Loretta's shoulders. In particular, Betty could be given greater legitimate and public responsibility for leading the sibship. Eileen and Akisha also need more and clearer responsibilities for self and home care. Loretta needs to lead the way in creating clear boundaries within the family about who is responsible for what.

For many patient systems, the presenting problems are organizational, as with the Christmans, or reflect organizational constraints, as with both the Butlers and the Christmans. In either case, organization constitutes the first place to look for constraints to problem solving as well as for critical components of what needs to be done to solve the presenting problem. At this point, both patient systems require a therapy that would at least address their organizational constraints.

Level 2: Biological Constraints

The second level of the problem-maintenance structure deals with biology. Biological constraints can limit the ability of the key members to solve the presenting problem or make the requisite changes on the organizational level that will lead to problem resolution. With the Christmans, there are no apparent biological constraints. On the other hand, with the Butlers, there may be numerous biological determinants. For instance, depression may in part constrain Loretta's ability to provide the required leadership for her daughters. A learning disability may constrain Akisha's ability to participate in and benefit from her educational opportunities. She may need more assistance than her mother and regular-track schooling can provide. Additionally, Akisha's obesity makes her an easy target of her sisters' and classmates' derision, which increases her already high level of frustration and masked depression.

The Butlers demonstrate that biological constraints that prevent resolution of the presenting problem do not have to be only within the identified patient. As in the case of Loretta, their most critical impact may be on the ability of a nonsymptomatic system member to perform the behaviors and provide the necessary experiences to help the identified patient and solve the presenting problem. In regard to identified patients, biological problems typically constrain their ability to absorb or benefit from attempted solutions.

At this point, the problem-maintenance scenario with the Butlers links the potential biological constraints to their hypothesized organizational constraints. For this scenario, the family would require a therapy that addresses both. In contrast, the Christmans, because of the lack of potential biological constraints within their problem-maintenance structure, would require a therapy that targets their organizational constraints only.

Level 3: Meaning Constraints

The third level of the problem-maintenance structure concerns the meanings that patient-system members attribute to themselves, each other, and their behavior. Meaning involves both cognitive and affective components. At this level, meaning is viewed as socially constructed and as the product of system members' participation in and adherence to different cultural contexts.

Building on Falicov's (1988) and Mac Kune-Karrer's (Breunlin et al., 1992) definitions, *culture* refers to the beliefs and practices that derive from a particular system's location in a set of biosociocultural contexts that define proper behavior and experience. Typical contexts include socioeconomic status, social class, race, ethnicity, religion, education, physical circumstances, and resources. In a heterogeneous society like the United States, each patient system is an interlocking set of microcultures that define meaning for its members. Different system members typically participate differentially in cultural contexts and therefore do not necessarily share similar beliefs and attribute similar meanings to events and behaviors. Thus, the problem-centered therapist is specifically concerned with the extent to which patient-system members' participation in and adherence to particular cultural contexts impairs their ability to solve their presenting problem.

A particularly critical set of culturally determined beliefs pertains to beliefs about gender: what it means to be male or female (Goodrich, Rampage, Ellman, & Halstead, 1988; Tannen, 1994). For the Christmans on this level, Joanne and Stewart's participation in various cultural contexts may play a central role in determining their organizational structure. More critically, these beliefs may play a primary role in constraining Stewart's ability to reorganize his marriage.

A meaning scenario for the Christmans might resemble the following: Stewart believed that as a male he should be the primary provider and protector of the family. Joanne's job as a female was to raise the children and to take care of the home and Stewart. Joanne's newfound aggressiveness, her desire to take leadership in reorganizing their marriage and family, and her direct challenge to his authority represent not only a violation of their implicit marital contract, but also, more profoundly, an abandonment of their cultural roots. Stewart's sense of who he is has been assaulted by Joanne's abandonment of proper female behavior in midlife. In his mind, what she is doing is not right.

With the Butlers, meaning constraints might take the following form: Loretta's feeling that she has to do everything may be a product of her sense of black motherhood—the powerful and nurturing female figure in black culture. Would the public delegation of more responsibility to Betty be a violation of her culturally defined sense of what she should be as a mother? Similarly, her failure to expect much for herself, her lack of a sense of entitlement, may also derive from the cultural icon of the selfless and uncomplaining black mother. Can the selfless and strong black mother admit her depression, express her anger at the lack of support she receives from her family and society, and ask for help for herself (medication, therapy, or both)? Or would such behavior violate her sense of who she is? Finally, to what extent does her lack of entitlement and expectation reflect an underlying despair and rage that is a response to the institutional racism of North American society?

Can the girls admit that they are not getting what they need from their mother and that she is failing in certain ways as a leader, or do they have to continue to turn their anger and sense of deprivation on each other? Would the open acknowledgment of their feelings of anger and loss traumatize their mother? Would explicit recognition of their sense of their mother's partial failure be a shameful experience for all of them? A black mother must be respected and admired. To say she is failing violates the essence of how she should be defined and treated. To be angry at her might reveal her fragility.

Finally, to what extent are all of the Butlers afraid to touch the issue of the dad's death 7 years ago? He was 15 years older than Loretta and worked as a supervisor in a steel mill in south Chicago. The family was told that he died of a heart attack at work, but the exact circumstances of his death were never made clear. Over the years, the girls got the message from Loretta not to ask about it. He was a strong presence in all of their lives; to what extent have they all avoided their feelings of abandonment, sadness, and anger about his premature and only partially explained death? Do these feelings and their fear of them prevent the family from becoming more cohesive and supportive?

The extent to which these meaning issues support the constraints on the organizational and biological levels of the problem-maintenance structure determines their status as constraints. As with all potential constraints, cultural (especially, beliefs and practices concerning gender) as well as emotional patterns should be addressed only insofar as they constrain the patient system's ability to solve the presenting problem (Pinsof, 1992b). If they are personally offensive to the therapist, that is the therapist's problem. As long as they do not jeopardize the mental and physical health of the system members, these beliefs become constraints only when they interfere with the system's ability to solve its problems.

For the problem-maintenance scenarios on this level, the Christmans would require a therapy that addresses their organizational as well as their meaning constraints. Organizational change that is acceptable to Joanne would probably necessitate at least some moderating of Stewart's gender beliefs. The Butlers would require a therapy that addresses their organizational, biological, and meaning constraints. For Loretta to do what needs to be done for her daughters and herself, she would need to moderate her sense of herself as an iconic black mother who can shoulder any burden without complaint.

Level 4: Transgenerational Constraints

The fourth level of the problem-maintenance structure addresses constraints that derive from the intimate social networks, families of origin, and transgenerational legacies of the adult members of the patient system (Boszormenyi-Nagy & Spark, 1973; Boszormenyi-Nagy & Ulrich, 1981; Bowen, 1978; Framo, 1992; Kerr, 1981; Kramer, 1985). Insofar as the organizational constraints on level 1, the biological constraints on level 2, or the meaning constraints on level 3 link to the current and historical "families" of the key members or to the transgenerational histories of their families of origin, issues on this level become constraints to problem resolution.

The Christmans' scenario on this level might focus on Stewart's mother and sister. His mother, Adele, a 78-year-old widow, has never been an admirer of Joanne. Similarly, Stewart's twin sister, Sally, has never been fond of Joanne. Both of them reacted with scorn and disdain to Joanne's new conflictual behavior as well as her desire to reorganize her marriage. Tenaciously allied with Stewart, they hope that the marriage ends and he can be free of this woman he never should have married.

On the other hand, Joanne, whose parents are recently deceased, receives strong support from her brother, Tim, and his wife, Monique. Additionally, Joanne's best friend, Pauline, has been urging her to do something with her life and her marriage for years. Tim, Monique, and Pauline form a strong support network for Joanne and are highly invested in her new course of action, even if it means the end of her marriage.

The presence of Pauline in the problem-maintenance structure highlights the broad definition of family of origin on this level and within the problem-centered model in general. It includes what anthropologists refer to as "fictive kin," or adopted family members, as well as blood relatives. These friends and allies constitute the intimate nonfamilial social network, take on the role of family members in the life of the key patients, and play critical roles in the problem-maintenance structure.

When the problem-maintenance structure includes this fourth level, it takes on two configurations. The first is that the constraints on the first three levels are embedded in the intimate social networks of the key patient-system members. Thus, in the case of the Christmans, their conflictual polarization may be sustained not only by their unbalanced organization, the beliefs and meanings they attach to that organization, and their conflicts about it, but additionally by the extended family systems that surround them. Stewart's mother and sister share his most polarized and negative beliefs and feelings. They support, if not actively promote, his rigidity and alienation from Joanne. Similarly, Joanne's brother, sister-in-law, and close friend share her new beliefs and feelings and passionately support her commitment to change her marriage or get out. Stewart and Joanne's involvement and investment in their families of origin and current social networks make these other members of the indirect patient system key players in their inability to resolve their conflict and reorganize their relationship.

The second configuration on this level ties the organizational, biological, and meaning constraints to the transgenerational legacies of the families of origin of the key patients. Whereas the family-of-origin/social-network configuration mentioned previously spreads out horizontally within the current intimate social network, this second configuration, legacy constraints, links back vertically into the histories of the key families of origin.

The Butlers' transgenerational scenario might take the following form: Loretta Butler is the eldest in a sibship of five. Her mother was a drug addict during most of Loretta's childhood and died at the age of 28 of an overdose when Loretta was 11. Loretta views herself more as her maternal grand-mother's daughter than her mother's. Several of her maternal aunts and uncles corroborate this view. Her maternal grandmother was a "very strong" person who led her family's migration from Mississippi to Chicago in the late 1940s. Working as a seamstress, she found jobs and housing for her siblings as they migrated to Chicago and brought her parents up North as soon as she was able to accumulate enough money to rent an apartment large enough for them, herself, and her children. Her husband was killed in a farming accident in Mississippi just before the family's migration.

Grandmother died in 1983 at the age of 60 of a heart attack after years of battling with hypertension. Tales of her strength and stoicism abounded within Loretta's family of origin. She worked at her dressmaking job until just before she died. She took care of everyone in her family and functioned as Loretta and her siblings' primary parental figure. Loretta had been her favorite grandchild and always felt a special bond and affinity with her. Loretta even looks like her maternal grandmother.

Loretta felt that she had to be like her grandmother and not like her mother. In fact, she felt she had to make up for her mother's failures—she had to be the daughter that fulfilled her grandmother's dreams. She wanted to be a doctor, but the births of her children and lack of money led her into nursing. She felt that she had to work, take care of her children, and be available to her siblings and their children just the way her grandmother had been. She also felt that she had to rise above her husband's death, just as her grandmother had appeared to transcend her husband's premature death. She had to be a first-rate nurse, single mother, sister, aunt, and friend. When she could not live up to these expectations, she felt like a failure.

Admitting failure was not acceptable. To fail, to complain, to be needy herself, was to be like her mother. Even now, the prospect of a psychopharmacological evaluation and the possibility of taking an antidepressant medication conjure up negative images of her mother's substance-abuse problems. For Loretta, needing antidepressant medication is equivalent to her mother's drug addiction. Facing her problems, Loretta feels as if she has failed in her efforts to fulfill her grandmother's dreams and make up to her family of origin for her mother's failures. The unfulfilled dreams of her grandmother and the frightening specter of her mother constitute a powerful legacy that constrains Loretta's ability to face her problems, get the help she needs, and eventually create a life structure that works for her and her children.

The critical contribution of this fourth level to the problem-maintenance structure is the anchoring of the organizational, biological, and meaning constraints in the extended-family systems and transgenerational legacies of the key patients. When the fourth level contributes significantly to the problem-maintenance structure, the therapy must address these family-of-origin and legacy constraints as well as the meaning, biological, and organizational constraints that prevent problem resolution.

Level 5: Object Relations Constraints

On this level, the functioning of the self and its constituent subsystems, such as the ego, can best be conceptualized in the language of object relations theory (Greenberg & Mitchell, 1983; Summers, 1994). From this perspective, the self contains a set of structures that represent the internalized and transformed early social environment of the person. These structures may be thought of as internal objects or intrapsychic parts. Usually, the person is represented by a subset of these objects; the other internal objects more or less embody the transformed and partial representations of key figures in the psychological development of the person.

The internal objects function dynamically in two ways—in relationship to each other and in relation to the external objects (people) that compose the person's psychosocial world. The ego can be conceptualized as the manager of these operations. It also performs other functions, including but not limited to the focusing of awareness, reality testing, self monitoring (observing ego), remembering, and organizing the self in relationship to time and space. The internal interactions can be characterized by the full variety of concepts that apply to social relations (Schwartz, 1995).

Additionally, a number of the classical psychoanalytic defense mechanisms can be used to characterize these internal interactions (Freud, 1966). For instance, the defense mechanism of denial reflects the maintenance of an internal object in an unconscious state, out of aware interaction with the other internal objects. Thus, the angry part of an individual may be denied as existing at all. Similarly, the defense mechanism of reaction formation reflects the use of an internal object to obscure the activity of its opposite, thereby maintaining the ego illusion that the latter, obscured object is not pertinent or does not exist at all.

Object relations theory is not just a theory of internal process; it also embodies a theory of interpersonal relatedness that is based on object relations. Other people constitute necessary and meaningful "objects" to which the self must relate. Additionally, the internal objects interact with external objects—other people. For instance, a part of the self can be projected onto another person and attributed to that person instead of the self.

In the Christmans' object relations scenario, Stewart does not experience himself as angry at his wife. He reports disappointment and some degree of scorn but denies being angry at her. On the other hand, he talks incessantly about how angry Joanne has become, even when her affect clearly reflects more sadness than anger. This scenario supports the hypothesis that Stewart is projecting his anger at his wife (and perhaps at others) onto Joanne.

The concept of projective identification reflects a more complex interaction between internal and external objects (Catherall, 1992). In this situation, the person not only projects or attributes his or her internal object to another, but also interacts with the other in such a way as to get the other person to experience the projected internal object as his or her own. Eileen Butler, the middle daughter, frequently uses Akisha in this way. Afraid to face her own feelings of deprivation in regard to her mother's lack of attentiveness and the loss of her father, she verbally attacks Akisha to the point that Akisha calls out to Loretta for support and protection. She then accuses Akisha of being a "baby," and in fact, at that moment, Akisha acts like an enraged baby. Akisha then becomes the "vessel" for Eileen's and perhaps even Betty's neediness and rage at their family's misfortune and their mother's failure to parent effectively.

The set of internal objects and their relations with each other and their external objects constitute a system that can constrain problem solving in two ways. The first occurs when the internal operations of the system do not permit key patients to recognize, experience, and ultimately integrate actions, feelings, and thoughts that would lead to changing the organizational, biological, meaning, or transgenerational constraints. Loretta Butler has denied an angry, deprived part of herself since her early, painful disappointments with her mother. Now that part is even less available because of the added biopsychological burden of her depression. For her to become a more effective leader and to move out of her depression, she needs to integrate psychologically this angry, deprived part. This integration would allow the anger, pain, and energy tied up in that part to help her become a more powerful and aggressive leader.

The second way that the object relations system constrains problem solving occurs when key patients take on object-management roles for each other. In this situation, the social relations of the patient system become linked to the intrapsychic organization of its members. Their social relations become a vehicle for the management of object relations. When this occurs, the object-laden social relations play a critical role in the object systems of the key patients. Insofar as implementation of the adaptive solution requires a change in these object-laden social relations and thereby threatens the key patients' object systems, it will be resisted.

For instance, insofar as Akisha Butler functions as the projective target of her sisters' neediness and rage at their mother, the sisters will be more likely to resist her movement out of the enraged, immature baby role. If and when she leaves that scapegoat role, her sisters will have to face their own neediness and anger. Similarly, Loretta's sisters and brothers may have to face their own feelings of loss and depression in regard to their mother's death as Loretta's depression moderates. Their discomfort at this prospect may lead them to discourage her from pursuing antidepressant medication or psychotherapy for herself.

In the Christmans' marriage, Joanne has projected her more masculine and assertive parts onto Stewart, and he has projected his more feminine and vulnerable parts onto her. Joanne's efforts to reclaim her projected parts and to become a fuller human being jeopardize their object-laden, overadequate–underadequate marital balance. Stewart now has to face in himself parts he projected onto Joanne that she no longer is willing to accept and experience. Insofar as the reowning of these parts threatens his intrapsychic organization, he will resist her moving out of the needed projective role.

An interesting and not uncommon twist that can occur in couple therapy may be seen if Stewart can reclaim his feelings of vulnerability and flexibility and Joanne finds that she has some difficulty reowning her power and relinquishing some aspects of her vulnerable role. This situation is particularly common when the problem-maintenance structure involves constraints from the next level, which is the level of the self.

The object relations scenarios on this level for both the Butlers and the Christmans require a therapy that addresses the object relations that link to the constraints on the higher levels. It would need to encompass the more contemporary constraints on the higher levels as well as the increasingly historical constraints on the transgenerational and object relations levels.

Level 6: Self-System Constraints

The last level of constraints moves beyond the internal objects and their relations to the most fundamental level of human experience. The *self* is the most basic psychological structure—the molecule of dynamic psychology. It contains the internal objects and their relations. It provides and is reflected in the most basic sense of identity—the felt sense of "me." Self psychology represents one of the newer developments within psychoanalysis in the last quarter of the twentieth century and builds on the work of its founder, Heinz Kohut (1971, 1978, 1984; Wolf, 1988).

A dynamic system in its own right, the self has a narcissistic balance, or homeostasis, that derives from its own innate vitality, the quality of its developmental experiences, and the quality of its current relationships with its self objects. Building on the object relations concept of an "object," a *self object* is a person or thing that has taken on psychological meaning for the person. In the old language of psychoanalysis, it is cathected with psychic energy. Self objects relate to the self through three types of normal transferences.

In the first narcissistic transference, *mirroring*, the self object reflects the self back to itself. In a positive mirroring transference, the reflection is reasonably accurate (corresponds to the self's sense of itself) and self enhancing. The different forms of the mirroring transference can be organized developmentally from a virtual merger in its most primitive form to an empathic I–Thou relationship (Buber, 1958) at its most developed form. The mirroring transference facilitates the development and maintenance of the ambition and initiative pole of the self structure.

In the second type of transference, *idealizing*, self objects function as idealized objects of the self. Developmentally, these transferences range from primitive adoration to deep appreciation and respect. The idealizing transference facilitates the development and maintenance of the pole representing ideals, morals, and integrity within the self structure.

Toward the end of his life, Kohut (1984) discussed a third transference, *twinning*, in which self objects provide a sense of similarity or identification ("we are alike") that is important to the development of talents and skills. Although Kohut did not explicitly link this third transference to a third pole of the self, his theorizing can logically be extended in that direction. Building on his concepts, twinning may be thought of as relating to a third pole of the self structure that deals with a sense of competence and self-efficacy.

The self can be conceptualized as a triangular structure with three linked poles dealing with ambition, ideals, and efficacy. To develop properly, each pole must be nurtured with a sufficient amount of its particular type of transference from appropriate self objects. A "sufficient amount" refers to the idea of the good enough self object. Such a self object performs its function, and at certain moments it also fails appropriately to perform its function. However, its failures are never catastrophic but just enough to force the self to develop some internal capacity to perform that function for itself.

Beyond their developmental function, self objects perform a critical ongoing maintenance function for the self. The self needs self objects over the course of the entire life cycle. The developmental ideal is not complete independence from self objects, but rather the development of a self with ambitions and aims, ideals and values, and a sense of efficacy and competence. This self can select and effectively relate to appropriate self objects and can tolerate vicissitudes in their performance without fragmenting. This tolerance relates to the self's capacity to perform that function for itself, the strength of the relevant part of the self, and the extent and nature of the self object's failure.

The greatest threat to the self is annihilation through fragmentation or falling apart. Symptoms are primarily mechanisms to restore and maintain the cohesiveness of a fragmenting self. The more narcissistically vulnerable the self, the greater the use of symptoms, the more desperate the dependence on certain self objects, and the less the capacity to relate to others as independent centers of their own aims and initiatives. Narcissistically impaired individuals who did not receive the mirroring they required; who did not have parental figures they could idealize; and who did not have parents, friends, or siblings with whom they could "twin," are more easily injured and have less narcissistic flexibility and resilience.

Insofar as solutions to the presenting problem require organizational or biological changes, meaning shifts, transgenerational/family-of-origin changes, or shifts in object relations that disrupt the narcissistic transferences and self systems of the key patients, these self systems and transferences must be addressed in the therapy. For the scenario on this level, there are no significant constraints for the Butlers. In contrast, Stewart Christman grew up with a very narcissistic mother, who wanted Stewart continually to mirror her. She adored Stewart insofar as he performed his narcissistic role as her supporter and empathized with her. As a result, Stewart did not receive adequate mirroring, particularly empathic mirroring that recognized his own needs and aims.

In his relationship with Joanne, Stewart's narcissistic needs emerged early and with tenacious force. She was to be his mirror, seeing his needs and interests, reflecting them back to him with caring and concern, and ultimately attending to them as he desired. Joanne performed her function for many years and now was stepping out of the role of mirroring self object for Stewart. Stewart momentarily felt as if he were falling apart when Joanne began to abandon her self-object role. He regained his narcissistic equilibrium by becoming coldly enraged, treating her with scorn and disdain.

He simultaneously turned to his mother and sister as mirroring self objects. They now performed the narcissistic functions for Stewart that Joanne was abandoning. However, their empathy was a manipulative sympathy designed to bring him back into their own narcissistic webs. Unfortunately, for Stewart and others with his level of ongoing and immediate narcissistic disability, the mirroring they feel they need is closer to a merger in which the other is at best dimly perceived beyond his or her role as a supporter. Such a relationship is frequently a devil's bargain that cannot last, because it is not based on any appropriate degree of narcissistic balance. One or both persons' investment in the other is primarily exploitative.

To make the changes that would be necessary to save his marriage, Stewart would need to become less narcissistically vulnerable. His self would need to be strengthened so that he could tolerate Joanne's differentiation without cutting her out of his life. The good news from self psychology is that a vulnerable self can be made stronger through therapy or a narcissistically therapeutic experience with another person. Self development is not a fate that is sealed in childhood. With the proper experiences, the self can grow throughout the life cycle, becoming stronger, more resilient, and less vulnerable to fragmentation in the face of self-object failure.

In conclusion, the critical point regarding the self and self objects from a problem-centered perspective is that when the self systems of key patients play significant roles in the problem-maintenance structure, they must be strengthened to the point that the key selves become strong enough to permit implementation of adaptive solutions. The criterion for self growth is not some acontextual ideal, but rather sufficient growth to permit problem resolution. Typically, such self growth requires a fairly lengthy therapy in which the relationship between the key patients and the therapist becomes meaningful and important enough to the patients to become the primary vehicle for self development.

CHARACTERISTICS OF PROBLEM-MAINTENANCE STRUCTURES

Typically, there is not an invariant or typical relationship between the type of presenting problem and the nature of the problem-maintenance structure. Sometimes, superficially similar problems have different problem-maintenance structures, and different problems may have similar problem-maintenance structures. Some problems have simple and superficial problem-maintenance structures with constraints from the top levels, in which case they are likely to respond to direct, interpersonal, behaviorally or biologically focused interventions. Other problems have deep and profound problem-maintenance structures with constraints from the lower levels that may respond only to more individually focused treatments that address key patients' families of origin, object relations, and self structures.

As hypothetical geometric spaces, problem-maintenance structures vary at least along three dimensions—depth, width, and darkness. The *deeper* the structure, the more the constraints that prevent resolution of the presenting problem are rooted in the past. The three lower metaframeworks contain these historical constraints. The more superficial the structure, the more the constraints that prevent problem resolution are rooted in the present biopsychosocial context. With the Christmans, the deepest problem-maintenance scenario would involve Stewart and Joanne's families of origin, the balance of their object relations systems, as well as their self structures. The most superficial would only involve organizational constraints.

Width introduces the spatial dimension of horizontality to the structure and reflects the number of constraints within a particular level. The greater the number of current organizational, biological, and meaning constraints, the wider the top part of the structure. The greater the number of transgenerational, object relations, and self-system constraints, the broader the depths of the structure. With the Butlers, a wide structure on the transgenerational level would reflect the involvement of a large number of Loretta's siblings, aunts, and uncles in the problem-maintenance structure. It might also reflect the involvement of members of her husband's family of origin. In such a scenario, everyone might be involved in trying to deny their unresolved feelings about the two premature deaths that have afflicted their system—that of Loretta's mother and that of her husband.

The *darkness* of various parts of the structure reflects the potency of the factors from that domain. The darker the area, the more powerful the impact of that factor on the problem-maintenance structure. Lighter areas reflect the presence of factors that do not contribute as much as darker factors to the problem variance. This darkness metaphor reflects a critical point in problem-centered theory: *The presence of a constraint does not reflect its power within the problem-maintenance structure.*

For instance, a 28-year-old pregnant professional woman, in therapy with her husband for problems pertaining to their anxieties about their changing roles when their first baby arrives, mentions to the therapist that she was sexually abused by the father of a friend when she was 12. Without getting to know her better, it is impossible to know the power of this experience in the problem-maintenance structure. It may be that the abuse was handled well by her family and responsible professionals and that at this point it does not play a major role in this couple's issues. Alternatively, it may have been handled terribly by her family, and the experience may now play a major role in the anxieties she and her husband present.

The shapes of problem-maintenance structures vary substantially. Some may be best conceptualized as an inverted pyramid—a structure with many interpersonal determinants and one or few intrapsychic determinants. Others may be viewed as a teardrop or regular pyramid—one or few interpersonal determinants and many intrapsychic ones. A horizontal bar near the surface of the problem-maintenance space would reflect a structure with many interpersonal determinants and no intrapsychic ones. A long thin column would reflect a structure with one or few interpersonal and one or few intrapsychic determinants. If the top of the column were much darker than the bottom, that would mean that the current interpersonal determinants were more potent contributors to the problem-maintenance structure than the lighter, intrapsychic ones. A relatively flat, inverted pyramid with a very dark lower tip that is located at the top of the problem-maintenance space might represent the problem-maintenance structure of a system in which one member is suffering a severe, biologically based depression that is wreaking havoc on the family.

The narrower, simpler, lighter, and more superficial the problem-maintenance structure, the quicker the problem is likely to respond to intervention. In contrast, the wider, darker, and deeper the structure, the more time and effort will be required to resolve the problem.

TREATMENT MATCHING AND PROBLEM-MAINTENANCE STRUCTURES

Just as each has a patient system, *every presenting problem has a unique problem-maintenance structure. This structure, not the superficial features of the presenting problem, is the most crucial determinant of the course and outcome of treatment.* This assertion challenges current psychiatric and psychological thinking about matching treatments to disorders. Most psychiatric and clinical psychological theorists and researchers view the primary task of psychotherapy research as the discovery of the best (most effective, longest lasting, and least costly) treatment for each disorder. The matching question—which treatment for which disorder?—has been the predominant concern of North American psychotherapy research for the last 20 years.

The predominance of the matching question, coupled with early research findings, has led to certain common assumptions within psychiatry and clinical psychology: The best treatment for sexual dysfunction is considered to be some type of short-term behavioral intervention (Masters & Johnson, 1970); the best treatments for phobic disorders are said to involve some form of systematic desensitization. This thinking has led to a research tradition searching for the best treatments for depression, schizophrenia, and drug addiction. Private insurance companies as well as federal insurers have eagerly awaited the results of such studies to determine which therapies will be funded to treat which disorders.

The problem-centered model, with the concept of problem-maintenance structure, challenges this "matching" thinking. It asserts that similar disorders can have different problem-maintenance structures and that, ultimately, it is the problem-maintenance structure that determines the nature and course of successful treatment. The superficial features of disorders will never produce a valid foundation for matching or predicting response to treatment within psychotherapy. It is the underlying features or the problem-maintenance structure that ultimately determines what will lead to problem resolution.

PROBLEM-MAINTENANCE STRUCTURES, DIAGNOSIS, AND EPISTEMOLOGY

The preceding sections dealt with problem-maintenance structures as if they actually existed. They do not. Problem-maintenance structures are a complex and comprehensive set of hypotheses about the factors that prevent the patient system from solving its presenting problem. Like patient systems, problem-maintenance structures can never be known definitively or conclusively.

Even more significantly, at this time there are few if any diagnostic instruments or procedures that can reveal the nature of a problem-maintenance structure short of direct intervention. Indicators like the multiplicity, chronicity, or severity of presenting problems do not accurately or consistently reflect the nature of the underlying problem-maintenance structures. Standard experimental assessment procedures like interactive testing (such as revealed differences or set task questions) do not accurately or consistently reveal the underlying problem-maintenance structure. Finally, these structures are not revealed through standard psychological or psychiatric testing. The problem-maintenance structure is like an onion that must be peeled, layer by layer, to determine the level or layer at which the primary constraints operate. Intervention becomes assessment within this framework, and the problem-maintenance structure becomes an evolving concept that changes its dimensions as therapy unfolds.

IMPLICATIONS FOR MANAGED CARE

Increasingly, psychotherapeutic services in the United States and elsewhere will be provided under the framework of managed care. The good news is that this trend will force psychotherapeutic services to be provided in as cost-efficient a manner as possible. The bad news is that managed-care companies are encouraged to save as much money as possible by offering the briefest and cheapest treatments available.

Problem-centered therapy has numerous implications for managed care, which are articulated at various points in this book. At this point, the main implication is that treatment is not effective unless it addresses the problem-maintenance structure, which ultimately determines what types of psychotherapeutic intervention are necessary to resolve a problem. As Chapter 2 illustrates, the briefest and cheapest therapies tend to be directed principally at the first three metaframeworks—organization, biology, and meaning—with the preponderance focusing on the first two. If the problem-maintenance structure of a problem primarily contains constraints from the top half of the structure and is relatively narrow, the problem should be amenable to relatively brief and inexpensive therapy. However, if a problem-maintenance structure contains numerous constraints from the first three levels, constraints from the lower three levels, or very powerful constraints at any level, it will not be amenable to brief, here-and-now treatment. The challenge to managed care is to provide for patient systems with broader, deeper, and darker problem-maintenance structures. Will such systems be denied treatment if they do not respond to the briefest and least expensive forms of psychotherapy? Hopefully not.

What is needed at this time is a model for offering managed psychotherapy services in as cost-effective and responsible a manner as possible. Problem-centered therapy provides such a model. Its problem focus and the concepts of the patient system and problem-maintenance structure represent three critical components of the model. Additional components are presented in Chapter 2.

CHAPTER 2

The Integration of Specific Psychotherapies: Contexts, Orientations, and Concepts

THE CHALLENGE

EVERY SPECIFIC FORM of psychotherapy has its own domain of expertise—the particular problems and populations for which it was developed. Generally, each form is most effective when applied to its domain of expertise. Most psychotherapeutic errors involve the application of a specific form outside of its domain of expertise. Additionally, psychotherapy research consistently indicates that any specific form of psychotherapy only helps approximately two-thirds of the people to whom it is applied (Smith, Glass, & Miller, 1980). This statistic decreases even further in follow-up studies (Snyder, Wills, & Grady-Fletcher, 1991). This means that even within their domains of expertise, specific approaches do not help a substantial number of patients.

The critical challenge facing the field of psychotherapy today involves two questions. The first, the effectiveness question, asks how the various specific forms of psychotherapy may be integrated to maximize their assets and minimize their deficits. What is the most effective way to link the therapies and their domains of expertise? The second, the cost-effectiveness question, asks how the specific therapies can be integrated with maximal cost-effectiveness.

These questions come together in a third: Can the specific approaches be organized so that the failures of a more cost-effective approach will be subsequently reversed by another, only slightly less cost-effective approach?

Integrative problem-centered therapy is a framework for organizing different specific approaches with maximal efficiency and effectiveness. This chapter defines the specific forms of psychotherapy addressed within this framework and the core concepts that underlie it.

CONTEXTS AND MODALITIES

A psychotherapeutic approach can be divided into context and orientation components. The *context* component, sometimes referred to as the modality aspect of a therapy, addresses the interpersonal structure of an approach, specifying who is consistently involved in the direct system of the patient system. Psychoanalysis, client-centered therapy, and rational emotive therapy specify the individual as the direct system. The direct context of couple therapy involves at least two people from the same generation within a patient system. Family therapy includes at least two people from different generations (parent and child) of the same patient system in the direct system. Classical group therapy includes at least two unrelated patients.

The *orientation* component of a psychotherapeutic approach specifies its theories of problem formation and problem resolution. The theory of problem formation, or the etiological theory, delineates how psychological and psychiatric problems are created and maintained. For instance, cognitive therapy attributes depression to maladaptive cognitions that affect emotional and behavioral patterns (Beck, Rush, Shaw, & Emery, 1979). These cognitions are usually learned in the family of origin and become self-reinforcing. Structural family therapy attributes problems to disordered family boundaries—the rules that govern who does what with whom (Fishman, 1993; Minuchin, 1974). The most critical boundary separates the generations; its violation produces and sustains disorders ranging from chemical dependency to anorexia and delinquency.

The theory of problem resolution of a psychotherapeutic approach, its theory of therapy, delineates the processes and procedures for resolving psychiatric and psychological problems. Cognitive therapy targets and transforms cognitions; structural therapy changes the boundaries that provide family structure; classical psychoanalysis increases awareness about unconscious experience and motivation; more recently, with the advent of self psychology, psychoanalysts provide "corrective," or healing, experiences that strengthen the self (Kohut, 1971, 1977, 1984).

INTEGRATION

The first, classical attempts at integration brought together psychoanalytic and behavioral orientations within an individual context (Dollard & Miller, 1950; Wachtel, 1977). More recent theorists have brought together other orientations within a single context, such as structural, strategic, and psychoanalytic orientations within an individual context (Wachtel & Wachtel, 1986) or strategic, behavioral, and psychoanalytic orientations within a couple context (Gurman, 1981).

Theorists have also pulled together multiple contexts within single orientations. For instance, Slipp (1988) and the Scharffs (Scharff & Scharff, 1987) bring together individual, couple, and family contexts within a psychoanalytic object relations orientation. Beck's recent work (1989) expands the cognitive orientation to couple as well as individual contexts. Other approaches bring together multiple orientations with multiple contexts (Feldman, 1985, 1992; Pinsof, 1983, 1994a).

THE PROBLEM-CENTERED CONTEXTS AND ORIENTATIONS

Figure 2.1 delineates the specific contexts and orientations brought together in integrative problem-centered therapy (Pinsof, 1983, 1994a). The problem-centered model draws on three contexts and six orientations. The contexts and orientations constitute generic categories that cover multiple specific approaches sharing major common features.

As illustrated by the matrix, the contexts cut across the orientations, creating 18 cells that represent specific domains of expertise. Each cell contains one or more psychotherapeutic approaches that primarily target that domain of expertise. These specific approaches represent one person or group's preferred method of working in that domain. In actual practice, each problem-centered therapist needs to find his or her own preferred method for working in each of the domains, which may or may not fit within any individual approach or combination of approaches mentioned in the following discussion.

The three direct contexts in Figure 2.1 can be superimposed on the six metaframework levels of the problem-maintenance structure shown in Figure 1.2 in Chapter 1. The constraints within each metaframework can be addressed from a family–community, a couple, and an individual direct context. For instance, organizational constraints can be addressed from a family, a couple, or an individual context. From this perspective, each metaframe-

Figure 2.1
Problem-Centered Orientation–Context Matrix

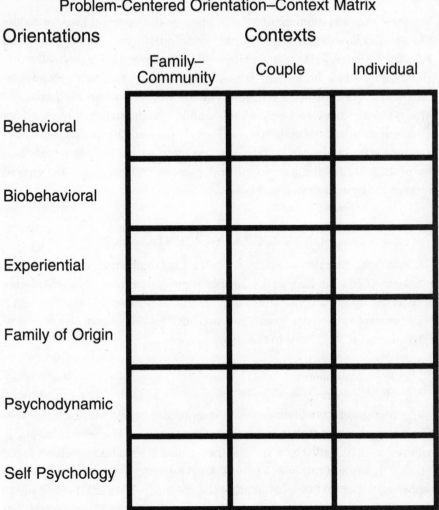

work embodies three domains of expertise—family–community, couple, and individual.

Each of the six orientation levels in Figure 2.1 roughly targets its corresponding metaframework level in Figure 1.2. This means that the theories and techniques of each orientation have been developed primarily to understand and modify the constraints from its corresponding metaframework. Thus, the behavioral orientations address the organizational metaframework; biobehavioral orientations target the biological metaframework; experiential orientations attend to meaning; family-of-origin orientations focus on the transgenerational metaframework; psychodynamic orientations deal with object relations; and self psychology orientations target the self.

CONTEXTS

The three direct-system contexts, identified as the three columns in Figure 2.1, are family–community, couple, and individual. *Family–community* includes the extended family and immediate community (e.g., school, work, friends) as well as the nuclear family. It is less concerned with blood relations and more concerned with individuals who constitute the functional family. *Couple* involves homosexual, sibling, premarital, heterosexual, or friendship couples. *Individual* targets a single person. That individual's relationships with others can be targeted, but intervention focuses primarily if not exclusively on the individual; interpersonal relationships are viewed through the eyes of the individual.

CONTEMPORARY ORIENTATIONS

The first three generic orientations—behavioral, biobehavioral, and experiential—focus on the here and now. For them, presenting problems derive from contemporary constraints: organizational, biological, and meaning. These orientations do not ignore the past, but they do not consider historical determinants to be central to the change process.

BEHAVIORAL

The first generic problem-centered orientation, behavioral, includes specific orientations that focus on interpersonal behavior. The term *behavioral* is not used in this context as a specific therapeutic orientation based on social learning theory, but rather as a generic label referring to approaches that target behavior per se. The goal of all of the specific behavioral therapies is to change action or behavior: what people do with each other. *The behavioral orientations have been developed primarily to address organizational constraints in patient systems.*

Within the behavioral domain, problem-centered therapy draws specifically on five orientations. The first is *social learning* (Bandura, 1977; Chamberlain & Rosicky, 1995; Jacobson & Margolin, 1979; Patterson, 1976); this orientation fits the classical understanding of the term *behavioral*. The social learning approaches emphasize a dyadic analysis of social interaction that examines reinforcement contingencies. Recently, behavioral analysts have focused on more extended interaction sequences, particularly in the realm of marital communication (Gottman & Krokoff, 1989; Hahlweg & Jacobson, 1984). Social learning therapists view themselves primarily as teachers. With families, social learning intervention teaches parents to reinforce increasingly their children's adaptive and prosocial behaviors and to ignore, or extinguish, maladaptive ones. Behavioral marital therapy teaches couples to modify communication patterns pertaining to conflict escalation, problem solving, and intimacy (Hahlweg, Revenstorf, & Schindler, 1984).

Problem-focused *strategic therapy* helps families modify maladaptive interaction patterns by bringing alternative and frequently paradoxical solutions to bear on presenting problems (Haley, 1976; Stanton, 1981; Watzlawick, Weakland, & Fisch, 1974). Strategic interaction analysis clarifies the patient's presenting problem and the ways in which the patient or the family has attempted to solve the problem. Symptoms regulate interpersonal systems. Strategic intervention targets the ways in which the system has ineffectively attempted to solve its problem and introduces alternative solutions that are more effective and less symptomatic and troublesome. Insight is not a therapeutic goal, and strategic therapists eschew formal educative roles. The strategic therapist is a change agent, not a teacher. Change is the goal, treatment is brief, and it is assumed that once the system has shifted, change will persist.

Coming out of a strategic tradition, *solution-focused therapy* rejects its predecessor's emphasis on problems and problem function, focusing instead on the search for solutions (de Shazer, 1988; O'Hanlon & Weiner-Davis, 1989). Emphasizing health, solution-focused therapists look for and examine exceptions to problem behaviors—periods of time in which the patient or family is symptom-free. On the basis of the understanding derived from this examination, therapists and patients collaboratively construct out-of-session tasks to increase these "exceptional" periods. With the positive emphasis on strengths and "what's good," the exceptional periods progressively become the norm, and the problem periods become the exception. Solution-focused therapists inspire their patients and families, leading them collaboratively in the construction of nonsymptomatic patterns of living. Solution-focused therapy frequently involves the use of a team of observers who intervene in the therapy at critical moments.

Merging social learning and strategic approaches, *functional family therapy* takes the strategic idea of systemic function and makes it the cornerstone concept (Alexander & Parsons, 1982; Barton and Alexander, 1981). Symptoms regulate interpersonal distance within families. Like strategic therapists, functional therapists help the system find less symptomatic and psychologically costly ways to regulate interpersonal distance. The need for particular distances is not necessarily addressed or modified. Intervention targets the family's strategies for maintaining particular distances. Insight is not essential, but consistent with a social learning perspective, the functional therapist teaches the family to respect its distance needs and to understand the role of its distance-regulation strategies. Functional therapy also frequently uses observing teams that intervene at key moments.

As mentioned previously, *structural family therapy* views psychopathology as the product of weak or rigid interpersonal boundaries, or both (Fishman, 1993; Minuchin, 1974). Although symptoms regulate distance, the target of intervention is not the symptom but the distance. In contrast to practitioners of the other four behavioral orientations, structural family therapists rely on a normative family model that asserts a strong need for hierarchy, clear generational boundaries, and proper interpersonal distances. Structural therapists rearrange the system, increasing closeness within certain dyads and distance within others. Intervention moves the family closer to the structural ideal. Of all the behavioral approaches, structural is the most explicitly organizational, focusing less on behavior per se than on the rules that organize it.

These five behavioral approaches differ in terms of the extent to which they use or eschew patient education, move patients toward a normative model, focus on problems or solutions, use observing teams, and focus on specific behavior patterns as opposed to underlying rules. However, they all attribute the formation and maintenance of psychological problems to dysfunctional behavioral patterns that reflect problems in social organization. Therapy replaces these behaviors with alternative, adaptive ones, and in doing so changes the organization of the patient system. Behavioral intervention in all five models is brief, and the therapist is active and directive.

None of the behavioral approaches exclusively targets behavior. Most have become more integrative and experiential, targeting cognitions (Baucom & Epstein, 1990) and affect (Kiser, Piercy, & Lipchik, 1993). However, they still fall within the behavioral orientation by virtue of their emphasis on behavior change as the primary target and goal of treatment. Although they may address thoughts and feelings, they do so secondarily, in the service of changing behavior and social organization.

Behavioral intervention with the Christmans would focus on changing the way in which Stewart and Joanne interact. A behavioral marital therapist might try to teach them problem-solving and communication skills, with special emphasis on negotiating as equals. A strategic therapist might paradoxically encourage them to polarize further, hoping that will trigger more affiliative and conciliatory behaviors. A solution-focused therapist might focus on the periods in which the couple collaborate and do not conflict, using these times as a foundation on which to build a less conflictual and more collaborative relationship. A functional therapist might reframe their conflict about power and participation as a distance-regulating mechanism that could be relinquished for a less contentious alternative. Finally, a structural therapist might attempt to redraw the boundaries that define their roles in regard to particular subsystems, such as children, and tasks, such as breadwinning and financial management.

BIOBEHAVIORAL

Biobehavioral orientations use either behavioral or biological interventions to change biological constraints. The first biobehavioral approach, *conditioning and training*, uses classical or operant conditioning, some form of systematic training, or both, to modify disorders with primary biological constraints. Classical conditioning, in the form of systematic desensitization, has been applied to most anxiety and phobic disorders (Bellack & Hersen, 1977). Operant conditioning, the basis for social learning theory, has been successfully applied to biologically based disorders such as autism and profound mental retardation (Lovaas, Koegel, Simmons, & Long, 1973; Lovaas & Simmons, 1969). Most treatments for learning disabilities involve some form of cognitive and behavioral training that may or may not be based formally on classical or operant procedures (Wong, 1991).

The second biobehavioral approach, *biofeedback*, applies classical conditioning techniques to biological constraints (Dicara, Barber, Kamiya, Miller, Shapiro, & Stoyva, 1975). Originally applied to anxiety-based disorders such as phobias and panic attacks, biofeedback more recently has been applied to obsessive-compulsive disorders and any biologically based disorder in which the autonomic nervous system can be conditioned. Using instruments to monitor a biological process such as heart rate or galvanic skin response, biofeedback provides feedback to the patient about the status of that process with some kind of visual or auditory signal.

The third biobehavioral orientation, *psychopharmacology*, uses psychotropic medication to modify biological constraints (Gitlin, 1990; Lawson & Cooperrider, 1988). Psychotropic medication has been generally accepted as an essential component in the treatment of schizophrenias and major mood disorders and is recommended for anxiety and obsessive-compulsive disorders. Stimulant medications have a long and successful history in treating attention deficit disorders and hyperactivity in children and even in some adults. Recently, antidepressant selective serotonin reuptake inhibitors like Prozac have been widely and controversially prescribed for dysthymia and other, less severe disorders (Kramer, 1993).

The last biobehavioral orientation, *psychoeducation*, represents a comprehensive approach to the treatment of psychiatric disorders with clear biological constraints. It was developed and has been used most extensively in the treatment of people with schizophrenia and their families (Falloon, Boyd, McGill, Williamson, Razani, Moss, Gilderman, & Simpson, 1985; Goldstein & Miklowitz, 1995; Hogarty, Anderson, Reiss, Kornblith, Greenwald, Ulrich, & Carter, 1991). More recently, it has been extended to the treatment of people with bipolar disorders and their families (Goldstein & Miklowitz, 1994).

The psychoeducational orientation involves three primary components: educational activities (lectures, workshops, written materials) to teach family members and patients the state-of-the-art knowledge of the disorder; psychotropic medication for the disorder; and behaviorally oriented family therapy to help the family learn to manage the person with the disorder. In most psychoeducational approaches, the family therapy emphasizes clear boundaries and low levels of expressed emotion (Hooley, Orley, & Teasdale, 1986). The expressed emotion intervention teaches family members to reduce the level of critical and angry interaction within the family and particularly in regard to the person with the disorder.

In their order of presentation, these four biobehavioral approaches use increasingly invasive procedures to modify the biological processes that underlie certain types of psychiatric, learning, and, more recently, medical disorders (for example, hypertension, migraine, connective tissue disease). They constitute a distinct psychotherapeutic orientation by virtue of their belief that the primary constraints for many of the problems patients bring to psychotherapy are biological and that intervention must address these constraints. The antagonism that many individual and family therapists have expressed toward these biobehavioral approaches, particularly psychopharmacology, seems to be waning in the face of multimodal integration (Patterson & Magulac, 1994).

A particularly important contribution of the psychoeducational approach to the biobehavioral orientations is the emphasis on educating the family about the disorder and the treatment. Historically, most biobehavioral interventions focused primarily on the individual. The research demonstrating the tremendous success of the psychoeducational approaches clearly shows that superior outcomes can be achieved when key patients are brought into the treatment process and educated about the problem and the treatment.

Biobehavioral intervention with the Butlers could take two or three forms. Loretta could be evaluated for antidepressant medication. Akisha could be evaluated for the presence of a learning disability and possibly given some tutoring or training to help her manage whatever emerges. Finally, Akisha should have a physical examination and a nutritional consultation for her obesity. Intervention might include a diet and an exercise program. Ideally, with each of these interventions, other key patients are involved and educated about the problem, the treatment, and their potential role in facilitating the impact of the intervention.

EXPERIENTIAL

The experiential orientations primarily address the metaframework of meaning. They all focus on some aspect of experience: cognition, emotion, or their integrated product, which is meaning.

The first specific experiential orientation drawn on by problem-centered therapy is *cognitive*. Articulated most fully by Beck (Beck et al., 1979), Meichenbaum (1977), Ellis (1974), and their colleagues, this approach focuses on people's thoughts. Most cognitive therapists modify maladaptive thought patterns with behavioral techniques, targeting cognitive patterns the same way that a social learning therapist targets a sequence of behaviors. With few exceptions, such as Beck's recent work with couples (1989), most cognitive therapists have focused exclusively on individuals.

With the exception of David Reiss's (1971) research on consensual experience in families, family therapists have been late in addressing cognition. Recently, neobehaviorists like Baucom (Baucom & Epstein, 1990) and Jacobson (Jacobson & Holtzworth-Monroe, 1986) have added cognitive components to their behavioral work with couples; nevertheless, their work is still primarily behavioral.

Although their primary goal was behavioral—to break up "dirty games"—the practitioners of the Milan model of family therapy (Palazzoli, Boscolo, Cecchin, & Prata, 1978; Tomm, 1987, 1988) can be placed within the experiential tradition. Their emphasis on hypothesizing, positive connotation, and circularity (circular questioning) reflected a primary concern with changing language and meaning structures within the families of schizophrenic and eating-disordered patients. They particularly attacked linear meaning structures that prevented a more systemic understanding of family process. Their emphasis on language and its impact on behavior, as well as their positioning of the therapist with the concept of therapeutic neutrality, created ideal conditions for the emergence of the narrative tradition.

Within the last decade, a narrative tradition has emerged within family therapy, which explicitly emphasizes attribution theory and the evolution of meaning within family systems. White and Epston's (1990) *narrative therapy* targets the meanings that family members attribute to events and behavior. Each person's reality rests on a story, or self-narrative, that constrains their ability to see and implement solutions to their problems. Therapy "restories" these self-narratives sufficiently to permit the family to resolve the problems for which they seek help.

In the narrative tradition, Goolishian and Anderson (1987) understand problems as socially created realities sustained by behavior and language. Their intervention changes family members' language systems and the meanings that rest on them. "The system to be treated includes those who are in a languaged context about a problem" (Anderson & Goolishian, 1988, p. 379). The narrative therapist is less an active intervenor than "a conversational co-participant in the social and dialogical creation of new meaning, narrative and social practice" (Goolishian & Anderson, 1992, p. 14).

The third experiential orientation addressed in problem-centered therapy is termed *emotionally focused*. It covers approaches that view emotion as playing a dominant role in problem formation and treatment. Greenberg and Safran (1987) reintroduced emotion as an explicit and primary psychotherapeutic focus. Johnson and Greenberg's work on emotionally focused marital therapy represents the most sustained effort in this direction within the family field (Greenberg & Johnson, 1988; Johnson & Greenberg, 1994). They emphasize the role of emotion in shaping interaction cycles and view the facilitation of emotional experience and expression in therapy as a tool, if not the major tool, in reorganizing interactional positions and self experience. Although they have been less explicit, other therapists within the field of family therapy (Satir & Baldwin, 1983) and individual therapy (Perls, 1973; Rogers, 1951) have emphasized affect.

The last specific experiential orientation within problem-centered therapy involves *interpersonal communication*, particularly the communication of feeling and thought. In fact, this orientation pulls the cognitive and affective approaches into a single experiential orientation emphasizing the management and sharing of thoughts and feelings within intimate systems. Many family-therapy approaches emphasize communication, but in particular, Satir (Satir & Baldwin, 1983); gestalt family therapists like Kempler (1971); and theorists in the area of marital enrichment (Guerney, 1977) work directly on facilitating the communication of thought, feeling, and meaning.

Although these experiential orientations differ from each other significantly, they all focus on meaning or the empathic communication and sharing of meaning within intimate systems. The critical questions from the experiential perspective concern what things mean to the participants in an interaction; to what extent these meanings can be changed in more adaptive directions; and finally, with certain experiential orientations, to what extent these meanings and the thoughts and feelings that compose them can be understood empathically and productively by the participants.

In treating the Christmans, the cognitive orientations would target Stewart's beliefs, particularly his beliefs about gender and family roles. The meaning of Joanne's desire to change their roles would be explored, positively connoting her desire to enrich each of their lives rather than destroy them. The "story" of each of their lives might be elaborated in an effort to enlarge their empathic understanding of each other and diminish their polarization. Her desire to change might be somewhat objectified and juxtaposed to her desire not to lose Stewart. Similarly, his rigidity might be objectified and juxtaposed to his desire for Joanne to be happy and fulfilled in their marriage. The goal of restorying might be to help Stewart and Joanne create their own story, which encompasses their hopes, their fears, and, most important, the complexity of their experience.

Emotionally focused therapy with the Butlers would attempt to clarify and facilitate the expression of their feelings. The daughters would be encouraged to express their sadness and grief about the death of their father and their fears about their mother's depression and inability to cope. Helping each of them talk about her needs for safety and attention might be a goal. Loretta might be encouraged to express her feelings of being overwhelmed and alone, her shame about those feelings, and the tremendous sense of burden she carries. Akisha might be encouraged to get beneath her defensive, angry posturing to her more primary and adaptive feelings of fear, shame, and loneliness.

The primary objective of both the more cognitive intervention with the Christmans and the more affective intervention with the Butlers would be the creation of less polarized, more empathic, and more collaborative patient systems. Within the context of problem-centered therapy, these more collaborative systems would facilitate the organizational changes that would lead to resolution of the presenting problems.

Although categorized as contemporary, the experiential orientations begin to shade into the historical orientations. The more narrative orientations in restorying attend to the history of the key patients. Concerning the Christmans, for example, it would be difficult to understand the meaning of Joanne's desire for change and Stewart's negative reaction without exploring the history of their marriage and possibly even their experiences growing up in their families of origin.

Emotions tend to be linked to particular events and experiences in patient systems. In the emotional work with the Butlers, it would be impossible not to go at least as far back into the history of the family as the death of the girls' father. In helping Loretta explore her feelings of burden and overresponsibility, it would probably be necessary and helpful to link those feelings to the role of her grandmother in her life and the impact of the death of her mother.

HISTORICAL ORIENTATIONS

The last three generic orientations within Figure 2.1—family of origin, psychodynamic, and self psychology—focus on meaning. However, their focus differs from the experiential orientations in that, for them, meaning is determined historically, and those historical determinants must be explicitly addressed to resolve the presenting problems.

Family of Origin

The family-of-origin orientations primarily target the transgenerational metaframework. This first historical orientation draws on the work of family therapists who emphasize transgenerational family patterns in the etiology, maintenance, and resolution of the problems patients bring to psychotherapy. The first specific approach within this genus, *contextual*, draws on the work of Ivan Boszormenyi-Nagy (Boszormenyi-Nagy & Spark, 1973; Boszormenyi-Nagy & Ulrich, 1981). In this work, transgenerational loyalties, legacies, and emotional entitlements and obligations constitute the primary targets of treatment. Boszormenyi-Nagy and his colleagues introduced to family therapy terms like *trustworthiness of relationship, multilateral caring,* and *accountability.* For them, therapy provides a context and impetus for rejunctive action that deepens empathic understanding and increases personal autonomy. The therapist flexibly takes sides ("multidirectional partiality"), alternating allegiances fairly and respectfully.

The second specific family-of-origin orientation, *Bowen systems theory,* is based on the work of Murray Bowen and his successors (Bowen, 1978; Kerr, 1981; Kramer, 1985). Bowen's theories of transgenerational family patterns and differentiation of self pioneered family-of-origin work. The genogram (McGoldrick & Gerson, 1985, 1986) has been a particularly important tool for family-of-origin therapists. Bowen's position asserts that current problems are the symptomatic expression of a psychosocial pattern elaborating itself over multiple generations within a family. That pattern involves a lack of differentiation of self for the individual family members and the use of projective processes and cutoffs to regulate the anxiety attendant on the prospect of differentiation.

The primary goal of Bowen's systems therapy is increasing differentiation of self. Patients learn to take responsibility for their own feelings, thoughts, and behaviors and get more comfortable thinking, feeling, and doing things that differentiate them from the other family members. Bowen therapy typically focuses on one key patient who is coached, through the use of out-of-session homework assignments, into increasingly differentiated positions with his or her family. The capacity to differentiate and to tolerate the differentiation of others without cutting off or getting cut off constitutes healthy behavior.

The last specific family-of-origin orientation, *direct family of origin*, draws heavily on Framo's (1992) work. This orientation involves direct engagement of adult patients' families of origin in therapy sessions. Typically parents or siblings of adult patients are invited to attend a relatively brief episode of sessions (one to three). Usually, this occurs in the context of individual therapy or conjoint marital therapy. These sessions are usually indicated when the couple has hit an impasse in their marital therapy or when the individual patient's resistance blocks progress.

Therapists who use direct family-of-origin sessions vary considerably in the way in which they define and organize them. Some include the spouse of the adult child, whereas others recommend exclusion. Some involve siblings of the adult patient along with parents, and others counsel against it. The amount of child–parent or patient–sibling confrontation also varies. Some therapists interview the parents and emphasize data collection, whereas others emphasize direct confrontation between family members on critical issues. All therapists who use these sessions agree, however, that it is extremely important to prepare the individual or couple carefully for these sessions and that they should not be engaged in precipitously.

The order of presentation of these three specific family-of-origin orientations reflects increasing levels of direct intervention into adult patients' families of origin. In contextual therapy, patients are encouraged to take rejunctive action with family-of-origin members, but directed coaching à la Bowen is not encouraged. The direct family-of-origin therapists go beyond encouraging and coaching to working directly with key family-of-origin members. All three approaches aim to modify patterns of meaning and action linked to patients' families of origin.

Family-of-origin work with the Butlers might involve all of the specific orientations. Initially, it would build on the experiential work that addressed Loretta's sense of overresponsibility. The emotional legacy she carries from her family of origin derives at least in part from her feeling that she had to make up for the sins of her mother. Her life is a debt to be paid on the loan of her mother. As well as helping her understand this legacy, rejunctive action might entail differentiating work with her family of origin as well as her children, in which she steps out of the debtor, overresponsible role. Mourning rituals might also be facilitative. Finally, it might be useful to invite some of her siblings or aunts and uncles for direct family-of-origin sessions in which Loretta could address the debt and unresolved mourning issues in which they all participate.

With the Christmans, a critical task at this point might be helping Stewart take a more differentiated position with his mother and sister without using his wife as the lever in the process. That work might involve coaching him in out-of-session homework assignments or direct family-of-origin sessions. It might also be useful to elucidate the way in which Joanne's experience in her family of origin predisposed her to take on the underadequate role in her marriage. At some point, family-of-origin sessions might be useful with her brother and sister-in-law or possibly with her friend Pauline. If Joanne and Stewart repair their marriage and work out a new organizational structure, some sessions with both of them and Pauline might be necessary to help Pauline come to terms with the new reality.

PSYCHODYNAMIC

The second major historical orientation addresses the object relations, or parts of the psyche, and the way in which they maintain their homeostasis. In contrast to the interest of the family-of-origin approaches in the history of patients' families over generations, psychodynamic approaches attend primarily to the history of the patient within his or her nuclear family of origin and the impact of that history on the organization and development of the patient's psychodynamics.

The principal specific psychodynamic orientation, *object relations* (Greenberg & Mitchell, 1983; Summers, 1994), originated in England (Fairbairn, 1952; Guntrip, 1969; Winnicott, 1965) after World War II and has intrigued family therapists almost from the inception of the field (Boszormenyi-Nagy, 1965; Scharff & Scharff, 1987; Slipp, 1988). Object relations therapists view the psyche as a set of objects that embody the internalized and transformed representations of the early attachment figures in a person's life. The self is also represented as part of the object system. This object system has its own homeostasis. Individual and interpersonal symptoms are defensive maneuvers of this object system to maintain its homeostasis in the face of various internal and external threats.

The object system uses various defense mechanisms such as denial, splitting, projection, and projective identification to regulate itself. These mechanisms are invariably involved in symptom formation and maintenance. Therapy involves the analysis and modification of these defensive and symptom-maintaining mechanisms. This entails changing the object-system homeostasis that has required their use. Object relations analysis applied to the interactions between family members looks at three phenomena: how family members function as projective and transferential objects for each other; how their individual object homeostases depend on this interpersonal object deployment; and the way in which the changes that need to occur within the family threaten their individual and interpersonal object relations.

Finally, the patients' relationship with the therapist becomes a primary vehicle for change in at least two ways in object relations therapy. The therapist eventually becomes a transference object for the patients, and their objects are projected onto the therapist–patient relationship. The analysis of this transference helps the patients become more aware of their objects and their deployment. In longer term therapy, if the relationship with the therapist is intense enough, the patients internalize the therapist. The therapist's internal representation changes the dynamics of the object system. It becomes a new salutary object in the system and changes the interaction of the objects and their homeostasis. Once this latter process occurs, termination of therapy becomes appropriate.

A variant of object relations theory, Schwartz's *internal family systems* model (Breunlin et al., 1992), involves the application of a structural-family-therapy model to the objects or parts of the psyche. In this model, the self is viewed as the leader of the parts. The therapeutic process in internal family systems therapy emphasizes helping the patients identify with and experience their parts through visualization and role playing.

The psychodynamic orientations attend to the various parts of the psyche. They look specifically at the parts that compose the psyche and the way in which their internal regulation and interpersonal deployment constrain problem solving and necessitate symptoms. Intervention aims to modify the parts, their internal regulation, and interpersonal deployment so that symptoms are no longer required and patients can engage in adaptive problem solving.

Psychodynamic work with the Butlers might involve helping the daughters, particularly Eileen and Akisha, to stop the projective identification process in which Akisha acts out the needy, demanding, and immature parts of her sisters. Depending on their degree of defensiveness, some of this work may have to be done in an individual context. Additionally, it might be appropriate to have some individual sessions with Loretta to help her work through with the therapist her struggles concerning taking responsibility and denying her needs.

The value of doing at least some of this work with Loretta in an individual context is that it would increase the likelihood that the struggle will emerge and be addressed in the transference with the therapist (Gill, 1982). An additional value is that it reinforces the generational boundary: She does the work she needs to do without putting her children into the position of having to take care of her emotionally. Finally, just creating the possibility of individual work for Loretta confronts her with her issues about going after and taking something just for herself.

The primary psychodynamic work with the Christmans would involve breaking up the mutual projective process that might underlie their overadequate–underadequate dynamic. Stewart needs to reown his more vulnerable, passive parts, and Joanne needs to reown her more aggressive and active parts. The issues and particularly the fears associated with this reowning process would probably need to be confronted. Ideally, as much of this work as possible would be done in a conjoint context, because their mutual projective and transference processes relate so much to each other.

SELF PSYCHOLOGY

The sixth generic orientation addresses the self metaframework that targets the organization of the self structures of the key patients. A more recent development within modern psychoanalysis, self psychology offers a model of the self as a self-organizing open system that is theoretically consistent with family-system models (Kohut, 1971, 1977, 1984). The self is the most basic psychological unit and the core of human identity. Its loss constitutes psychological death, and the anxiety attendant on its fragmentation feels like death anxiety. The self contains the internal objects discussed previously, and its resilience strongly influences their homeostatic range and flexibility. The self develops and is sustained throughout life by self objects, which are people or things that are emotionally important to the person. Self objects relate to the self through three normal narcissistic transferences: mirroring, idealizing, and twinning (Kohut, 1984). Small failures in these transferences facilitate the growth of the self and the partial internalization of the self objects.

The self is not fixed; it has the capacity to grow in any meaningful relationship. A strong marriage or a good therapeutic relationship can strengthen a weak self. Generally, the most important self objects in a person's life are family members. Self psychology examines and attempts to improve the self-object transferences within family systems. The therapist as self object can strengthen patients' self structures sufficiently to help them engage in narcissistically threatening adaptive activities. Self psychology has hardly begun to penetrate family-systems theory (Cleghorn, 1987), where it has been primarily used to understand and treat narcissistic vulnerability in marriage (Solomon, 1992).

If Stewart and Joanne Christman cannot do the work they need to do on their object relations constraints, the therapeutic focus needs to shift to their self constraints. To accomplish this, it probably would be necessary to have individual sessions with each spouse, but in particular with Stewart. His narcissistic vulnerability may be such that the work that needs to be done on the higher levels of the problem-maintenance structure constitutes a disruptive narcissistic injury. In that case, Stewart probably would not be able to do that work without strengthening his self system and thereby decreasing his vulnerability. For that to happen, the therapist probably would have to become a self object for him. In working through the frustration–internalization process with the therapist, Stewart's self can become internally stronger and more capable of tolerating and even facilitating the changes that need to occur to solve the presenting problems.

MODALITY–ORIENTATION SUMMARY

Modalities cut across orientations, and vice versa. Thus, problem-centered therapy contains behaviorally oriented family, couple, and individual therapy (the top row in Figure 2.1) as well as behavioral, biobehavioral, experiential, family-of-origin, psychodynamic, and self psychological family intervention (the first column in Figure 2.1).

The context dimension specifies who is to be directly and consistently engaged in therapy, whereas the orientation dimension specifies the focus, content, and temporal orientation of intervention. From this perspective, the critical task becomes identifying the best contexts for particular interventions with particular problems and systems. For instance, is it better to do a psychodynamic transference interpretation in a family, couple, or individual context with a depressed father with adult children and a supportive wife? Potential answers to such questions will be addressed throughout this book.

The specific suborientations identified previously are not meant as an exclusive or closed list of the potential specific orientations addressed within problem-centered therapy. Rather, they are specific and relatively well-known orientations that naturally fall within the generic orientations and that meet a basic systemic criterion that is articulated in the next section. Additionally, the order in which the generic and specific orientations within them, as well as the contexts, have been presented is not coincidental and will also be explained in the next section.

The inclusion of so many generic and specific orientations is not meant to imply that a competent problem-centered therapist must know and be proficient in every orientation, context, and cell of the matrix. In all likelihood, such a therapist does not exist. In fact, the inclusion of multiple specific orientations within most of the generic categories reflects the fact that there are multiple ways to work within that orientation. As mentioned previously, each therapist must find his or her own preferred way of understanding and working each metaframework, which will probably include some components from one or more of the specific approaches as well as idiosyncratic components unique to the therapist. Finally, the problem-centered model is also a model for referral and consultation. When a therapist lacks the knowledge or skills associated with a particular generic orientation, referral to a knowledgeable and skilled therapist in that orientation is appropriate. A more detailed and comprehensive presentation of problem-centered therapy with the Christmans and Butlers is presented at the conclusion of the book in Chapter 8.

CORE INTEGRATING CONCEPTS

Two sets of concepts inform the matrix in Figure 2.1 and integrate the different contexts and orientations. The first is a unifying and *underlying theoretical framework*. The second is a set of *principles of application* that specify rules for sequencing and organizing the contexts and orientations. These principles specify what should be done when and with whom.

UNDERLYING THEORETICAL FRAMEWORK

An integrative psychotherapy should be based on an underlying conceptual framework that applies to each of its modalities and orientations (cells of the matrix in Figure 2.1). This framework functions as a common base language for the approach and specifies its fundamental assertions about reality, knowledge, and causality. Each of the orientations identified previously was selected in part because it either explicitly embodies this conceptual framework or is implicitly compatible with it.

The underlying core theory framework for problem-centered therapy has three primary components. The first concerns epistemological and ontological premises and is called interactive constructivism; the second, systems theory, specifies premises about the basic structures and organization of living systems; the last component, intimately linked with the second, is mutual causality.

Interactive Constructivism

Constructivism asserts that human beings construct reality. Theorists can be located at various points on a constructivist continuum, ranging from the metaphysical realist pole, which asserts that there is a knowable, independent reality, to the radical constructivist pole, which proposes that the world that is constructed is an experiential world that consists of experiences and makes no claim whatsoever about "truth" in the sense of correspondence with an ontological reality (von Glasersfeld, 1984).

The metaphysical realist position denies that humans create their realities. Reality exists and can be known through either science (objectivism) or revelation (religious fundamentalism). In contrast, the radical constructivist position denies the existence of any objective world. All that exists is your reality and my reality. For the radical constructivist, all that matters about an orientation's theory of problem formation and problem resolution is that it fits the patient's "reality," or construction of the world.

Problem-centered therapy rejects radical constructivism and takes an interactive constructivist position. This position, at the midpoint of the constructivist continuum, asserts that there is an independent, objective reality but that human beings can never know it objectively. Our knowledge of the world, including ourselves, is ineluctably subjective. Science is just a more systematic extension of our subjective capacity to know (Pinsof, 1992a). Perception and cognition are defined and conditioned by our biology, the learned impact of our cultures and languages, and the social structuring of our environments. Human reality is the product of the interaction between our limited and conditioned perceptual–cognitive apparatus and objective reality.

There is no such thing as ultimate or direct knowledge of reality; it is always relative and indirect. This is not to say that there is no knowledge of reality; it is just limited and partial. We can "know" reality vaguely through our senses, but it is most apparent when it conflicts with our theories, plans, and projects sufficiently to disconfirm or disrupt them. "We never get to see the constraints of the world, with which our enterprises collide" (von Glasersfeld, 1984, p. 37); but we experience the collision and know that we have bumped into something real.

There are two major implications of the interactive constructivist position for psychotherapy. The first is that a specific psychotherapeutic approach not only must "fit" the patient's reality, but also must fit objective reality to some extent. If the approach only fits the patient's reality but differs too much from the "objective" reality, failure results. Similarly, if it fits the "objective" reality but is not congruent with the patient's, it is not acceptable. A structural approach may best fit one system, whereas a functional approach may be most congruent with another. If the core constraints are not behavioral, none of the behavioral approaches will work, and biobehavioral, experiential, or historical approaches will have to implemented.

The second implication of interactive constructivism for psychotherapy is that diagnosis–assessment and intervention are coextensive processes spanning the entire therapy. Because knowledge is always partial but cumulative, the therapist will know more about a patient system after ten sessions than after one, and more after twenty than ten. Thus, a therapist's diagnosis, or assessment, of a patient system is an evolving set of hypotheses that are continually refined on the basis of the feedback from interaction with the system. Splitting therapy into an assessment phase followed by an intervention phase arbitrarily cuts off the assessment process and disqualifies it as an active intervention into the patient system.

Systems Theory

The second major component of the underlying theoretical framework of problem-centered therapy, systems theory, derives from general systems theory (Buckley, 1968; von Bertalanffy, 1968). Human life consists of *hierarchically organized living systems*. The lowest viable level of organization is the living cell; the highest is human society. The family exists as a social system in the intermediate levels. The self is a psychological system within the individual. Most systems are subsystems of larger ones and host hierarchically organized subsystems. A hierarchically organized system can be relatively integrated (healthy) or disintegrated (unhealthy). The Christmans and the Butlers represent moderately disintegrated patient systems in which specific subsystems fail to collaborate.

A system is a set of entities that are interrelated such that a change in one affects the others. These effects impact the initial entity, and so on. The impact process is circular or, more accurately, mutual. Effects feed back and influence the general state of the system, which has been referred to as homeostasis or morphostasis. There are two forms of feedback—negative and positive (Watzlawick, Jackson, & Beavin, 1967).

Problem-centered therapy takes change as a given. Everything is constantly in motion. The essence of life is self-sustained motion. Death is lack of such motion. The cause or mechanism of movement is *positive feedback*, which amplifies deviation (Hoffman, 1971). To anthropomorphize, positive feedback greets change or deviation in a variable with a green light. In terms of couples, positive feedback always drives the partners closer or further apart. In relation to the self, positive feedback drives toward greater cohesion or fragmentation. Unchecked, positive feedback leads ultimately to chaos and randomness. Positive feedback is necessary for systemic change and adaptation.

Negative, or error-activated, *feedback* occurs when a variable exceeds permissible deviation limits and violates its host system's stable state, or homeostasis. Negative feedback signals that a deviation has gone too far, and a healthy system deploys negative feedback mechanisms to stop the change and restore homeostasis. Metaphorically, negative feedback is the red light of systemic traffic regulation. Negative feedback is necessary for systemic stability.

Subsystems develop and transform. To survive, every system periodically reorganizes itself around internal changes driven by its own and its subsystems' inherent developmental processes. A family reorganizes instrumentally and affectively when a child is born and when a child leaves home. A system must also adapt to changes in its environment. A father's job loss requires adaptive reorganization on the family-system level as well as on the marital and individual psychological levels.

Systemic adaptation to internal and external changes requires ongoing regulation of the balance between negative and positive feedback. There are two types of systemic pathology. In *positive feedback pathology*, the negative feedback mechanisms have broken down, and change destroys the system's homeostasis. Biologically, cancer represents positive feedback pathology. The quest for a cure searches for negative feedback mechanisms that can "turn off" cancerous cells. Within a family, murder represents positive feedback pathology; the family cannot deploy negative feedback mechanisms to contain escalating rage and violence.

Rigidity is the primary characteristic of *negative feedback pathology*. The rigid system cannot adapt to internal and external changes. Most systems resist change at first. After this initial constraining response, they incorporate what must be incorporated and function adaptively. The rigid system does not soften after this initial negative reaction. It continues to employ negative feedback mechanisms to minimize change. If the change is so powerful that it cannot be denied, the system will disintegrate or become symptomatic. Disintegration involves the collapse of the system's brittle negative feedback mechanisms and the dominance of its positive feedback capacities. Symptoms may serve the function of maintaining systemic homeostasis in the face of the disintegrating change process.

Negative feedback pathology is particularly evident with the Christmans. The changes within their system are being driven primarily by the developmental processes within the system—the fact that the children have all left home and Joanne is experiencing a greater desire for control, power, and autonomy. Stewart's reaction to these changes represents the rigid deployment of negative feedback mechanisms. The pressure for the changes coupled with the rigidity of response results in symptomatic behavior: conflict and hostile disengagement. The conflict symptom also links Joanne and Stewart and prevents their marital system from disengaging and disintegrating even more.

Crisis intervention programs treat positive feedback pathology. They restore stability by creating or activating negative feedback mechanisms to constrain the variable exceeding permissible deviation limits. A psychotic break, a biopsychosocial runaway, can be contained with hospitalization, medication, and family intervention. Crisis intervention restores homeostasis.

Outpatient psychotherapy clinics primarily treat negative feedback pathology. In such cases the system's symptoms at least in part reflect a failure to change. More specifically, the system cannot recalibrate itself around new developments in its internal or external ecologies. In the face of negative feedback pathology, therapy modifies the negative feedback mechanisms sufficiently to permit systemic adaptation to internal and external changes.

The Butlers have rigid rules around the expression of grief and sadness. These rules, or constraints, block the grief work necessary to come to terms with the losses of great grandmother, grandmother, and father. Akisha's immature behavior and school problems, coupled with the chronic conflict among the sisters, particularly between Eileen and Akisha, may help the family avoid grieving about their losses and thereby maintain the family's homeostasis. Effective intervention requires changing the grief rules as well as finding more adaptive and less symptomatic methods to maintain the family's emotional balance.

Psychotherapy modifies the balance of negative and positive feedback mechanisms within human systems to facilitate survival, adaptation, and growth. A critical task involves determining the particular systems that are most pertinent with particular patients and problems, and intervening to modify the positive–negative feedback balance within those systems. This task typically involves helping the conflicted subsystems within the patient system become less polarized and conflicted. With the Christmans, this entails interrupting the subsystemic confrontation and helping Joanne and Stewart explore the constraints that prevent them from working more collaboratively on the change process.

An implication of systems theory is that it is not sufficient to view therapy as the interaction between the therapist and the patient system. From a systemic perspective, therapy is the interaction between the patient system and the therapist system. *The therapist system consists of all of the people involved in providing therapy to the patient system.* For a therapist working in a clinic, team members, supervisors, and consultants are members of the therapist system. Typically, there is only one member of the direct therapist system—the therapist; the other members of the system constitute the indirect therapist system. If supervisors or consultants join the therapy, they temporarily become members of the direct therapist system.

When other therapists work concurrently with different subsystems of the same patient system, those therapists constitute members of the direct therapist system. For instance, concerning the Christmans, if Stewart began individual therapy while he and Joanne were in couple therapy, both his individual therapist and their couple therapist would be members of the therapist system.

Together, the therapist and patient systems constitute the *therapy system*. The interaction of the parts of each system as well as the interaction between the two systems can be understood in the context of mutual causality and interactive constructivism.

Mutual Causality

Many family therapists have rejected the concept of linear causality in favor of circular causality. Linear causality stems from a nineteenth-century Newtonian model of the physical universe in which effects have specific causes and responses have specific stimuli. Circular causality is viewed as the alternative to linear models and equates with systems theory and the concept of feedback.

The problem-centered theory of causation, mutual causality, embodies several propositions. The first, *multicausality*, asserts that all processes involve multiple causes (Kaplan, 1974). Simplistic unicausal theories such as the schizophrenogenic mother overlook the contribution of other family members and, most significantly, biology. Consistent with interactive constructivism, it is possible to know some of the causes of a particular phenomenon, but that knowledge is always partial, and some causes invariably remain unknown.

The second proposition asserts that *causality is mutual*. Another way of saying this is that causality is bidirectional or, more accurately, omnidirectional. With a three-person family, everyone constantly affects everyone individually and collectively. The mother affects her husband and her daughter, and each of them affects her. However, she does not just react to each of them individually; she also reacts to her husband and daughter as a subsystem, or unit. Similarly, the father affects and is affected by his wife and daughter individually and collectively. The same assertions apply to the daughter.

The word *mutual* is used rather than *circular* because the latter connotes an influence process in which causation moves around the circle of the family: Mother affects father, who in turn affects daughter, who in turn affects mother, and so on. The connotations of circularity obscure the omnidirectional and simultaneous aspects of mutual causality. At times causal processes in systems may take on a circular form, but circularity is viewed as one type of mutual causality.

The third causal proposition, *differential causality*, asserts that different subsystems contribute differentially to particular causal processes. Each of the multiple causes of a phenomenon are not equally powerful. For instance, in the context of incest between a father and his young daughter, the father is far more powerful and accounts for much more of the variance in the phenomenon than the daughter. In fact, for the sake of simplicity, it may be useful to think of phenomena like sexual and physical abuse as linear, realizing that such an assertion is a shorthand way of attributing responsibility.

Another implication of differential causality is that disorders are determined to differing extents by different variables. For instance, with particular disorders such as schizophrenia, autism, and manic depression, biological systems may account for more of the variance than psychological and social systems. This is not to deny the importance of psychosocial systems in these disorders, as the research on expressed emotion has demonstrated (Goldstein & Miklowitz, 1995), but rather to recognize that their contribution is smaller. With other disorders, such as school phobia or marital conflict, psychosocial systems may contribute more than biological ones.

The last causal proposition asserts that *interactive processes cannot not be punctuated*. The concept of punctuation, originally proposed by Watzlawick et al. (1967), means that people perceive, divide up, or interpret interaction sequences according to their perspective and their needs. Everyone punctuates. One cannot *not punctuate*. Stewart Christman punctuates his marital problems as beginning with Joanne's demands for more power and authority in regard to finances. Joanne punctuates the problems as beginning with

Stewart's offensive rigidity. Like most patients, Stewart and Joanne both experience themselves as victims of the other's behavior. Helping each of them see their role in the dysfunctional conflict process typically would involve a restorying of their relationship that is more consistent with a mutual causality punctuation.

Underlying Theory Summary

Systems theory and mutual causality offer a common language for describing and analyzing systems and the interaction between them. They use similar terms to describe the functioning of biological, psychological, and social systems, as well as the interaction among them. No longer is it necessary to choose among the biological, the psychological, and the social. With a hierarchically organized systems model informed with the concepts of mutual causality, the pitfalls of biological, psychological, or social reductionism can be avoided.

Interactive constructivism, systems theory, and mutual causality constitute the three components of the underlying theoretical framework of problem-centered therapy. They apply to each cell of the problem-centered orientation/context matrix (as indicated in Figure 2.1) as well as to each metaframework layer of the problem-maintenance structure in Figure 1.2. Additionally, they define the therapeutic process as the mutual interaction of the patient system and the therapist system.

PRINCIPLES OF APPLICATION

An integrative psychotherapeutic approach should have explicit principles of application. These principles specify what theories and techniques should be used with which patients at specific points in the treatment process.

Shifting Down the Matrix

The primary principle of application in problem-centered therapy is illustrated by the large arrow in Figure 2.2. This arrow has been superimposed over the matrix originally depicted in Figure 2.1 to illustrate graphically the universal and preferred sequence of problem-centered conceptualization and intervention. Progressing from the upper left to the lower right quadrant of the matrix, this sequence moves from the interpersonal, here-and-now approaches to the individual, historically focused approaches.

This movement is termed a *universal and preferred* progression because it is intended to be used more or less in every case. This principle of application is

Figure 2.2
Problem-Centered Principle of Application

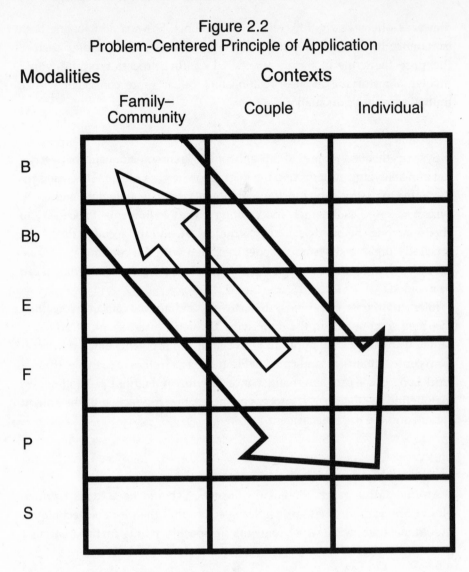

not meant to be a rigid ideal, but rather a starting point and point of reference throughout the course of therapy. The universal progression is intended as a flexible guiding structure for organizing approaches in integrative treatment.

Within problem-centered therapy, this progression occurs in the process of addressing particular presenting problems. In fact, it is best conceptualized as a problem-centered progression. The rationale for shifting from the upper-left toward the lower-right quadrant rests on three criteria. The first is *resistance*, which refers to the patient system's failure to respond successfully to interventions that are more immediate, interpersonal, behavioral, or biobehavioral. This resistance typically takes the form of a block: The system cannot implement an adaptive solution or some part of an adaptive solution to the problem for which it is seeking help. When a block emerges at any particular point, treatment moves closer to the lower-right quadrant of the matrix and addresses constraints in lower metaframeworks.

The second criterion is *lack of success*. In this situation, the patient system responds to behavioral, family-based interventions, but these responses do not lead to problem resolution. The patient system does not resist doing what needs to be done; the members do what apparently needs to be done, but it does not work. Usually, the therapist and patient system try several different interventions on a particular level before concluding that shifting to the next one is appropriate. In other words, the first response to failure on one level is to try different interventions on that level. For instance, if narrative interventions lead to changes in meaning but the presenting problem persists, it would be appropriate to try emotionally focused interventions before shifting out of the experiential orientations to the family-of-origin level.

The third criterion for shifting is *lack of diagnostic evidence*. The problem-centered progression provides a framework not only for the sequential application of psychotherapeutic theories and techniques, but also for the consideration of different types of diagnostic or etiologic hypotheses. The problem-maintenance hypotheses of the upper-left quadrant assert that the primary constraints that prevent resolution of the presenting problem are interpersonal, organizational, behavioral, biological, experiential, or some combination of these. In contrast, the hypotheses of the lower-right quadrant view the primary constraints as historical, relating to transgenerational, object relations, or self variables.

The ideal progression involves consideration of social interaction and biological hypotheses before intrapsychic ones. Interpersonal–interactional or biological hypotheses, or both, are abandoned when initial intervention, based on such hypotheses, fails to provide clear evidence in support of the hypothesis. Such failure to support leads to the active evaluation of more historical, intrapsychic, and individually focused hypotheses. This evaluation usually involves intervening into the relevant direct system as if the new hypothesis were true.

Treatment for most presenting problems begins on a problem-solving, behavioral level. This involves techniques and theories from the behavioral orientations, the first orientation listed in Figure 2.1. These theories and techniques are applied within a family or dyadic context, depending on the nature of the presenting problem. If the therapist encounters a block, failure to change, or a clear lack of evidence to support a behavioral, family-system hypothesis, treatment shifts to the biobehavioral level. If there are no indications of biological constraints, or if the patient system is blocked or fails to change, intervention moves to the experiential orientations, focusing on cognitive and affective communication within dyadic systems. If blocks, failure to change, or lack of evidence emerges on this level, intervention shifts to the historical orientations.

Entering the historical realm, the therapy addresses transgenerational constraints in interpersonal contexts. If this type of intervention is unsuccessful, becomes blocked, or fails to produce supportive evidence, treatment moves to the psychodynamic orientations in a family or dyadic context. When treatment on the psychodynamic level fails, is blocked, or produces insufficient evidence, the focus shifts to self psychological orientations. Initially, this work should be done in a dyadic or larger context. However, if the work is unproductive, the context should increasingly shift toward the individual. Ideally, a problem-centered therapist begins treatment like a behavioral or structural family therapist and, if necessary, concludes treatment like a psychoanalyst. Along the way, the therapist may function as a psychopharmacologist, an experiential couple therapist, or a family-of-origin therapist.

This progression involves shifts in the role of the therapist. As the therapist moves down the matrix, the focus and quality of therapeutic behavior change. The therapist typically becomes less active, less directive, more exploratory, and more reflective. This shifting requires different therapeutic skills in different cells of the matrix; it requires therapists with extensive skills in working in different orientations in different contexts. As mentioned previously, no therapist is likely to possess all the requisite skills; therefore, the progression can function as a referral framework. Additionally, the method argues for the use of a formal or informal treatment team with members who have different skills that can be offered to patient systems as they traverse the matrix.

The smaller arrow shown going back up the matrix in Figure 2.2 graphically represents several concepts. First, as the therapy progresses down the matrix, the process does not abandon the upper levels that have been traversed. The lower-level perspective is added to the attention that continues to be directed to the upper levels. For instance, as the therapist works on the psychodynamic level, attention continues to be paid to the constraints on the experiential and behavioral levels that prevent resolution of the presenting problem.

The second concept represented by the smaller arrow is that the progression is, in actual practice, more like an oscillating process that moves down toward the lower-right quadrant and back up to the upper-left quadrant and back down toward the lower right and so on until the presenting problem is resolved. As the oscillating process goes on, the swings get longer and longer as they expand toward the lower-right quadrant. The critical point is that the progression is not rigidly linear and should be viewed as a rough guideline for the conduct of integrative problem-centered therapy.

THE PROGRESSION, COST-EFFECTIVENESS, AND MANAGED CARE

The orientation and context matrix shown in Figure 2.1 embodies many of the most well-known and researched psychotherapies in use at this time. The arrow in Figure 2.2 reflects the problem-centered principle of application. This principle organizes these psychotherapeutic orientations so that they will be deployed sequentially in the most cost-effective fashion.

The specific orientations in the top three generic categories are generally short term and typically involve more than one patient in the direct system. These contemporary orientations serve more people in less time. The large progression arrow specifies that these orientations should be used first, before turning to the more historical specific orientations within the lower three generic orientations. These historical orientations, particularly the psychodynamic and self psychological approaches, tend to be longer term and rely primarily on individual contexts. They cost more because they typically involve more sessions than the higher orientations and serve fewer people directly.

The cost-effectiveness distinction does more than dichotomize the top three and lower three generic orientations. The order of presentation of the generic orientations and, to some extent, the specific categories within them reflect even finer grained cost-effectiveness considerations. Thus, the behavioral and biobehavioral therapies tend to be shorter term and more cost-effective than the experiential therapies. Similarly, family-of-origin therapies tend to be shorter term and more cost-effective than psychodynamic therapies, which tend to be shorter term and more cost-effective than self psychological therapies.

The positioning of biobehavioral, particularly psychopharmacological, orientations after behavioral orientations reflects not so much cost-effectiveness concerns as concerns about the potential hazards of psychopharmacological intervention. Biological interventions frequently have serious side effects and frequently are only effective as long as the patients continue to be medicated. Problem-centered therapy would rather address a biological constraint with a nonpharmacological treatment than a pharmacological one, if the treatments are equally effective. The behavioral treatments do not run the risk of potentially dangerous side effects and tend to "train" patients to regulate the biological process independently of treatment.

The order of presentation of the contexts also reflects cost-effectiveness considerations. Clearly, a unit of therapy that involves more people directly costs less per person. Thus, in general, family contexts should be tried before couple contexts, and couple contexts should be tried before individual contexts. There are a number of considerations that moderate this recommendation, however, such as the nature of the presenting problem and patient system and the alliance requirements of the system. These considerations are addressed in greater detail in Chapters 3 and 5.

As stated in Chapter 1, it is the problem-maintenance structure, not the superficial features of the presenting problem or the patient system, that ultimately determines which therapeutic orientations need to be used. At this point in the development of the science of psychotherapy, there are no consistent and reliable methods for determining in advance the nature of the problem-maintenance structure and the therapeutic requirements of a case; therefore, problem-centered therapy recommends that therapy progress theoretically and technically from more to less cost-effective orientations.

The sequential implementation of the orientations in problem-centered therapy progressively reveals the problem-maintenance structure. The orientations constitute diagnostic probes as well as attempts to help the patient system solve the presenting problems. The problem focus of this approach confines the exploration of the patient system to features that appear to be linked to the presenting problem: the problem-maintenance structure. Once the patient system can solve the problem, the problem-maintenance structure for that problem has been resolved, and therapy stops or moves on to other presenting problems. The therapy goes just as far into the problem-maintenance space as necessary to resolve the presenting problem.

Problem-centered therapy offers managed care a framework for responsible and comprehensive therapy. Care managers should encourage therapists to try the higher orientations and more interpersonal contexts listed in the matrix in Figure 2.1 before proceeding to the more expensive and historically focused orientations and the less interpersonal contexts. If the more interpersonal and more cost-effective intervention succeeds, the therapy is over. If it is not successful, the next most effective and inclusive intervention can be tried. If that works, therapy terminates. If it does not, therapy progresses to the next lower treatment in the matrix. With this model, no patients have to be abandoned psychotherapeutically before their presenting problem can be resolved, and therapy lasts just as long as necessary.

Finally, the definition of the therapist system includes the care manager as a member of the indirect therapist system. The therapist and the care manager are part of the same team and need to work as allies to help the patient system. Their collaboration is essential to effective care-managed psychotherapy.

INTEGRATION SUMMARY

This chapter had four objectives. The first was to delineate the major orientations and contexts in problem-centered therapy. The second was to present the underlying theoretical components of problem-centered therapy: interactive constructivism, systems theory, and mutual causality. The third objective was to identify the primary principle of application in problem-centered therapy: the progression from the interpersonal and the here and now to the intrapsychic and historical. The last objective was to link the orientations and the progression to cost-effectiveness and to delineate the implications for managed care.

CHAPTER 3

The Therapeutic Alliance

THERAPY IS the interaction between the therapist system and the patient system. The relationship between the therapist and patient systems critically determines the process and outcome of treatment. The therapeutic alliance, a component of that relationship, plays a crucial role within problem-centered therapy. This chapter delineates the nature, role, and progressive unfolding of the therapeutic alliance over the course of therapy.

THE PRINCIPLE OF APPLICATION AND
THE THERAPEUTIC ALLIANCE

The problem-centered principle of application recommends progressive shifts in the structure and focus of therapy in the face of the patient system's failure to resolve presenting problems. As a guide to a cost-effective and health-promoting therapy, this principle delineates what is ideal; however, it is not sufficient. It must be tempered and at times even superseded by the therapist's understanding and management of the therapeutic alliance. The application progression should never be rigidly implemented independently of the alliance.

To illustrate, if the mother of a 5-year-old "unmanageable" boy insists that he be seen individually, rather than in the context of the family, creating an adequate alliance with her may require that the therapist see the child individually or arrange for another therapist, perhaps a child psychiatrist, to see the child. If the moderately paranoid husband in a highly conflictual couple feels blamed to the point of discontinuing marital therapy by the therapist's attempts to focus on his family of origin, the therapist should focus primarily on the here and now or on the history of the couple. *Maintaining the alliance between the therapist and the patient system takes priority over principles of application.*

The alliance priority applies until the compromise neutralizes the treatment. When sacrificing the principle of application in the service of the alliance reaches the point at which change is no longer possible, the therapist should either begin the process of termination, without demeaning or blaming the patients, or empathically insist on sufficient implementation of the application principle to make treatment viable. However, the therapist should work hard and creatively to avoid such a confrontation and use it only as a last resort.

THE THERAPEUTIC RELATIONSHIP AND THE THERAPEUTIC ALLIANCE

The relationship between the therapist and patient systems consists of the feelings, thoughts, and response predispositions that the members of the therapist and patient systems have toward each other (Pinsof & Catherall, 1986). The relationship includes everything that exists between the two systems, from feelings of sexual attraction or a sense of ethnic or racial identification to feelings of trust and respect. It begins, like the therapy, with the first contact between the therapist and the organizing family member, usually over the phone.

The therapeutic alliance constitutes the clinically relevant part of the relationship between the therapist and patient systems. The alliance "consists of those aspects of the relationship between and within the therapist and patient systems that pertain to their capacity to mutually invest in and collaborate on the tasks and goals of the therapy" (Pinsof, 1994b, p. 176). The two critical components of the alliance are the psychological *investment* that each system brings to the relationship and the capacity of each system to *collaborate* to bring about change within the patient system. The alliance views therapy as a collaborative endeavor, defining the therapist and key patients as players on the same team. The alliance unites the patient and therapist systems to create an inclusive and effective therapy system.

The therapeutic alliance constitutes a necessary condition for successful psychotherapy; however, the alliance does not constitute a sufficient condition for effective treatment. On the part of the therapist, specific perceptual, conceptual, technical, and personal skills are also essential. On the part of the patients, a willingness and capacity to change are necessary. Without an alliance, however, no array of therapist skills and patient capacities can lead to change. The alliance is the vessel within which therapy occurs and creates the necessary context for change.

FLUCTUATIONS IN THE ALLIANCE—THE TEAR AND THE REPAIR

A dynamic phenomenon, the alliance differs from therapeutic system to therapeutic system and changes over the course of therapy within the same system. As therapy progresses, the alliance usually becomes "deeper" and more intense. Different types of therapy and different therapists form different types of alliances with similar patient systems. The alliance varies with the phases of therapy within the same system. An alliance crisis between the patient and therapist systems can occur at any time. Such a crisis tears the alliance and creates a turning point in the relationship between the therapist and patient systems. It either strengthens or destroys the alliance and makes or breaks the therapy.

The Rosenbergs sought family therapy when their 19-year-old son, Charlie, returned from college saying he did not know what he wanted to do with his life. The alliance crisis occurred after the family (Al, Rosalie, Charlie, and Charlie's 13-year-old brother, Mark) had been attending weekly family-therapy sessions for 2 months. The therapist also had seen Charlie individually several times and had episodic conjoint sessions with Al and Rosalie. The sessions with Al and Rosalie touched on, but did not address in any depth, their obvious marital problems. The sessions focused on Charlie. Clearly depressed, Charlie spent long periods of time in his room and made no effort to get a job or take classes at a local college. Al favored getting tough with Charlie, whereas Rosalie felt he needed time and understanding. Al and Rosalie were deadlocked and could not form an effective team to help Charlie, who was deeply triangulated in their marital conflicts and tensions.

In his individual sessions, Charlie articulated fears that his parents' conflictual marriage was about to break up. He spoke of his guilty fantasies of going away to college and abandoning Mark to the "druids"—his parents. He blamed his problems on their "horrible" marriage, for which he ironically felt overwhelmingly responsible. He alternated between believing that his depression derived from the despair he had felt in his family since early childhood, to thinking that if he had been a better son and person, he could have made his parents happy.

Charlie left school because he could not concentrate on his work and had no idea what he wanted to do with his life. He felt bitter and "down." The only energy he manifested was in family sessions, in angry defiance of his father's attempts to motivate him to get a job, call friends, or take a course at the local community college. Charlie refused a psychiatric evaluation for medication, saying, "I'm not crazy and I don't believe in taking any kind of drugs." In an individual session, he confided bitterly to the therapist that "my parents are the people who really need medication."

After 2 months, it became clear to the therapist that Al and Rosalie's marital problems interfered with their capacity to set effective and consistent limits on Charlie. They used him to stabilize their marriage: Al expressed his anger at Charlie instead of dealing directly with his feelings of dissatisfaction with Rosalie, and Rosalie offered the compassion and sensitivity to Charlie that should have gone toward Al. Additionally, Charlie had substantial identity and autonomy problems compounded by a biologically loaded depression.

When Charlie or the therapist brought up the marital problems, the parents denied their seriousness and accused Charlie of evading or minimizing his emotional problems, which was partially true. Eventually the therapist decided that continuing therapy with the Rosenbergs, in the face of their denial of their marital issues, not only was unproductive, but also increased Charlie's frustration to the point that he was becoming more depressed and withdrawn. At this point, the therapist decided to take a risk—to confront the parents and point out the destructive consequences of their failure to address their relationship.

Before the confrontation session, the therapist felt frightened that the confrontation could lead the parents to withdraw angrily from therapy. During the session, she prompted, supported, and seconded Charlie's revelation to his parents of the effect of their marital distress on him and Mark. She also added her professional weight to the confrontation by saying that it was imperative for the mental health of everyone in the family that the parents face at least some of their issues. The prior 2 months of therapy had convinced her that Al and Rosalie would not be able to help Charlie confront his depression and get his life back together unless they faced the marital issues that prevented them from working as a more effective parental system.

The parents left the session angry at the therapist, accusing her of putting ideas in Charlie's head and of not understanding the family. This confrontation tore the fabric of the alliance. Al and Rosalie felt abandoned and accused. Charlie also felt confronted by the therapist's comments about his depression and his need for his parents' help to deal with it. Although he felt moderately irritated, he was also impressed by the therapist's willingness to speak frankly with his parents and to set a limit on her involvement with their destructive behavior.

The anxiety that the therapist experienced before the confrontation and her concern after the confrontation that Al and Rosalie would discontinue treatment are typical therapist experiences when the alliance is about to be torn. In the face of this fear, however, the therapist was convinced that the therapy was going nowhere and that without the confrontation, change was unlikely, if not impossible. She also felt that her alliance with the Rosenbergs was strong enough to tolerate the confrontation. These fears, convictions, and feelings are important if not essential experiential precursors of successful therapist-induced alliance crises.

To the therapist's surprise and relief, the Rosenbergs were early for their next session. Al and Rosalie began by talking about how upset they felt after the last session, commenting that they had even discussed the possibility of discontinuing therapy. Three days after the confrontation session, Charlie got wind of this; he told his parents that if they quit therapy, it would mean that they did not care about him, Mark, or ultimately themselves. After thinking it over and having some uncharacteristically frank discussions between themselves, Al and Rosalie decided that the therapist was right and that they were willing to try to change their marriage and the way they triangulated Charlie into it. They knew their relationship was extremely troubled and they feared divorce, but they felt that the consequences of avoiding the subject, which they had begun to see over the last several months, were too high a price to pay. Charlie was somewhat stunned and frightened by his parents' turnaround, but he felt hope for his family and himself for the first time in many months. Mark expressed relief that finally his parents might get help and that Charlie might get better.

This vignette illustrates an alliance tear and repair episode stimulated by a therapist's planned confrontation. Tears occur in many ways. The most common disruptions derive from unintended and ethical therapist failures, such as misunderstandings, logistical or scheduling errors, and failures to know something patients expect the therapist to know. *After such tears, the therapist should relate empathically to the patients' experience of the disruption. Defensive behavior deepens the tear and diminishes the likelihood of repair.*

Bordin (1980) hypothesized that in individual therapy, the most successful cases involve at least one alliance tear and repair episode. Cases in which tears never occur are not as powerful therapeutically. For Bordin, the tested and repaired alliance is stronger than the untested one. Bordin's theory resembles Kohut's (1984) concepts of optimal frustration and progressive de-idealization.

Kohut asserted that the therapist's small and manageable failures to gratify and live up to the idealized expectations of the patient create self structure, particularly when the therapist acknowledges and empathizes with the patient's experience of the therapist's "failure."

Clearly, together with the possibility of increased benefit is the risk of premature termination. Alliance disruptions may be too large and irreparable for various reasons, some of which may pertain more to the patient and others more to the therapist. Patients may be too narcissistically vulnerable to handle the disappointment and may reject treatment. The therapist's response after the disruption may not be sufficiently empathic with the patients' experience, exacerbating the tear and undermining treatment. Finally, the therapist's failure may be so grossly inappropriate and disruptive that patient flight becomes a healthy and adaptive response in the face of the therapist's unethical, unprofessional, or incompetent behavior.

Usually the alliance is torn at some point in any extended therapy, regardless of therapist intent or expertise. Tears are inevitable. Almost every therapy contains episodes in which the patients feel misunderstood or disappointed by the therapist. Alliance tears do not need to be created and should not be created just for the purpose of creating an alliance disruption. As with the Rosenbergs, the only rationale for intentionally tearing the alliance occurs when the therapy cannot progress otherwise. Even in such a case, the confrontation needs to be done with sensitivity.

A CLINICAL–THEORETICAL MODEL OF THE ALLIANCE

Since the mid-1970s, the concept of the therapeutic or working alliance has experienced a resurgence of interest within the psychotherapy research community. A number of research groups throughout North America developed scales to measure the alliance in individual therapy and, more recently, in family and marital therapy (Greenberg & Pinsof, 1986; Horvath & Greenberg, 1994). These groups have had surprisingly encouraging results with their various indices of the alliance, consistently finding positive correlations between their measures and patient outcomes. Much of the early thinking and instrument development of these groups were spurred by Bordin's alliance theory (1979).

Most alliance theory derives from individual therapy and views the alliance as a phenomenon between the therapist and the patient. However, once the theorist enters the integrative domain and views therapy as the interaction between patient and therapist systems (Pinsof, 1989), the notion of the therapeutic alliance must be expanded. The systems perspective asserts that regardless of the number of people directly involved in therapy, the therapeutic alliance exists simultaneously on multiple levels between and within the patient and therapist systems.

For problem-centered therapy, the alliance embodies two primary dimensions (Pinsof, 1994b). The *interpersonal system dimension* focuses on four levels and loci of the alliance between and within the therapist and patient systems. The *content dimension* addresses three qualities of the alliance that cut across the four interpersonal dimensions. Figure 3.1 graphically depicts this 3 × 4 model of the *integrative systems alliance*.

THE INTERPERSONAL SYSTEM DIMENSION

The interpersonal system dimension of the alliance contains four dimensions. The first three interpersonal dimensions in Figure 3.1, the top three rows, address three increasingly inclusive levels of the alliance between the patient and therapist systems. The fourth dimension, the last row in Figure 3.1, does

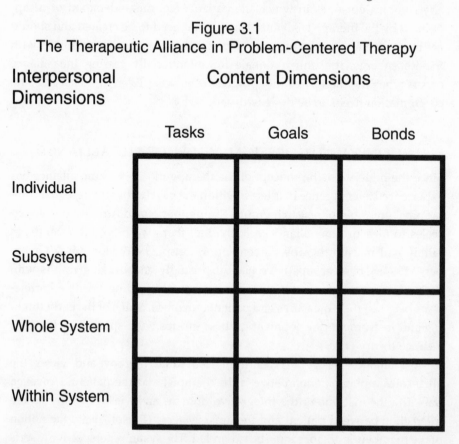

Figure 3.1
The Therapeutic Alliance in Problem-Centered Therapy

not target a level but focuses instead on a different locus of the alliance. It addresses the alliances within the therapist system and the patient system, rather than the alliance between them.

The systemically lowest alliance level, the top row in Figure 3.1, occurs between the individual members of the therapist and patient systems—the *individual alliance*. With the Rosenbergs, the therapist had individual alliances with each of the four members of the direct system. The therapist and other subsystems of the therapist system (the supervisor or supervisory team, consultants, receptionists, and administrators) also have alliances with various subsystems (such as parents, siblings, or school personnel) within the patient system. These constitute the next level, depicted in the second row of the figure, the *subsystemic alliances*. The therapist has a subsystemic alliance with Al and Rosalie as the parents and another subsystemic alliance with Charlie and Mark. Rosalie's mother and father have been supportive of the therapy and, as members of the indirect patient system, have an alliance with the therapist. The alliance between the therapist system and the patient system constitutes the highest level, depicted in the third row, the *whole-system alliance*. The entire Rosenberg patient system, including extended-family members, has an alliance with the therapist that is more than the sum of their individual and subsystemic alliances.

The *within-system alliances*, depicted in the fourth row of Figure 3.1, pertain to the alliances between the individuals and subsystems within the patient system and within the therapist system. They address the extent to which Al and Rosalie are allied with each other concerning the therapy. In regard to the therapist system, within-system alliances address the alliance between the therapist and supervisor or the alliances between the members of a therapeutic team. When therapy occurs under managed care, the alliance between the care manager and the therapist constitutes a critical determinant of the success of the therapy. Finally, when different therapists work with different subsystems of the same patient system, the within-system alliance between them can play a decisive role in the outcome of the therapy.

Each alliance level and locus influences, through mutual causality, every other level and locus. These levels and loci together constitute a system—the *total alliance*. However, differential causality asserts that some levels of the alliance may play a more critical role than others in determining the strength of the total alliance. In some cases, individual alliances may account for most of the variance within the total alliance. Of all the alliances in the Butler case, probably the most critical is the alliance between the therapist and Loretta. In other cases, subsystemic alliances may predominate. With the Rosenbergs, the alliance with the marital subsystem, Al and Rosalie, most critically determines the total alliance.

The key determinant of which subsystems contribute most to the variance in the total alliance is the amount of power the subsystems have to facilitate adaptive changes within the patient and therapist systems. That person or subsystem may be part of the direct or indirect system. For instance, Moises and Lupe Portillo, a Mexican-American couple, are in therapy with their 6-year-old son, Tomas, who has recently been extraordinarily aggressive at school and with his friends. The Portillos live in the top apartment in a two-flat building in Chicago. Lupe's parents live in the bottom apartment and provide most of the child care in the afternoon and early evening for Tomas. They have noticed his recent aggressiveness, came in for the first session, and are mildly supportive of the therapy. They do not speak much English and were not enthusiastic about coming in again with Moises, Lupe, and Tomas. The grandparents play a critical role in Tomas's life, as well as in the lives of Moises and Lupe. If the grandparents do not support the therapy and the changes it might bring about in their lives, they can undermine it.

THE SPLIT ALLIANCE

Conceptualizing therapy, regardless of context, as the interaction of patient and therapist systems opens a new possibility—that of the split alliance. A familiar peril for family therapists, this phenomenon occurs when the therapist has a positive alliance with one subsystem and a negative alliance with another subsystem of the same patient system. With some split alliances, therapy can still be viable, whereas with others, therapy cannot proceed. There are two critical determinants of therapeutic viability with split alliances. The first is the relative power of the subsystems with which the therapist has the split alliance. The second is the relative strength or intensity of the alliance with each of the relevant subsystems.

In terms of subsystemic power, the positive alliance must be with the stronger, or more powerful, subsystem of the patient system. If it is with the weaker subsystem, therapy is not viable. For instance, with the Portillos, if the therapist has a strong alliance with Tomas and a poor alliance with his parents or his grandparents, therapy will not work. The grandparents have the power to undermine the therapy, and Moises and Lupe have the power to discontinue the therapy altogether.

Subsystemic power is usually a function of age, economic resources and control, and psychological influence. Parents usually are more powerful than children in maintaining the therapeutic alliance; however, there are exceptions. Ruth and Ed Samuels, both in their late 40s, were required to seek marital therapy by their three children, who ranged in age from 10 to 19. The children were annoyed with their parents' continual bickering and decided to confront them with a constructive ultimatum: to get into therapy or the children would move out of the house and go to live with a maternal aunt. The aunt supported the children's ultimatum, adding weight to their confrontation. The children, at their insistence, attended the first therapy session with their parents and moved into the indirect system thereafter. Their alliance with the therapist constituted the barrier that kept their parents in treatment long enough for the parents' involvement to become self-sustaining.

The principle of ensuring the viability of the alliance with the most powerful subsystems in the patient system should not be used to justify a lack of concern about the alliance with weaker subsystems. The ideal goal is positive alliances with all subsystems on all levels. However, in rare circumstances when split alliances present the therapist with Solomonic decisions, the therapist should ally primarily with the more powerful subsystem, attempting simultaneously to maintain as positive an alliance as possible with the weaker subsystem. This guideline applies even when the therapist is in greater agreement with the weaker subsystem, unless, of course, allying primarily with the more powerful subsystem endangers the weaker subsystem or fundamentally compromises the therapy.

Split alliances become particularly problematic when they involve two equally powerful subsystems or individuals within the same patient system. This situation highlights the second determinant of therapeutic viability with split alliances: the relative strength of the negative and positive alliances. The negative–positive distinction is a continuum, not a dichotomy. With two equally powerful subsystems, the overall alliance can still be viable if the negative alliance is not stronger than the positive alliance. If the strength of the negative alliance exceeds that of the positive alliance, the total alliance deteriorates to the point that therapy cannot be effective.

Larry and Charlotte Roty were in couple therapy for 10 weeks at a university clinic. Married for 4 years with a 2-year-old daughter, they were both graduate students in molecular biology. They entered couple therapy because Charlotte recently had a brief affair with a professor, her research mentor. Their therapist was a second-year female graduate student in clinical psychology specializing in family and marital therapy. She was not married but lived with her boyfriend.

From the beginning of therapy, Larry had an extremely difficult time believing that the therapist could empathize with his feelings of outrage and humiliation. He sensed that the therapist sympathized with Charlotte. He also felt that because the therapist had never been married and had no children, she did not intuitively grasp his commitment to marriage, fidelity, and monogamy. He discussed these feelings with Charlotte but was reluctant to bring them up directly with the therapist.

Charlotte felt quite comfortable with the therapist. She also believed that the therapist understood Larry's pain and commitment. She worked with Larry between sessions, encouraging him not to quit therapy and urging him to talk about his feelings with the therapist. The therapist sensed that something was not right with her alliance with Larry, but every time she brought it up, Larry would say, "No, everything is fine between you and me. I just can't get over what Charlotte has done." Eventually, with Charlotte's insistence, Larry brought up his negative feelings. The therapist was able to hear, acknowledge, and empathize with his experience. In fact, she talked about her own desire for a monogamous marriage and her own belief in the importance of fidelity. Larry felt greatly relieved and subsequently was able to engage more openly and actively in the therapy.

Charlotte's strong alliance with the therapist contained and neutralized Larry's weak alliance. Eventually, the strength of Charlotte's alliance became the stimulus for Larry to express his concerns and develop a more positive alliance with the therapist. This vignette shows that a split alliance does not necessarily weaken a therapy to the point of rupture.

Split alliances are complicated, ubiquitous, and problematic. They require the therapist to monitor and evaluate the alliance continually with each individual and subsystem as well as with the whole patient system. Specifically, the therapist needs to monitor shifts in the relative power of the key members and subsystems within the patient system, as well as shifts in the relative strength of the various alliances within the alliance network with each patient system. These ongoing assessments delineate the alliance guidelines within which the principles of application can be employed with any particular system. They set the relational parameters of the therapy.

THE CONTENT DIMENSION

Bordin's (1979) tripartite concept of the therapeutic alliance provides the conceptual underpinning for the content dimension of the alliance (Pinsof, 1994b; Pinsof & Catherall, 1986). Building on Bordin's theory, the three primary content dimensions are labeled tasks, goals, and bonds.

TASKS

The tasks dimension addresses the major activities, or tasks, that the patient and therapist systems engage in over the course of therapy. Specifically, it refers to the extent to which the patients find the task requirements of the therapy comfortable and consistent with their expectations. If a patient expects to have a conversation with the therapist and the therapist seldom says anything, the therapist's behavior is not consistent with the patient's expectations of therapy. The patient expects a dialogue, and the therapist expects the patient to talk with minimal therapist feedback. The tasks component of the alliance would be relatively low in this situation.

The comfort component refers to the degree of comfort or anxiety that the patients experience in relation to the task requirements of therapy. For instance, a therapist might strongly encourage Louise, a 17-year-old hospitalized for a suicide attempt, to tell her older siblings and parents that her uncle sexually abused her from the age of 10 to 14. If Louise is too frightened to engage in this task, however, fearing that it might destroy the vestige of a family that she has left, Louise and her therapist will be in conflict. The therapist's task expectations exceed Louise's comfort threshold. Even if Louise thinks telling her siblings and parents is theoretically a good idea, even if her task expectations are congruent with the therapist's, emotionally the task is beyond her at this point. If the therapist insists that she engage in this task, the tasks component of the alliance will be severely jeopardized.

GOALS

The second major dimension of the alliance, goals, refers to the extent to which the patients experience the therapist as working with them on the problems for which they are seeking help. Is the therapist trying to help them achieve their goals for therapy, or is the therapist focusing the therapy on goals that do not address their concerns? For instance, the Rosenbergs sought therapy for Charlie's depression and to get him back on some kind of appropriate developmental course—working and possibly living independently. Improving their troubled marriage was not a goal. Focusing prematurely on their marital problems would have severely diminished their alliance and jeopardized the therapy.

The problem-centered approach maximizes the likelihood that the therapist will be aligned with the patient system on the goals dimension. At least one goal statement exists within every presenting problem. Teasing out the specific goals implicit in the presenting problems helps the therapist better understand their specific meaning for the patient system. Because every goal also embodies specific objectives, fleshing out the goals facilitates the delineation of specific and shared objectives for therapy.

From a goals perspective, the problem-centered linkage of presenting and secondary, or nonpresenting, problems means that if they are going to be pursued, therapist-identified goals must be linked to the patient system's goals. The Rosenbergs' therapist eventually had to link her concern about their marital problems to their inability to function as a unified team to help Charlie. Her goal becomes theirs insofar as they perceive its achievement as a necessary step to achieve their primary goal.

Goals are particularly critical in regard to within-system alliances. For instance, Arnie O'Brian came to therapy to separate from his wife, whereas his wife, Peggy, came to therapy to save their marriage. Arnie and Peggy are not allied on the goal dimension. The critical task for the therapist is to help the O'Brians find a common goal. The risk is that the therapist might side with one or the other in such a way as to create a split alliance that negates the therapy. With the O'Brians, the first task is to help them find a problem they can agree about, and then to help them address it. They both agree that the future of their relationship is uncertain, and they both would like to find some way to reduce that uncertainty. Their alliance with each other may have to be built around certain problems and goals, while other goals are left at least temporarily unresolved.

BONDS

The third subdimension of the content dimension, bonds, addresses the affective quality of the alliance and includes aspects of the patient–therapist relationship like trust, caring, and involvement. The dimension of bonds covers the extent to which the therapist becomes a meaningful and charged emotional object for the patients, as well as the patients' felt sense that the therapist is committed to and cares about them.

What some psychoanalysts refer to as transference falls within the category of bonds (Freud, 1912; Gill, 1982; Kohut, 1971). From an alliance perspective, transference pertains to those aspects of the patients' experience of the therapist that are primarily determined by experiences in "other" past and current relationships, particularly intimate relationships with parents, siblings, spouses, and children. Transference does not encompass all aspects of the bonds subdimension, but particularly captures aspects of deep meaning—the evolving sense of what the therapist means as an intimate psychological object for the patients over the course of therapy.

Transferences can strengthen or destroy therapeutic alliances. A powerful negative transference can destroy an alliance with adequate task and goal components, whereas a strong positive transference can overcome an alliance with inadequate task and goal components. The development and elaboration of the transferences constitute key elements of the process of problem-centered therapy and are addressed in detail later in the chapter in the section on the progressive bonding process.

ALLIANCE PROFILES

Every case has a unique alliance profile that usually changes over the course of therapy. The two alliance dimensions presented previously provide a useful framework for conceptualizing different profiles.

INTERPERSONAL PROFILES

As discussed earlier, alliance systems may be whole or split, and if they are split, they may range from disastrously fragmented to mildly fractious. Beyond splits, there are other interpersonal profiles that can be elaborated, such as the individual and whole-system profiles. In the individual profile, individual patients experience the therapist as positively allied with them as individuals but not as a group or family. The reverse configuration pertains to the whole-system profile, in which the patients experience the therapist as more allied with their relationship than with them as individuals. With the whole-system profile in couple therapy, the patients might feel that the therapist cares more about saving their marriage than about helping them as individuals. In contrast, with the individual profile, the patients might feel that the therapist cares more about helping each of them find the right path for themselves than saving the marriage.

The critical question is, What kind of interpersonal dimension profile is best with what kind of system, problem, and problem-maintenance structure at what point in treatment? For instance, the whole-system profile might help stabilize certain polarizing couples during crises, whereas the individual profile might help open up constricted couples who are terrified of conflict and differentiation. In contrast, the whole-system alliance profile might "turn off" a more differentiated couple, or the individual profile might increase the alienation of a disengaging couple. The issue is what kind of alliance to promote in what context.

Content Profiles

The triadic structure of the content dimension also provides a framework for conceptualizing and identifying different types of therapeutic alliances. The task–goal alliance is high on tasks and goals but relatively low on bonds. In this alliance, patients feel comfortable with the task demands of the therapy and believe that the therapist is committed to helping them achieve their goals. With this type of alliance however, the patients may not feel a high level of trust in the therapist and might not experience the therapist as caring about them personally. This task–goal alliance typifies the early stages of a viable therapy in a clinic setting in which patients are assigned a competent therapist they did not know previously. In general, the task–goal alliance is more common in the behavioral and biobehavioral orientations.

In contrast, the bonds alliance is of course high on bonds and relatively low on tasks and goals. In this type of alliance, the patients have high levels of trust and confidence in the therapist but may feel moderately threatened by the task demands of the treatment and their sense that the therapist wants to work on issues and goals beyond the presenting problems. The bonds alliance is more common in the experiential, family-of-origin, psychodynamic, and self psychological orientations.

The bonds alliance is usually more common in private-practice settings with a high-profile therapist whom the patients have sought out and to whom they are willing to extend considerable benefit of the doubt. Even though they sense that the therapist has a different agenda and is asking them to do things that make them uncomfortable, their belief that the therapist is competent allows them to suspend their discomfort and invest in the treatment. Their confidence and trust in the therapist overcomes their unease with the task and goal components.

Seeking help for their troubled marriage, Tom and Lois Winter called a highly renowned family therapist in their hometown in August. He had been recommended by their family doctor, their minister, and close friends who had been in therapy with him several years before. The therapist had no openings in his practice at that time and referred them to a colleague. Tom and Lois decided to wait until the therapist had an opening. They finally entered therapy in mid-October.

Neither Lois nor Tom had ever been in therapy before. Tom was extremely practical and wanted advice and guidance. Lois felt that Tom was out of touch with her, his feelings, and their children. In the second session, the therapist asked them about their sexual relationship. Tom wisecracked, "What is this, sex therapy?" The therapist did not relent, but in fact reiterated his question and explained that information about their sexual and intimate relationship could help him understand them better and could expedite the therapy. Tom looked uncomfortable and replied, "Sex is fine—no problems." The therapist did not challenge this assertion.

On the way home, Tom told Lois that he did not understand why the therapist asked about their sexual relationship. He was not interested in disclosing intimate details of their sex life with a stranger in this therapy; he wanted to fix the marriage and get on with their lives. He did not want to end up like his sister-in-law, Janet, who loved to disclose intimate details of her life to everyone and had been in and out of different kinds of therapy for much of her adult life.

Without Lois's intervention, Tom proceeded to challenge his own doubts, commenting that if their minister thought this therapist was so great and if he had been able to help their friends who had been on the brink of divorce, he must have something going for him. Tom decided to continue in treatment and suspend his unease as much as he could. He even began to bring up their sex life in therapy, without going into any intimate details. Four sessions later, however, he came into therapy and brought up the issue of his sexual frustration with Lois. He expressed his fears that she might feel hurt by what he had to say. Lois reassured him that she wanted to hear and could handle whatever he needed to say. Tom began to talk about the lack of spontaneity and creativity in their lovemaking, and Lois responded that she too felt frustrated by that but was afraid saying so would hurt his feelings.

The content profile of the therapeutic alliance tends to change over the course of therapy. The most common change in a "good" therapy is a progressive deepening of the bond component of the alliance. Shorter term therapies tend to involve more task–goal alliances, and longer term therapies, more bond alliances. In general, the more psychosocially and psychodynamically invasive the therapy, the greater the need for a strong bond component.

The delineation of alliance profiles in relationship to different types of patient systems at different points in therapy is barely in its infancy. Research has just begun to take a complex and differentiating look at the different types of alliances that therapists form with different types of systems and the extent to which different types of alliances facilitate or impede therapy. Clearly, the interpersonal profiles interact with the content profiles to yield a complex framework for studying different types of alliances. The specific alliance profiles mentioned here represent just a few of the possible configurations.

THE INSTITUTIONAL ALLIANCE

Because the alliance occurs and evolves in the interaction between the therapist and patient systems, patients have an alliance not only with their therapist but also with the system of which the therapist is a part. Frequently the systemic or institutional alliance plays a critical role in facilitating treatment.

Elmer and Eileen Bancroft were in their late 60s. After 44 years of marriage, Elmer began to have some problems with episodic impotence. Through much of their life in Chicago, they had various contacts with the hospitals at the University of Chicago. Even though Elmer had never gone to college, he respected universities, and he felt that the University of Chicago was one of the finest, if not *the* finest, university in the United States. He had even managed to select health insurance policies that he knew would include services at the university hospitals.

Eileen called and made an appointment for Elmer and herself at the sexual dysfunction clinic at the university. Elmer had never spoken explicitly with anyone about sex, including Eileen. During their first session with their sex therapist, who happened to be a woman in her early 30s, Elmer was agitated and inarticulate. Not only shy about sex, Elmer was also extremely embarrassed about his episodes of impotence. Furthermore, talking to a relatively young woman therapist about sex added extra anxiety to the whole experience. He could hardly reply to the therapist's questions about his sexual experience and problems. Nevertheless, he struggled to answer her questions and overcome his embarrassment and shyness. After the session, Elmer's only comment to Eileen was that they must know what they are doing at the University of Chicago and therefore he would go along with the treatment despite his discomfort and doubts.

This example illustrates how an institutional bond can provide a sufficient alliance for a therapy in which the required patient tasks frighten and embarrass one or more key members of the patient system. It also illustrates how the institutional bond can even compensate for a weak or problematic bond with the therapist. The imprimatur of the university on the young female therapist sufficiently neutralized Elmer's fear and doubts so that he could continue in treatment.

THE PROGRESSIVE BONDING PROCESS

The problem-centered principle of application entails a shift not only in the temporal focus and topic of the therapy, but also in the nature of the therapeutic alliance. It involves the progressive deepening and elaboration of the bonds component of the alliance. The alliance and bond required to work on historical intrapsychic issues with an individual differs from what is required to work with that individual in a family context on fairly direct and simple behavioral tasks. Diagnostically, the critical alliance question becomes, What are the necessary alliance requirements to engage in particular types of therapeutic tasks with particular types of patient systems with particular problem-maintenance structures at particular points in treatment?

This progression also requires a shift in the quality of the within-system alliance between the key patients. As the bond between the therapist and each patient deepens, the relative intensity of the bonds between the patients diminishes, at least in therapy, if not at home. The progression makes the therapist an increasingly important self object to the key patients. Concomitantly, but not commensurately, the patients become relatively less important to each other as self objects when they are with the therapist. As therapy progresses into later stages and, eventually, termination, this relational progression reverses: The therapist becomes progressively less important and the patients more important to each other. The patient system is restored, one would hope with a more adaptive affective structure and improved problem-solving capacity. This progression reflects the process by which the therapist enters, becomes part of, and eventually leaves the affective patient system.

The fullest conceivable alliance progression is depicted in Figure 3.2 in a series of hypothetical relational structures between the therapist and two patients. Although two patients are used to illustrate the relational dynamics, the progression of structures does not solely apply in couple therapy; it applies in all therapies. A patient dyad is used as opposed to a triad or four patients for ease of illustration. The theory reflected in Figure 3.2 applies to any problem-related relational structure.

The full relational progression depicted in Figure 3.2 is not an ideal progression. It is the progression of relational structures required in treating patient systems with the deepest and most complex problem-maintenance structures. The simpler and more superficial the problem-maintenance structure, the fewer the stages or structures that need to be traversed. The full progression is presented to illustrate all of the relational structures that could be required in treatment. How far into the progression any therapy

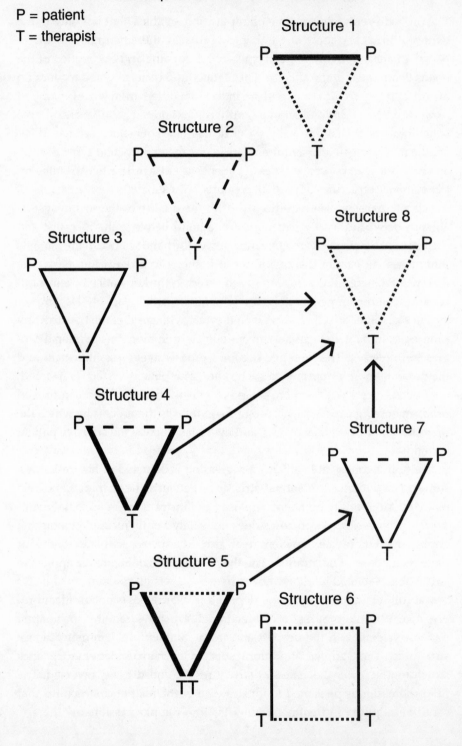

Figure 3.2
The Progressive Bonding Process in Problem-Centered Therapy:
The Sequence of Relational Structures

P = patient
T = therapist

Structure 1

Structure 2

Structure 8

Structure 3

Structure 4

Structure 7

Structure 5

Structure 6

system needs to go depends on the depth and complexity of the problem-maintenance structure.

Although presented as discrete structures within a progressive stage sequence, the actual structural progression within therapy is usually experienced as a seamless process. The only major experiential discontinuities occur within the later structures, when the intervention context shifts from conjoint to individual.

FACILITATING THE PROGRESSION

There are four primary tools that the therapist can use to facilitate this relational progression. These tools, or procedures, derive primarily from psychoanalytic theory and technique. The first is the *relational focus* of the therapy. Explicitly increasing the focus on the patients' individual and collective experiences of the therapist tends to make the therapist more salient and important psychologically (Gill, 1982). It explicitly defines the relationship between the patients and the therapist as an important vehicle or component of the therapy.

The second tool is the *frequency of the sessions*. Increasing the frequency of the sessions tends to strengthen and deepen the bond between the patients and the therapist; it intensifies the therapy and increases psychological and, ultimately, therapeutic dependence on the therapist.

Shifting the context of the therapy is the third tool. Systematically decreasing the number of people in the direct patient system frequently increases the bond between the therapist and the patients. Ultimately, seeing a key patient individually and often over an extended time period is the surest way to increase and strengthen the therapeutic bond. It defines the therapist structurally as being there for the patient, as the patient's ally in therapy.

The fourth tool hardly deserves to be called a tool. It is *time*. Some patients, no matter the frequency, focus, and context of therapy, will not allow the therapist to become a self object until they have spent a substantial amount of time with the therapist. They need to go through several tearing and repairing episodes and repeatedly disconfirm their fears about trusting the therapist. Only the passing of months, and in some cases years, will facilitate the development of the bond.

These tools for facilitating the deepening of the therapeutic bond tend to be used in the sequence presented. They are the mechanisms that the therapist can employ to move the therapeutic system through the sequence of structures delineated in Figure 3.2. Of course, they must be used empathically and sensitively, to avoid jeopardizing the task dimension of the alliance.

STAGES AND RELATIONAL STRUCTURES

The eight structures depicted in Figure 3.2, corresponding to stages of therapy, fall into two broad categories. Stages 1 through 6 constitute a deepening sequence. As therapy moves through these structures, sessions become more frequent, intrapsychically focused, and individual. The bond to the therapist becomes progressively more intense, and the therapist becomes a major player in the emotional system. Concomitantly, the bonds between the patients become less intense, and the patient system is therapeutically disengaged.

Stages 7 and 8 constitute a reconnecting and surfacing sequence. In these stages, the patient system is put back together, and the therapist becomes increasingly peripheral. These are the terminating structures. As indicated by the arrows in Figure 3.2, the terminating structures can be accessed from different points in the deepening sequence. For instance, Structure 8, the last stage of therapy, resembles Structures 1 and 2 and can be accessed directly from Structures 3 and 4. Therapy has not gotten so deep that more than one termination stage and structure is required.

In contrast, if therapy progresses as far as Structure 5, the termination and surfacing process ideally requires two stages—7 and 8. To progress from 5 to 8 would be too abrupt and would not do justice to the intensity of the patient–therapist alliance developed in Stage 5. If therapy gets to Stage 5, Stage 7 is a necessary transition to the final structure—8.

Stage 6 is somewhat anomalous. In this stage, all of the key patient-system members typically have their own therapists and are primarily engaged in relatively intensive individual therapy. Commonly, Structures 7 and 8 do not follow 6 because the individual treatments take on an independent life of their own. The conjoint aspects of treatment frequently terminate before the individual therapies end if treatment has progressed to Structure 6. Consequently, the individual therapies may not be followed by a surfacing sequence. This is particularly the case when the patients are fairly stable and accepting of the changes that derive from the individual therapies.

THE DEEPENING SEQUENCE

Within *Structure 1*, the first stage of the bonding process, patients are seen primarily conjointly. Sessions during this stage seldom occur more frequently than once a week. Stage 1 structure characterizes the early stages of therapy or of the relational dynamics in brief family and marital therapy. It usually involves task- or goal-type alliances. In this alliance, the primary affective bond is between the patients. They are only minimally related to the therapist, who seldom becomes significant emotionally. In self psychological terms, the therapist does not function as a self object for the patients. During this stage, the therapist is viewed more as a technician than a person. This structure is usually sufficient to facilitate problem solving with healthy patient systems with relatively superficial problem-maintenance structures and characterizes interpersonal work in the behavioral and biobehavioral orientations. Few if any exchanges during this stage explicitly address the patient–therapist relationship.

In *Structure 2* the patients are still highly charged self objects for each other, but the therapist becomes more salient affectively. Patients are still seen primarily in a conjoint structure with weekly sessions. However, each patient relates more to the therapist and may even begin to direct some needs, concerns, and fantasies toward the therapist. In this structure, patients typically care whether the therapist understands them and their concerns and may also be interested in the therapist's approval and support. The bond component of the alliance begins to be relevant. This structure is usually necessary to work experientially and affectively with couples and families. Some of the therapeutic conversation within this stage begins to address the patients' relationship with the therapist.

Although the therapy is still primarily conjoint, the bond between the therapist and the patients begins to approximate the bond between the patients in the third stage, in *Structure 3*. The therapist becomes a self object for the key patients, capable of containing and reducing anxiety. Within this structure, the bonds component of the alliance becomes at least as important as, if not more important than, tasks and goals. Although the connection to the therapist is stronger in this structure, the patients still function actively as self objects for each other. Structure 3 is usually necessary to begin work on the historical orientations of the orientation–context matrix. To engage in meaningful family-of-origin work or to open up historical issues and wounds requires a significant degree of trust and comfort in the relationship with the therapist. Structure 3 provides the necessary relational context to work successfully with systems presenting moderately complex and deep problem-maintenance structures. This structure involves a balanced focus on the relationship between the patients and each of their relationships with the therapist. Often the frequency of sessions within this stage and structure increases to three every 2 weeks or two per week.

The big change in *Structure 4* is that the salience of the relationships between the family members begins to dim in contrast to the power and intensity of the relationships to the therapist. Much of the work is still done conjointly (in the presence of the relevant other), but the focus of the work is on the individuals and their object relations. The exploration of the therapist as a significant transference object becomes relevant and useful within this structure. The therapist is used as a mirroring, idealizing, or twinning (sibling) self object for the key patients. Structure 4 is usually necessary to work effectively on individual, psychodynamic issues within a conjoint context. In this fourth stage, sessions typically occur twice a week.

In the fifth stage, the emergence of *Structure 5* is associated with a shift to individual intervention contexts. Key patients who play central roles in preventing the system from solving its presenting problems are seen individually. It may be a husband in couple treatment who has been unable to reliably sustain intimate contact with his wife or a mother who cannot empathize with and manage her 14-year-old disabled daughter.

Within this structure, the relationship between the patient and therapist becomes the central relationship; it becomes the charged emotional context. During this stage, therapy resembles relatively intensive psychodynamically oriented psychotherapy. The only difference is that the individual sessions may be interspersed with occasional conjoint sessions.

Frequently, the therapist in Structure 5 maintains intense individual relationships with multiple family members. For instance, the therapist may see each partner in several individual sessions punctuated by occasional conjoint sessions. Alternatively, the therapist may see a single parent and his or her adolescent child each in individual sessions. The focus of these sessions is on the here-and-now transference between the therapist and the patient; on significant historical relationships in the patient's life; or on the patient's experience of and role within problematic day-to-day interactions. Significant others are only of moderate concern. The self-object transferences mentioned in the discussion of Structure 4 become even more intense. The psychological demands on the therapist to fulfill narcissistic functions for the patients increase significantly.

Structure 5 is undoubtedly the most demanding and complex relational structure for therapists to manage. It requires considerable skill on the part of the therapist to conduct concurrent individual therapies with members of the same patient system, interspersing them as needed with conjoint sessions. The therapist needs extensive psychodynamic and interpersonal skills.

A key issue that can be thought of as a fifth tool for intensifying the therapeutic bond becomes pertinent in Structure 5. That tool is *confidentiality*. Typically, up to this point in the therapeutic progression, most problem-centered therapists operate with a no-confidentiality contract. Whatever one member of the patient system says to the therapist is potentially accessible to other appropriate and relevant members of the patient system. This no-confidentiality contract protects the therapist and the family against pathological attempts to triangulate and neutralize the therapist's effectiveness.

Coupled with the movement to predominantly individual sessions, instituting a confidentiality contract intensifies the therapeutic bond. It draws a stronger and more distinct boundary around the relationship and creates a more unique bond with the therapist. It also complicates the therapist's role, particularly when a patient shares information that is potentially hurtful to another member of the patient system with whom the therapist is also working. The critical confidentiality task is to make sure that all of the key patients understand the nature of the therapeutic contract (confidential, nonconfidential, or confidential to a limited extent); understand the rationale for the contract; and accept the contract even if they do not like it. If they do not accept the contract, other options should be explored, such as introducing other therapists into the system. These and other confidentiality issues are addressed in greater detail in Chapter 5.

Structure 6 entails a shift to the exclusively individual treatment of key system members. If the treatment has progressed to this point, it is clear that one or more of the key patients require an intensive, relatively long-term, exclusively individual therapy experience aimed at the core vulnerabilities of the self to permit successful resolution of the presenting problem. With reference to the orientation–context matrix, most of the therapy in Structure 6 occurs in the lower-right cell of the matrix: the self psychology–individual cell.

The same therapist seldom does all of the therapy with the individuals and subsystems of the patient system during this stage. Other, secondary therapists should be introduced. Once the primary therapist enters into the type of therapeutic alliance required in Structure 6, that therapist cannot sustain adequate alliances with the other key patients. The narcissistic transference requirements of the individual will be continually violated by the therapist's involvement with and allegiance to other members of the system. Patients who have gotten this far in the therapeutic progression need their own therapist and their own therapy. They need the protection, intimacy, safety, and intensity of the exclusive, confidential one-to-one relationship.

At this point the primary therapist confronts a choice point—to continue as the system's therapist or to become the individual therapist of one member of the system. The therapist cannot do both. If the primary therapist chooses the individual path, depending on the condition of the patient system, a system therapist may need to be introduced into the therapy system. If the therapist chooses the system path, another therapist should be introduced into the therapy system to conduct the individual treatment.

This decision is usually made with the key patients, who in many circumstances are the final arbiters of the decision. In certain circumstances, it may be easier to find a therapist for one patient than to find a replacement for the primary therapist, who has established viable alliances with all of the key members of the patient system. Alternatively, some patients have such difficulty establishing a trusting therapeutic alliance with a therapist that the idea of entering into an intensive individual treatment with someone else is unacceptable.

Ron Severn, a 46-year-old structural engineer, was in family therapy with his wife, Sherry, and the their two sons, Burt, 14, and Lamont, 9. The major presenting problem was Ron's angry and abusive behavior. He was violent with the children on three occasions and slapped Sherry several times in the year before entering treatment. Ron and his family were frightened that he was losing control of himself, and they sought help. After approximately 12 conjoint sessions, Ron was seen on a regular, individual basis by the therapist at the same time that the therapist saw the whole family and had occasional couple sessions with Sherry and Ron. This structure and the associated interventions reduced the level of overt violence, but Ron still felt troubled by his potential for violence. After a year in therapy, the family situation was stable and relatively safe, but Ron wanted to stop feeling like a time bomb about to explode.

Ron had never opened up to anyone in his life. He had been raised in an abusive home and had always kept his feelings hidden and controlled. The death of his father about a year and half before the family entered therapy was the event that shook his defenses and led to his violent outbursts. When he entered therapy, he was extremely wary of the male therapist, but his desperate desire to control his feelings and behavior pushed him over the threshold of involvement. He opened up and began to talk. Therapy was slow, and Ron reported remembering virtually nothing from his childhood.

After a year of therapy, Ron was blocked. He could control his overt behavior, but he felt tortured inside. He and the therapist both felt that he needed to go further, and the therapist recommended that he and Ron meet alone twice a week and that the therapy with the rest of the family terminate for now. Sherry and the boys were comfortable with this option, but Sherry wanted to have the option of coming back to see the therapist with one or both of the boys and Ron if she felt scared or worried that Ron might become violent again.

The therapist felt that if he started working intensely and exclusively with Ron, interrupting that therapy with conjoint sessions with other family members might precipitate the very type of violent outburst the conjoint sessions were intended to prevent. The therapist proposed the following alternative: He would introduce the family to a highly respected female colleague who had worked extensively with abused and abusive families. At some future point, while he was working with Ron, if Sherry or one of the boys felt any need for therapy or consultation, they could call the therapist, and he would arrange a session for the family with his colleague. The female colleague joined the therapy for a session before the family terminated, and the consultation structure and procedures were arranged.

This example illustrates the kinds of decisions that need to be made as well as certain aspects of the process of making them at this stage in therapy. Unfortunately, at this structural point in treatment, the therapeutic requirements of the patient system necessitate a painful decision—someone has to lose or at least diminish his or her relationship with the primary therapist. That decision is ideally made with the full participation of the key patients, with the therapist functioning as an expert consultant. However, it is ultimately the therapist's responsibility to ensure that whatever decision is made has a decent probability of bringing about the desired changes and does not harm the patient system.

The most extreme intervention in this stage is psychoanalysis. In this form of intervention, one or more members of the patient system are seen individually three to four times a week over a period of 4–6 years or longer. Confidentiality is essential, although some limited and patient-approved communication with other members of the patient system may be indicated and permissible. It would be inadvisable and virtually impossible for the same therapist to be simultaneously engaged in treating an adult in psychoanalysis and his or her family in conjoint sessions. The transference with the individual would be vitiated, and the jealousy stimulated in other family members would jeopardize their alliances with the therapist. Most often, if an analysis seems indicated, the primary therapist recommends that the individual patient see another therapist who is an analyst. Ideally, that analyst should be at least sympathetic to the idea of prior and future systemic interventions that may involve the patient with other system members during the analysis. In particular, it may be important for the analyst to communicate directly and fairly openly with the primary therapist if the need arises.

THE SURFACING STRUCTURES

In *Structure 7* the primary therapist begins the process of putting the system back together and extricating him- or herself from the system. The stage resembles a mixture of Structures 4 and 5, in that the therapist gradually diminishes the individual and increases the conjoint sessions. The focus of these sessions shifts from the historical toward the here and now.

The duration of this stage can vary greatly. If the presenting problems were resolved in prior stages of therapy, this stage is usually relatively brief. As well as functioning to bring the key system members back together, this structure functions as a transition phase during termination of individual treatments. The task of this phase is to bring everyone up-to-date and to set the stage for termination.

If the treatment structures and processes of the preceding phases have not resolved the presenting problems or have only led to partial resolution, this phase may be longer. The primary task then becomes helping the key patients accept the constraints under which they will have to operate in the future. Alternative solutions may have to be pursued that may be less than desirable, but necessary.

Laura Abas, a 37-year-old widowed mother, was in individual treatment with her female therapist, Karen, for almost 2 years. During that time, Karen had also been seeing Laura's 14-year-old depressed daughter, Carol. Carol had become symptomatic 3 years before, shortly after her father, Tom, committed suicide. The three major presenting problems when Laura and Carol entered family therapy were Carol's verbal abusiveness to her mother, her school failure, and Laura's depression following her husband's suicide. Major secondary problems that eventually became primary foci of therapy were Laura's inability to empathize with, to nurture, and to be consistently available to Carol. Laura and Carol did not connect emotionally, and Carol was desperately in need of parental engagement.

After 2 years of individual treatment, Laura was still blocked. She understood the constraints behind the block but had been unable to overcome her inability to truly care for Carol. The closer involvement with Karen had been helpful to both Laura and Carol, but Carol was still moderately symptomatic and in need of greater support and nurturance. After much soul searching, Laura, with Karen's help, decided to send Carol to a small, structured, and very supportive boarding school.

Structure 7 for Laura and Carol involved a mixture of conjoint and individual sessions. The conjoint sessions involved focused discussions about the plan for Carol to go away to school and some processing of Carol and Laura's feelings about this decision and plan. The individual sessions with each of them dealt more focally with the pain and guilt about not being able to work out living together at this time in their lives. The intense emotional processing of their separation was done within individual contexts to protect Carol from the additional pain of opening up and sharing her pain and resentment in a nonempathic context and to protect Laura from the increased guilt, resentment, and bewilderment she tended to experience in affective encounters with Carol.

Structure 8, the last stage in the progressive bonding process, resembles Structures 1 and 2. The major task of this stage is termination of direct contact between the patient and therapist systems. Conjoint sessions typify this stage and are seldom held more than once a week. The therapist focuses the therapy during this final stage primarily on the interaction among the patients and minimally on the interaction with the therapist.

The exact distribution of focus (patient–patient versus patient–therapist) during this final structure depends on the length of treatment and number of structures that the therapy has traversed. Structure 8 can be accessed from Structures 3 and 4 as well as from Structure 7. If the therapy did not require Structures 5 through 7 (individual sessions), Structure 8 focuses minimally on the patient–therapist relationship.

In contrast, if the therapy required Structure 5, this final stage necessitates greater attention to the patient–therapist relationship. In getting to Stage 5, patients develop intense bonds to the therapist, and termination requires some attention to saying goodbye. Termination entails not only ending the therapist's direct relationship with the direct patient system, but also ending the individual relationships the therapist has developed with key members of the patient system. From the patient's perspective, it is not only that *we* are losing and going to miss the therapist, but also that *I* will lose and miss the therapist. A balanced patient–patient and patient–therapist focus is appropriate in Structure 8 to do justice to the emotional process when therapy has progressed beyond Structure 3 or 4.

SUMMARY AND OVERVIEW

Focusing on the concept of the therapeutic alliance, this chapter has delineated the relationship theory and practice of problem-centered therapy. The collaborative aspect of the relationship between the therapist and patients, called the therapeutic alliance, is a necessary ingredient in problem-centered therapy. Without it, therapy does not work. It takes priority over the problem-centered principles of application, and its progressive deepening provides the means for accessing and resolving deeper and more complex problem-maintenance structures. Its tearing and repair constitutes a critical and potentially positive event in any therapy. The alliance changes from case to case and from phase to phase within each case. It is an evolving phenomenon that creates the relational context for therapy.

CHAPTER 4

Assessment and Intervention: Premises and Roles

ASSESSMENT AND INTERVENTION are the essential components of psychotherapy. Assessment activities are primarily intended to increase therapist and patient understanding of the patient system, its presenting problems, and its problem-maintenance structures. Intervention activities are primarily intended to change the patient system by modifying its problem-maintenance structures sufficiently to resolve its presenting problems.

Intervention and assessment are inseparable activities. Every therapist behavior has intervention and assessment characteristics. Whether a behavior should be categorized primarily as assessment or intervention becomes a meaningless question. For instance, family-of-origin therapists routinely use genograms to gather individual and family histories (McGoldrick & Gerson, 1985, 1988). Typically, the therapist's primary intent is assessment; however, constructing a genogram is also a potent intervention. Transgenerational family patterns illuminated in this process lead patients to new ways of looking at themselves, each other, and their families of origin. From an assessment perspective, the genogram and the process of constructing it with the family tell the therapist about the rules, roles, and structure of the immediate family as well as the families of origin.

Similarly, a forceful therapist intervention like detriangulating (blocking and redirecting) a precocious 11-year-old daughter who continually interrupts her parents' efforts to communicate directly with each other ("I want you to stop interrupting your parents when they talk with each other") does more than change the family's structure and communication process. It also sets in motion an illuminating sequence of events. The family's response to this intervention tells the therapist about the family's problem-maintenance structure. The parents may respond by defending the daughter and criticizing the therapist for excluding her. From this reaction, the therapist might hypothesize that the parents are invested in maintaining the weak generational boundary with their daughter and that it may serve a regulatory function for the couple and the family.

Every therapist intervention, regardless of intent, from the first phone call to the last good-bye, has both assessment and intervention value. The genogram, typically understood as an assessment device, impacts the patient system as it reveals the nature of the system and the problem-maintenance structure. Blocking and redirecting, therapist behaviors typically regarded as interventions, reveal the problem-maintenance structure as they impact it. Every intervention impacts and reveals.

Not only are intervention and assessment inseparable, *assessment spans the entire course of therapy*. It does not end after a discrete phase at the beginning of therapy. According to interactive constructivism, as therapists get to know patient systems, they learn more and more about them, but the systems can never be known definitively. The learning process never ends, not even with termination. A therapist learned with surprise that a sensitive and perceptive husband in a couple she had successfully treated 8 years previously had callously left his wife and children for a childhood sweetheart after his father died. From her previous contact with the couple, which had lasted for more than a year, the therapist never would have predicted that the husband would behave this way.

As mentioned in Chapter 1, it is the problem-maintenance structure underlying the problem and not the problem itself that determines the requirements of successful therapy. The only way a particular problem-maintenance structure can be assessed is through intervention. The patient system's response to intervention yields a process diagnosis that tells the therapist about the problem-maintenance structure and the requirements of subsequent intervention (Greenberg & Pinsof, 1986; Ruesch, 1973). These structures only reveal themselves as they are worked with and probed. Patient systems teach us about themselves as we get to know them. They reveal themselves in their responses to our active and progressive penetration.

A CLINICAL SCIENTIFIC METHODOLOGY:
TOWARD A SUFFICIENT ASSESSMENT

If knowledge is always evolving and partial, when is it enough? The answer is pragmatic: when the therapy has helped the patient system solve all the presenting problems. At that point, therapy can terminate. An assessment, a set of hypotheses about the problem-maintenance structure, is sufficient when it generates therapist interventions that help the patient system resolve the presenting problem. The sufficiency of an assessment can only be determined post hoc, after the interventions derived from it have either helped or hurt patient-system progress toward problem resolution.

For instance, in the case of the Butlers, the therapist may hypothesize that the primary constraints that block Loretta from taking more effective leadership pertain to her feelings of guilt about her children. She feels that she has not been able to provide for them as she had hoped to and therefore does not feel entitled to expect more responsible behavior from them. On the basis of this constraint hypothesis, the therapist intervenes by asking the girls to respond. Betty and Akisha both assert emphatically that their mother should expect more from them, not less, and that she should stop feeling sorry for them.

In the weeks after this interaction, Loretta's behavior does not change appreciably. Even with her daughters' encouragement and the therapist's coaching, she still does not take charge. Based on this feedback, the therapist begins to revise the problem-maintenance premise according to the problem-centered progression and begins to consider biological constraint hypotheses linking her leadership block to a nonclinical, chronic depression.

Problem-centered therapy embodies a clinical experimental methodology that progressively tests, through intervention, increasingly refined hypotheses about the problem-maintenance structure of the presenting problem. Within this methodology, assessment and intervention exist in a circular feedback relationship to each other. The feedback loop that links them forms not a circle but a narrowing spiral that reflects the progressive nature of assessment and intervention within the problem-centered model. This progressive process ends when the presenting problem is resolved.

Within problem-centered therapy, every intervention ideally derives from and tests a hypothesis about the problem-maintenance structure. The sequential framework delineated in Chapter 2 and graphically depicted by the large arrow in Figure 2.2 represents a framework for progressively testing clinical hypotheses about patient systems and problem-maintenance structures. After initial intervention, if the data either do not support an organizational hypothesis or suggest the presence of additional factors, treatment progressively tests hypotheses pertaining to biological, meaning, transgenerational, object relations, and self constraints. The arrow links the vertical shifts with the metaframeworks to horizontal shifts from family to couple and, eventually, to individual context hypotheses.

The problem-centered therapist begins to formulate hypotheses about the patients, the problem, and the problem-maintenance structure from the intake information sheet and the first phone call. The more the therapist makes use of the assessment potential of every intervention by making sure that each intervention tests at least one hypothesis about the problem-maintenance structure, the more cost-effective and efficient the therapy. Ideally, every intervention should generate data that support, refute, or modify the major hypotheses that are under consideration at the time.

As therapy progresses, some hypotheses are ruled out, others are modified and refined, and eventually some are supported. The therapist's picture of the problem-maintenance structure gets clearer and more detailed. The assessment–intervention spiral feedback process culminates in a *sufficient assessment* leading to problem resolution. That sufficient assessment is the therapist's hypotheses about the problem-maintenance structure just prior to implementing the interventions that lead to problem resolution.

Does the success of the intervention confirm the validity of the assessment that generated the intervention? Because the intervention moved the system closer to problem resolution, does that mean that the hypotheses that generated the intervention were "true" or accurately reflected the problem-maintenance structure? The answer is, only partially. The systemic principle of equifinality asserts that different means or pathways can lead to the same end point. Thus, different sets of hypotheses about the problem-maintenance structure can generate the same or a different set of interventions that would resolve the presenting problem. The success of a particular intervention strategy only means that the assessment that generated it was pointed in the right direction; it was not wrong. It was sufficient. As is the case with hypotheses in scientific research, data do not prove or confirm the truth of a hypothesis. They either support or refute it. Once again, our knowledge is always partial. Reality can only be dimly known through the veil of our particularity.

ASSESSMENT–INTERVENTION PREMISES

Four premises guide assessment–intervention in problem-centered therapy. These premises provide the rationale for the clinical progression (the large arrow) from the upper-left to the lower-right quadrant in Figure 2.2 in Chapter 2.

Presumptions of Least Pathology

The first two premises constitute presumptions of least pathology. The first and most comprehensive, the *health premise*, asserts that *the patient system is healthy until proved sick*. Healthy means that the patient system is capable of solving its presenting problem with minimal and direct assistance from the therapist. Sick means that the patient system requires extensive, indirect, and prolonged assistance from the therapist to resolve the presenting problem. This premise encourages the therapist to approach the patient system, regardless of the severity, chronicity, and multiplicity of its problems, as if the most cost-effective interventions would be sufficient to facilitate resolution of the presenting problem.

The *problem-maintenance premise*, a corollary of the first premise, presumes that *the problem-maintenance structure is simple and superficial until proved otherwise*. This premise encourages the therapist to approach the patient system as if its problem is not rooted in a deep and complex problem-maintenance structure. Together with the health premise, the problem-maintenance premise maximizes the likelihood that the therapist will look for and elicit the healthiest capacities and resources within the system. These premises "load the dice" in the direction of health and competence, minimizing the extent to which the therapist might inadvertently encourage underachievement and overemphasize pathology. Together, they create the emphasis on strength rather than pathology in problem-centered therapy.

As a word of caution, it is essential that these premises and their presumption be used with sensitivity and good clinical judgment. With an insensitive or inexperienced therapist, these premises can be clung to with dangerous tenacity well after they should have been abandoned in the face of convincing evidence about the depth and breadth of particular problem-maintenance structures. Although the therapist should look for strengths, that search should not naively blind the therapist to indications that the system is more profoundly impaired and requires modification of the health and problem-maintenance premises.

It is essential to temper these premises when there is any risk of destructive behaviors such as suicide, homicide, and physical or sexual abuse. Particularly with otherwise high-functioning individuals and systems, it may be easy to use the presumptions of least pathology to minimize dangerously the likelihood of such destructive behaviors. Jerome and Penny Nichols, two highly successful corporate attorneys without children in their late 30s, presented their conflictual relationship for what they described as brief couple therapy. In the early sessions, Penny mentioned that before they were married, Jerome had gotten into several physical fights with other men but had never been violent to her. She never worried about Jerome hurting her.

Presuming health, the therapist began to confront Jerome directly with his destructive behavior with Penny. He pointed out to Jerome how he selectively perceived Penny's behavior and tended to emphasize the negative. Jerome appeared to listen attentively to the therapist without protest and said that he would try to work on that before the next session.

Late that night, the therapist got an emergency phone call from a distraught Penny. Jerome had picked a verbal fight with her in a restaurant after the session and stormed out saying he was going to walk home. Before dinner Jerome drank a double scotch, and during dinner he split a bottle of wine with Penny. Several hours later, she got a call at home from the police, saying that Jerome had been arrested. Apparently, he had gone to a bar near the restaurant and continued drinking. After about an hour, he picked a fight with another patron. In the fight, he broke the man's nose and even tried to assault the police when they arrived. She went down to the police station, but the police would not even consider releasing Jerome on bail because he was still so drunk.

The therapist underestimated Jerome's fragility and potential explosiveness. The presumptions of least pathology are not meant to justify psychopathological naivete. They are intended to encourage the therapist to err slightly on the side of health at the myriad decision points that emerge in the course of therapy. Informed by good clinical judgment, they safely maximize the strength-enhancing component of problem-centered therapy.

COST-EFFECTIVENESS PREMISE

The third premise concerns the sequencing of interventions. Based on the principle of parsimony, the cost-effectiveness premise asserts that *the therapist should try the simplest, most direct, and most cost-effective interventions before more complex, indirect, and expensive interventions.* Interventions or types of therapy from the top rows of the matrix in Figure 2.1 usually are less costly, less complex, and more direct than the orientations in the middle and lower rows. In fact, the orientations and contexts in Figure 2.1 are sequenced by the large arrow in Figure 2.2 in order of increasing cost.

The following example illustrates the implementation of the cost-effectiveness premise, as well as the use of the health and problem-maintenance premises. After consulting his internist and ruling out biological determinants,

Joe Delaney, 46 years old, and his 43-year-old wife, Sally, sought behaviorally oriented sex therapy for sexual impotence. Their problem-centered therapist, also trained as a sex therapist, initially hypothesized that the problem-maintenance structure was simple and superficial.

In this initial scenario, Joe's impotence was seen as deriving primarily from performance anxiety that had been increasing since a sexual encounter with Sally about a year ago in which he was unable to get an erection. According to the couple's account, this episode occurred late in the evening after Joe and Sally were out at a party at which Joe had been drinking heavily. His fear of failure, coupled with Sally's fear of embarrassing Joe, led the couple to avoid intercourse. On the rare occasions when they attempted sex, Joe's anxiety interfered with his capacity to get and maintain an erection. A vicious cycle emerged in which avoidance supported anxiety, which interfered with performance.

On the basis of this set of hypotheses, brief, behaviorally focused intervention was attempted to systematically rebuild sexual security and comfort with progressive exercises and a temporary ban on intercourse. The exercises linked masturbation and erotic tasks with relaxation, building to the point when successful intercourse might be possible. Eight sessions of short-term behaviorally oriented sexual therapy were not successful. Joe was unable to relax with the "sensate focus" exercises (Masters & Johnson, 1970), and Sally was troubled by feelings of resentment when called on to "pleasure" Joe (Kaplan, 1974). These reactions led to an avoidant pattern, in which Joe and Sally could not "find the time" to do their homework.

At this point, their therapist recommended shifting the focus of therapy to work on whatever was preventing them from taking advantage of the sex therapy. Initially, Joe and Sally both felt reluctant to broaden the scope of the therapy. However, after three more unproductive sessions, they agreed to explore some of the aspects of their marriage that might be getting in the way of the sex therapy.

As the couple got into more experientially focused couple therapy, the therapist developed the following hypothetical problem-maintenance scenario: Joe and Sally have been drifting apart for the past 3 years, since their youngest child, Linda, left for college and Sally decided to return to a local college to finish her own undergraduate education, which was suspended when she and Joe married 22 years earlier. Joe felt abandoned in the face of Linda's departure and Sally's return to college. He lost his "baby" and his wife at the same time.

Joe resented coming home at night to an empty house when Sally had late classes and did not like to go to bed alone when she had to study. Vaguely aware of his resentment, Joe expressed it in masked ways, characterizing Sally's professors as "eggheads" and her student friends as "immature." Sally reacted with defensiveness to Joe's put-downs and stopped sharing her new experiences with him. In the course of 3 years this pattern escalated to the point that Joe and Sally did not communicate openly about most things. Their sexual encounters became less frequent, and Joe's impotence finally emerged about a year before the first visit.

In this scenario, Joe's impotence performs multiple functions. It covertly expresses his anger at Sally without his having to take responsibility for the feelings of frustration, inadequacy, and anger he stimulates in her. Joe's symptom also places him in the patient role, which pressures Sally into a complementary caretaker role that resembles her role in their marriage before her return to college. Sally also vaguely understands that Joe is unhappy with her new independence and self-focus, but she is afraid to confront this situation for fear of his open anger and possible rejection. She is also frightened that open conflict may somehow jeopardize her new independence and derail her education. She would rather focus her concerns and their attention on his "problem."

These issues were addressed, and communication appeared to improve between Joe and Sally. Joe's feelings of abandonment and his subsequent anger were identified and explored. Sally's discomfort with his feelings was examined and diminished. Her fears of destructive and derailing conflict were defused. As Sally and the therapist came to understand Joe's feelings, his sense of abandonment appeared to diminish, but something still prevented them from reestablishing intimacy. When erotic tasks were attempted, Joe found various reasons not to do them. After 12 experiential marital therapy sessions, the therapist expressed puzzlement about their lack of progress in the sexual area and speculated that all of the cards might not be on the table.

In the next session, Joe admitted that he had been having an affair with his secretary, Mary, for approximately the last year and a half. Mary, a 25-year-old single woman, had worked for Joe for a year before the beginning of their affair. She looked up to Joe and sought his advice about personal problems. A good listener, Mary was always interested in anything Joe wanted to talk about. Joe's impotence with Sally got worse as his affair with Mary developed. He had no sexual dysfunction with Mary.

Joe claimed that he loved Mary. She understood him in ways Sally never did. In therapy, he also implied that sex with Mary was fantastic and problem-free. Sally was devastated. She felt as if this were her punishment for having pursued her own interests. Initially, she became solicitous of Joe and begged him to stay in the marriage. Joe refused to terminate his affair with Mary. Sally became depressed, and Joe and Sally became distant and alienated. His refusal to relinquish his affair with Mary was an ongoing insult to the integrity and viability of the marriage.

In special individual sessions with each partner, the therapist began to understand the depths of alienation in Joe and Sally's marriage, as well as some of their transgenerational, object-relations, and self constraints. This understanding coalesced into a third set of hypotheses about the problem-maintenance structure. Joe, an extremely narcissistically vulnerable man, sustained his marriage so long as Sally and his daughter, Linda, took care of him by looking up to him and catering to his physical and emotional needs. When they diminished these self-object functions to pursue their own appropriate interests, Joe collapsed psychologically. He turned to Mary to fill the gap and get himself back together.

Joe's narcissistic vulnerability and passive-aggressive rage are rooted in his early experience in his family of origin. Joe grew up in an early dual-career family. His father was an insurance salesman, and his mother worked as a nurse. Joe was cared for as a toddler by a grieving maternal grandmother who had recently lost her husband. Alone much of his childhood, Joe seldom experienced his caretakers as physically or emotionally available. He took care of his grandmother emotionally and tended to his younger siblings. His fantasy life alternated between fantasies of adventurism and fantasies of a loving woman tending to him as he imagined his mother tended to her patients in the hospital. He occasionally indulged in sadistic daydreams in which horrible accidents happened to his mother's patients in the hospital. Frequently, these patients were older women.

Sally spent most of her growing-up years tending to her overly involved and moderately depressed mother. Her father left her mother when Sally was 5 and was only marginally involved with her during most of her early years. He reinvolved himself when Sally was in high school and was relatively active in her life since then. Sally had always been a "good girl," taking care of her parents, her siblings, her husband, and her children. Going back to school and starting to fantasize about a career as a teacher represented her first efforts to pursue her own interests and ambitions. Her fantasies ranged from becoming a school principal with a supportive husband who encouraged her autonomy and success, to being a defender of abused and exploited women.

To help Joe and Sally, these historical constraints needed to be addressed and worked through enough to permit resolution of their marital impasse. This working through required some degree of insight development about each of their pasts and how their previous experiences influenced their current behaviors. Second, some degree of corrective emotional experience with the therapist was required to strengthen Joe and Sally's individual self structures. This self strengthening ultimately facilitated the establishment of an empathic framework between Joe and Sally that began repairing their ruptured relationship.

This psychodynamic and self-psychological therapy was done primarily in extended conjoint treatment, but it required substantial amounts of individual work. When Joe and Sally could not open up in the conjoint context, the therapist temporarily worked with each of them in individual contexts. At one point, even the individual sessions were not sufficient to get some constructive movement with Joe and Sally, and the therapist considered the possibility of finding individual therapists for each of them. After discussing that possibility with Joe and Sally, however, they started to move.

Joe discontinued his affair. Subsequently, Joe and Sally started meeting mostly in conjoint sessions. After several months dealing primarily with the consequences of the affair, they began to focus on reestablishing trust and empathy. As their genuine empathy grew and each understood the meaning of their own and each other's behavior over the past 3 years, they decided on their own to resume the pleasuring sexual task. With hardly any explicit effort, Joe's impotence disappeared. After several more months of therapy, feeling wiser, bruised, but more solid than ever, Joe and Sally terminated. Their more historically oriented and mixed-context therapy lasted approximately 9 months.

This example illustrates the use of progressively more costly and complex interventions to explore and modify the problem-maintenance structure underlying a symptom, in this case, Joe's impotence. Initially, the therapist proceeded as if Joe's impotence had a simple and superficial problem-maintenance structure and would respond to brief, conjoint sexual therapy. After the data disconfirmed that set of hypotheses, the therapist hypothesized a deeper and broader problem-maintenance structure in which the marital problems impeded the resolution of the presenting problem. On the basis of this second set of hypotheses, intervention required marital treatment as well as behaviorally oriented sex therapy.

As the experientially focused marital therapy failed to bring about change, the therapist hypothesized a third problem-maintenance structure in which object-relations and self constraints impacted the marital system and influenced the presenting problem. Successful psychodynamic and self-psychological intervention, in both conjoint and individual contexts, addressed these historical constraints sufficiently to resolve the marital problems enough to permit the couple to resolve the problem for which they sought treatment in the first place, Joe's impotence. The therapy only moved to more extensive problem-maintenance hypotheses and more costly interventions in the face of failure to resolve the presenting problem.

INTERPERSONAL PREMISE

The fourth premise underlies the large arrow in Figure 2.2 and asserts that *therapy should progress from the interpersonal to the individual.* An intervention is usually more effective and productive in the long run if it can be done in an appropriate interpersonal context rather than in an individual context. The rationale behind the interpersonal premise involves five propositions.

The first proposition pertains primarily to the beginning of therapy. *Therapists will generally learn more about patient systems if they meet as many of the key patients as soon as possible.* They will be better able to form their own impressions about key players and thereby know with whom they are dealing as quickly as possible. Involving key players in the direct system at the beginning of treatment gives the therapist a quicker and clearer snapshot of the interpersonal dimensions of the patient system.

The second proposition is that *the therapist usually will establish a stronger therapeutic alliance with the patient system if that alliance is based on direct, face-to-face contact.* Involving the baby-sitting grandparents in the first session with the Mexican-American Portillo family reassured them that their daughter and son-in-law were taking their 6-year-old son to a "simpatico" therapist at a benevolent organization.

The third proposition concerns the concept of the collective observing ego: the capacity of the patient system to observe, understand, and modify its own behavior. *Doing as much of the work as possible in front of the key patients maximizes the likelihood of creating a wider, more stable, and more empathic collective observing ego.* More people understand what is going on and why. If one person loses perspective, another may help him or her to regain it if that person understands the processes at work. For instance, 6 months after Joe and Sally formally terminated therapy, Joe began to get sullen and withdrawn. Because she was present when Joe explored his reaction to her increased involvement outside the home and his early experience in his family of origin, Sally quickly understood Joe's withdrawal as a response to her recent diminished availability caused by her efforts to complete her undergraduate honors thesis. Using the tools and knowledge she had gained in conjoint therapy with him, she moved closer emotionally and sexually and obviated the need for his withdrawal. This step minimized the impact of what previously would have been a regressive and destructive episode.

The fourth proposition is that *the transforming impact of major breakthroughs is usually greater when they occur in the presence of key patients.* When Sally finally saw Joe's pain concerning her diminished availability and the related pain regarding his early experiences in his family, she not only cognitively understood what happened to him, but also felt what these events meant to him. It allowed her to begin to forgive him for the affair. Seeing his tearful sadness softened her rage.

The fifth point behind the interpersonal premise is that, on an ongoing basis, *the therapist will have a more accurate understanding of the problem-maintenance structure if key patients are directly involved in ongoing treatment.* Furthermore, the clinical opportunity to use this understanding constructively will be maximized. To illustrate, if Sally had responded to Joe's tearful rendition of his early experiences in his family by criticizing him for feeling sorry for himself, the therapist would immediately observe the emergence of this new block. On the basis of this information, the therapist can shift the focus of the therapy to address the constraints that prevent Sally from responding to Joe in a more supportive fashion. If Sally had not been present during Joe's breakthrough, the therapist would not have been able to see her reaction so immediately. Even more important, the therapist would not have been able to minimize the extent of Sally's maladaptive response and help Joe and Sally understand what prevented her from responding more adaptively.

Like the first two premises, the interpersonal premise should be used with sensitivity and good clinical judgment. Although it is usually better to do as much of the work as possible in the presence of as many of the appropriate key patients as possible, *there are many legitimate situations in which patients should be excluded from the direct system or types of clinical work should be done individually.* If the work can be done in an interpersonal context, it should be done that way. If it cannot or should not, the therapist should not delay shifting to a more limited or individual context. Chapter 5, Defining the Direct System, elaborates additional guidelines for deciding when and whether to work in an interpersonal or an individual context, or both.

The four assessment–intervention premises are not just useful at the beginning of treatment. They are valuable whenever the therapist confronts one of the many decision points that emerge in any sustained therapy. They encourage the therapist not to approach these decision points neutrally, but to lean with sensitivity in the direction of the premises. The premises encourage the therapist to work in such a way that treatment proceeds as effectively and efficiently as possible. Strengths and the possibility of rapid response are maximized, costs are reduced, and the likelihood of regression or under-achievement is minimized.

THERAPY AS EDUCATION AND THE THERAPIST AS TEACHER

Problem-centered therapy is fundamentally an educational endeavor. This is not to deny the therapist's role as a problem solver, change agent, or healer. Rather, it asserts that the primary role of the therapist is to teach the patient system more effective problem-solving rules and mechanisms. This educational emphasis in problem-centered therapy constitutes a broad fifth assessment–intervention premise that informs the therapeutic process from beginning to end.

As teachers, problem-centered therapists give away their skills and expertise in human problem solving. They empower and strengthen patient systems so that the patients will be more capable of solving future problems. *Problem-centered therapists should leave patients stronger than they were before therapy.* Problem-centered therapy strives to strengthen specific problem-solving skills within the patient system that relate to the class of problems for which the system sought help.

The problem-solving skills that problem-centered therapists teach fall into two broad categories. In the first, *pattern identification*, the therapist teaches the patient system to identify its maladaptive problem-solving patterns. These maladaptive patterns can be behavioral, biobehavioral, cognitive, affective, or a combination of these and are usually driven by unconscious problem-solving rules.

Dorothy and Fred Kalmas did not recognize their 16-year-old daughter's increasing depression over the course of 6 months. Initially, they attributed Andrea's suicide attempt and subsequent hospitalization to the influence of bad friends and the loss of a boyfriend. Their failure to recognize Andrea's depression was the product of affect-recognition rules precluding identification of sadness and depression. Furthermore, if they had been able to recognize Andrea's depression, Dorothy and Fred would have been unlikely to address it effectively. Neither parent learned any productive affect-management skills in their families of origin, and they were at best unnerved by displays of sadness or despair. Thus, their behavioral rules about permissible activities would have precluded addressing Andrea's depression even if they had been able to recognize it.

Consistent with the health and problem-maintenance premises, problem-centered therapists also teach patient systems to identify their adaptive problem-solving skills. For instance, Loretta Butler functions effectively as the charge nurse on a surgical floor at her hospital. Her staff respects her, and the doctors and hospital administrators are pleased with her management style. However, Loretta has not been able to provide proper leadership and set consistent boundaries with appropriate consequences for her three daughters.

In this situation, the therapist points out that Loretta seems able to be an effective leader and set appropriate limits with her staff and patients at the hospital. Looking for the constraints, the therapist asks Loretta what prevents her from engaging in similar behavioral patterns with her daughters at home.

LORETTA: I feel sorry for them. They've had a rough time. I work so much, I'm not home that much, and I feel guilty for leaving them alone too much. Then there's daddy's passing. No father makes it even harder.

THERAPIST: So if you didn't feel sorry for them, you'd be able to be the kind of leader you obviously can be and are at work?

LORETTA: Yeah, that may be true. I just hate to come home and have to be on top of everybody the whole time. Did you do this? Well why not? They don't need more hassles.

THERAPIST: Do you have to be on top of everybody at work, telling them what to do and checking up on them all the time?

LORETTA: No, I don't.

THERAPIST: Why, what's the difference between the hospital and home?

LORETTA: The nurses that work for me know what I expect, and they know that if they don't do it I'll hear about it and they're gonna get into trouble.

THERAPIST: So at work, you delegate. People know what's expected and what's gonna happen if they don't do it. Why isn't it that way at home with the girls?

AKISHA: Momma doesn't make us do hardly anything.

EILEEN: Shut up Akisha, you don't know what you're saying.

BETTY: She's right, Eileen. Momma let's all of us get away with a lot.

In this vignette, the therapist identifies Loretta's adaptive behavior at work and contrasts it with her maladaptive behavior at home. The therapist is assisted by Akisha and Betty, both of whom support the proposition that Loretta does not expect enough from them at home.

The second set, or category, of problem-solving skills taught by the problem-centered therapist pertains to *pattern modification*. The therapist not only teaches key patients to identify their adaptive and maladaptive problem-solving patterns, but also, perhaps even more important, teaches them to modify these patterns. This job encompasses two types of tasks. The first is helping the patient system to transfer adaptive patterns from one context to another, as was illustrated previously with the Butlers. This transfer task assumes that the patient system possesses the necessary pattern-modification skills in its problem-solving repertoire.

The second pattern-modification task pertains to patient systems that lack the requisite adaptive problem-solving skills in their repertoires. In this situation, the therapist must teach the patient system new skills, patterns, and rules. If the problem-maintenance structure in a skill-deficit situation is simple and superficial, the therapist may determine that the skill deficit is primarily the result of lack of modeling and training. For instance, Fred and Dorothy's difficulties in addressing Andrea's depression may derive primarily from a lack of modeling and training in their families of origin. In this case, the therapist will probably have a relatively easy time modeling, coaching, and training them to deal more effectively with their daughter's depression.

If the skill deficit has a deeper and more complex problem-maintenance structure, however, the therapist's work becomes more complicated. Fred and Dorothy's skill block may not be due to lack of modeling and training but to some deeper fear about the catastrophic consequences of addressing and expressing sadness and despair. These deeper fears and their attendant anxieties would need to be addressed in therapy for the parents to be able to help Andrea.

This example illustrates another major aspect of the therapist as teacher. As well as teaching new adaptive patterns of thought, feeling, and action in regard to presenting problems, problem-centered therapists teach patient systems about their problem-maintenance structures. Fred and Dorothy need to understand and work through their deeper anxieties about depression and sadness before they can help Andrea. They need to develop a cognitive and affective understanding of their individual and collective psychologies sufficient to free them to learn new ways of helping Andrea. This entails knowledge about the constraints that have prevented them from helping their depressed daughter: knowledge about their problem-maintenance structure.

From the dual educational and problem-solving perspective of problem-centered therapy, the problem-maintenance structure is a set of hierarchically organized rules that pertain to cognition, emotion, and behavior. These rules specify what is permissible: what can be thought, felt, and done. The more these rules link to transgenerational, object-relations, and self con-straints, the deeper and wider the problem-maintenance structures and the more difficult the task of modifying them.

In teaching patient systems about problem-maintenance structures, the therapist creates a *collective observing ego* within the patient system that under-stands and can modify the constraints at all levels of problem-maintenance structure. Patients learn to understand and manage these superficial as well as deeper constraints so that the constraints will not interfere with their efforts to solve the presenting and other, similar problems. Although the problem-maintenance structure around Andrea's depression may be modi-fied sufficiently for Fred and Dorothy to help her, the fears and anxieties that let the problem get out of hand are not necessarily extinguished. Fred, Dorothy, and at some point Andrea need to understand their collective prob-lems with affect recognition and management as well as some of the roots of these problems. This understanding ideally serves to inoculate the system against future regression to the state that led to Andrea's depression in the first place.

A major difference between problem-centered therapy and more conven-tional individual therapies lies in the concept of the collective observing ego. Initially Freud delineated the concept of the observing ego along with the concept of the therapeutic alliance. The observing ego is the healthy part of the patient that allies with the therapist to work on the patient's more dis-turbed parts. The individual observing ego is not only the therapist's ally within the patient psychodynamically, it is also that part of the ego that will eventually take over the role of understanding and managing the patient's conflicts and issues once therapy is over. Problem-centered therapy builds on Freud's original concept in targeting the collective observing ego: the part of the patient system's collective object relations that allies with the therapist and represents the shared healthy management capacities of the patient system.

The problem-centered therapist strengthens the collective observing ego as well as the individual observing egos of the key patients. This goal derives from the assumption that individuals are generally less stable problem-solving systems than small groups. As discussed previously in regard to the interpersonal premise, if understanding about the nature of the problem-maintenance structure can be disseminated within the patient system beyond a specific individual, that understanding can be drawn on and used by multiple individuals. If Dorothy Kalmas misses a signal from Andrea at the beginning of a depressive episode, Fred may pick it up, or Andrea may even be able to increase the clarity of her request for help. When Loretta Butler gets induced into the role of trying to do everything for her daughters and not delegating responsibility, one or more of her daughters can identify the maladaptive pattern and stimulate more adaptive behavior.

SHIFTING RESPONSIBILITY:
THE GOOD ENOUGH THERAPIST

Teaching pattern identification and modification typically involves a progressive process in which the therapist increasingly relinquishes responsibility to the patient system for recognizing and modifying maladaptive patterns linked to the presenting problem. Initially, the therapist takes primary responsibility for these tasks. As soon as the patient system is able, however, the therapist starts to shift the locus of responsibility to the system.

At times the therapist tests the system's readiness by failing to respond as expected or by asking the patient system to identify what has just happened or what needs to happen. These questions convey the metamessage to the system: "I expect you to work in this therapy." They clarify the *definition of the key patients as active learners: students in problem-centered therapy*.

The problem-centered therapist can also put pressure on the system to perform as competently as possible by becoming increasingly and skillfully "incompetent." This incompetence is generally not the result of therapist skill or expertise deficits, but a capacity for passivity or nonaction in the proper context. The therapist's goal is to be "just good enough"—not too competent or incompetent. Excessive therapist competence leads to an underadequate and underachieving patient system; excessive therapist incompetence leads to a frustrated, possibly traumatized, and frequently prematurely terminating patient system. The trick is to find the good enough point that places as much responsibility on the system as it is capable of handling at any particular moment.

The process of shifting responsibility for pattern identification and modification, like any psychological growth process, is an oscillating process with progressive and regressive phases. The system takes on more responsibility and then regresses, requiring the sensitive therapist to become more active and "competent" until the regressive phase is worked through and progress continues. The good enough therapist becomes more competent when the system regresses and less competent as the system progresses. This up-and-down process characterizes the entire course of therapy, although it is most intense during the middle phases. It clearly diminishes in the termination phase of therapy, as the patient system takes full responsibility for managing its problem-solving rules and mechanisms.

ASSESSMENT AND INTERVENTION: SUMMARY AND OVERVIEW

This chapter defined assessment and intervention as two co-occurring processes that span the entire course of therapy, from the first phone conversation through the last session. The assessment and intervention processes are driven by a clinical experimental methodology that tests increasingly refined hypotheses about the problem-maintenance structure. The process is continually informed at key decision points by four premises that promote health and cost-effective intervention. Finally, problem-centered therapy is education. In the assessment and intervention processes, the good enough therapist teaches the key patients pattern identification and modification skills, expanding the collective observing ego and progressively shifting more and more of the responsibility for problem solving to the patient system.

CHAPTER 5

Defining the Direct System:
The Interpersonal
Context of Therapy

E VERY PATIENT SYSTEM approaches therapy with a distinct *mode of presentation* that specifies the presenting problems and the way they should be addressed: "These are the problems we want to address in this therapy; these are the people we want you to see and how we want you to work with them." Beyond specifying the presenting problem, the most critical aspect of the mode of presentation is the patient system's definition of the interpersonal structure of the therapy: who will be included in the direct system. Systems' modes of presentation, particularly the interpersonal structure component, vary in explicitness and flexibility. Some systems boldly say that they want to be seen individually, whereas others whisper that they want to be seen conjointly.

Most cases fall into one of four mode-of-presentation categories. Category 1 includes *nuclear families* with one or two parents presenting with a *child as the identified patient*. They may be seeking child or family therapy, or both. *Binuclear, divorced families* presenting with a *child as the identified patient* constitute Category 2. They may be seeking family or child therapy, or both. Category 3 encompasses *couples*, with or without children, seeking conjoint treatment with their *relationship as the primary presenting problem*. Category 4 includes *individual adults*, presenting with either individual or interpersonal problems, who are not currently cohabiting (Category 4a) or who are currently cohabiting with another adult and/or children (Category 4b).

The stance of problem-centered therapy toward a patient system's preference for a particular interpersonal context differs from its attitude toward the presenting problem. The patient system determines the presenting problem. In contrast, the patient system is *not* the primary determinant of the interpersonal context of therapy. Guided by the structural principles of problem-centered therapy represented by the large arrow in Figure 2.2, *the therapist primarily determines who will be involved in what way at each point in treatment.* Of course, the key patients must agree with the therapist about the intervention context or the alliance will be jeopardized. Nevertheless, the patient system's desire for a particular context is just one factor in the therapist's decision making about the interpersonal structure of therapy.

Therapy can be broken into four phases, each with its own goals and special tasks. At first, the therapist, in consultation with the key patients, decides which patient-system members should be invited to the *initial session* (Phase 1). Subsequently, the therapist and key patients decide on the direct participants in the *early sessions* (Sessions 2–5; Phase 2), in the *middle sessions* (Phase 3), and during *termination* (Phase 4). Although these phases are presented separately, in actual practice they flow together. Duration estimates should be modified to fit each system.

This chapter presents theory and guidelines for structuring patient systems in the four modes of presentation in the four phases of therapy. The 4 × 4 matrix in Figure 5.1 illustrates this organizational structure. The chapter operationalizes the context aspect of the problem-centered principle of application.

PRELIMINARY INTERVENTION AND THE INITIAL SESSION: PHASE 1

The first phase of therapy contains the first interview and prior contacts between the therapist and patient systems. *Its twin goals are to establish a preliminary alliance with the patient system and to develop a preliminary understanding of the presenting problems.*

Treatment commences when someone—the identified patient, a family member, or a professional—refers the patient system for treatment. This person constitutes the *referral source.* Usually, the identified patient or another key patient functions as the *organizing patient,* making arrangements with the therapist and organizing key patients to get them to therapy.

Typically, the therapist conducts initial interviews over the phone with the

Figure 5.1
Modes of Presentation and Phases of Therapy

Phases of Therapy

Modes of Presentation	Initial (Session 1)	Early (Sessions 2–5)	Middle	Termination
1 Nuclear family with a child as identified patient				
2 Binuclear family with a child as identified patient				
3 Couples with their relationship as a presenting problem				
4a Noncohabiting adults seeking individual therapy				
4b Cohabiting adults seeking individual therapy				

referral source as well as the organizing patient. For instance, a pediatrician refers the Jensens, a married couple with a 5-year-old, Danny, who allegedly has an attention deficit hyperactivity disorder (ADHD). Over the phone, the therapist gets as much information as possible about the child and family from the pediatrician. Subsequently, the therapist talks with the mother, Marie, to find out more about the child and family as well as to make arrangements for the first session. In some systems, the referral source and the organizing patient are the same person. A husband may refer himself and his wife for marital therapy, or a young single adult woman may seek therapy for herself.

These initial contacts are important diagnostically and therapeutically. The referral source and organizing patient are invariably important members of the patient (and possibly the therapist) system, and these initial contacts provide useful data in forming preliminary hypotheses. They are also the first interactions that shape the alliance with key patients.

Three questions inform the decision about whom to include in the direct system initially and in the later phases. The first is, *What are the presenting problems?* The therapist should collect initial data about the presenting problems before the first session to maximize the assessment and intervention value of that session. The therapist needs to ask the referral source as well as the organizing patient about the presenting problems. A thorough understanding is not essential. At this point, the therapist only needs to know enough about the major presenting problem or problems to decide who should come in.

Once this preliminary understanding has been achieved, the next question is, *Who should be involved in the first session?* The theoretical and ideal answer, regardless of mode of presentation, is that *all of the relevant members of the patient system who actually or potentially play central roles in the maintenance or resolution of the presenting problem should be involved in the first session.* With a "school-refusing" 9-year-old boy from a divorced family, at least the following should be invited: the boy, both parents, their new spouses if they have remarried, siblings, and extended family members (such as grandparents, aunts, or uncles) who are living with the identified patient. With a couple seeking marital therapy, both partners should attend. For a depressed wife and mother, her husband, her older children, and possibly some highly involved extended family members and fictive kin would be invited.

In extending invitations, there are two lists: an essential and an optional one. People clearly involved with the identified patient and the presenting problem as well as those who are likely to play a role in resolving the problem constitute the essential list. The optional list contains patients whose presence may be helpful but not essential. The therapist assertively attempts to involve the members of the essential list in the first interview.

Multiple phone contacts with different key patients may be required. With the Jensens, the therapist spoke with the mother, requesting that she bring her husband, Dan, and her son and daughter. The mother responded that Dan did not want to be involved and did not believe in therapy. In response, the therapist suggested that she tell Dan that the therapist requested his direct involvement, at least for the first session, to understand his perception of the problem and thoughts about how it should be handled. The therapist asked Marie when she would be able to talk with Dan and made an appointment to call her back after that time.

When the therapist called, Marie informed him that her husband still refused to be involved. With Marie's permission, the therapist called Dan that evening, asking him to come in for just one session to help the therapist better understand the problems his wife was reporting about their son. In the face of this direct and limited request for assistance, Dan agreed to come in for the first session.

In the early interactions, the therapist should not expand the problem beyond what is presented. Key patients are invited to assist the therapist in understanding and treating their presenting problems. The therapy is intentionally *not* defined as family therapy, which minimizes the extent to which family members feel blamed for the problems. As well as aiding in key patient recruitment, this problem focus facilitates the establishment of the therapeutic alliance: "We are getting together to work on the same goals."

If Dan Jensen had refused the direct request, the therapist would have accepted politely. The phone call would have ended with the therapist informing him that at some point, if it was absolutely essential, he might be invited in again. Additionally. if Dan had any thoughts or feelings about the therapy or Danny's problems, the therapist would express the hope that he would call or come in; his input would be valued at any point.

This scenario with Dan Jensen illustrates aspects of the third question guiding contacts, *What are the alliance requirements of this patient system during this initial and each subsequent phase of therapy?* The therapist continually elaborates the answer to this question by careful analysis of the feedback to interventions from key patients. A more specific variant of the alliance question permeates all of the therapist's interactions with the system: Is the alliance best served at this moment by including or not including this person in the direct system?

The guiding principle in pursuing resistant key patients is to *push hard but to back off at the point at which the therapeutic alliance appears to be in jeopardy.*

After direct contact, if the alliance appears to be threatened by continuing to try to move patients into the direct system, the therapist should support their temporary membership in the indirect system.

The therapist should attempt to make recalcitrant patients reasonably comfortable in the indirect system, from a face-saving point of view, and definitely should not depreciate them to the patients in the direct system. Sometimes direct-system patients are angry at a patient's refusal to join them. Particularly at the beginning, it is important not to reinforce negative stereotypes of reluctant patients. Furthermore, therapists should contain negative counter-transference reactions to recalcitrant patients, even when they feel demeaned or abused. A negative alliance with an indirect-system member may critically damage the total alliance.

The therapist cannot compromise the viability of the therapy initially by not insisting that key resistant patients attend. It is impossible to determine that a therapy is fundamentally compromised at this early stage by the refusal of any patient to attend, even the identified patient. If the therapist creates a positive alliance with the direct system and at least a nonantagonistic alliance with the indirect system, therapy is viable. The therapist's "foot is in the door," and change is possible.

NUCLEAR FAMILY WITH A CHILD AS IDENTIFIED PATIENT

In this first mode of presentation, the identified patient is a child or adolescent living in a nuclear family with one or two cohabiting parents and possibly other relatives. Frequently, this type of system is referred by a teacher, guidance counselor, or physician. A parent is usually the organizing patient.

As stated previously, the guiding principle in engaging these systems is to get as many of the key patients as possible to attend the first session. This usually includes the parents, the identified patient, siblings of all ages, and extended family members living at home or actively engaged with the identified patient. Occasionally, school personnel may be invited, although it is usually better to bring them in during the early sessions, after the therapist has had a chance to meet and get to know the family.

As indicated previously, the therapist should be as tenacious as possible without jeopardizing the alliance. With Jerry, a 17-year-old bright but extremely depressed adolescent referred by his family physician, the therapist aggressively attempted to get him to come in with at least both of his parents, if not his three younger siblings. With equal tenacity, Jerry refused. Eventually, the therapist relented and saw Jerry alone for the first session.

The therapist had already established a relationship with the parents in phone calls trying to make arrangements with Jerry. After the first session, Jerry permitted the therapist to arrange a meeting with his parents during the next couple of weeks. He even reluctantly attended the meeting after the therapist said he preferred to talk with Jerry's parents about Jerry in front of Jerry rather than behind his back.

Binuclear Family with a Child as Identified Patient

This mode of presentation involves a child or adolescent as the identified patient living primarily with one custodial parent or, alternatively, with each of two joint-custodial parents. These families can be thought of as binuclear (Ahrons, 1994) and typically involve two households. The biological parents are separated or divorced. The parents may or may not be remarried. The organizing patient is usually one of the parents, most often the one with primary custody. Undoubtedly, these systems require the most contact and work prior to the first interview. Much of this work can be done by the organizing patient, unless he or she refuses to interact with the ex-spouse.

As in nuclear families, the organizing principle with binuclear families for the first session is to include as many of the key patients as possible. This diminishes the likelihood of actual or perceived coalitions between the therapist and various family factions and increases the likelihood that everyone will feel equally allied with the therapist. Ideally, the identified patient, parents, stepparents, siblings, and stepsiblings should be invited to the first interview, which allows the therapist to meet with and directly assess as many of the key patients as possible.

Frequently with divorced systems, this structural ideal is unattainable. The divorced parental systems may be so alienated that bringing them together precludes getting any meaningful work done. In the face of such intense alienation, the therapist must decide which subsystem to meet with first. The therapist may have two or three "first sessions" with the different subsystems of a divorced system. With intensely conflicted divorced systems, it may be possible to bring key patients together for a specific task once they have established adequate alliances with the therapist and have some insight into their role in the conflict. This is seldom the case at the beginning of therapy.

Once again, the therapist pushes for the structural ideal but backs off in the face of intense resistance or compelling evidence that certain key patients should not be brought together. Creation of therapeutic alliances with all of the key patients in binuclear systems is the initial goal. The fair, flexible, and creative use of the direct- and indirect-system boundary is essential in achieving that goal with most divorced systems.

COUPLES WITH RELATIONSHIP PROBLEMS

The simplest mode of presentation involves cohabiting heterosexual or homosexual couples presenting with relationship problems. The partners should be seen together for the first session. This precludes the possibility of one partner being seen alone initially and being perceived by the other partner as more closely allied with the therapist. An unbalanced alliance early in couple treatment is always perilous.

Seeing both partners together also prevents the therapist from receiving secret information from one spouse that could jeopardize the incipient alliance with the other spouse. For the same reason, the therapist has to be careful during preliminary phone contacts to avoid receiving information from the organizing partner that could jeopardize the alliance with the other partner (e.g., affairs or plans to separate that have not been shared).

It may be necessary to inform the organizing partner over the phone that nothing at this point is confidential. This "warning" should not be issued routinely, because it can communicate a sense of therapist suspiciousness that could jeopardize the patient's ability to trust the therapist. It should be offered only if the therapist suspects he or she is about to receive "hot," alliance-damaging information. Beyond gathering information, the primary goal of the preliminary contacts and the first session is to create a context in which the alliances with each partner and with the couple can develop. If that objective is compromised at this point, therapy is not viable.

INDIVIDUALS SEEKING INDIVIDUAL TREATMENT

Consistent with the structural principles of problem-centered therapy, the general operating rule concerning adults seeking individual treatment is that it is preferable to see them in the first interview with developmentally and diagnostically appropriate members of their patient system. In operationalizing this rule, a distinction must be made between noncohabiting (Mode of Presentation Category 4a) and cohabiting adult patients (Category 4b).

Usually, it is not necessary or practical to include other key patients in the initial interview of *noncohabiting adults*. These patients may present with individual or interpersonal problems, but the lack of a relevant "cohabiting other" makes it difficult to readily discern key patients who should be included in the first session. Lorraine, a 38-year-old lawyer, divorced for 9 years and childless, sought therapy for intense feelings of depression and loneliness. The therapist saw her alone initially and during the early sessions.

Of course, there are situations in which noncohabiting adults may seek conjoint treatment. In these situations, it is generally appropriate to see them with a noncohabiting relevant-other for the first session. Robert, a 45-year-old bachelor, sought therapy because he and his father were in great conflict about the disposition of the family business. Robert wanted to be seen with his father, and the therapist saw both of them for the first session.

Within problem-centered therapy, married or cohabiting adults (Category 4b) are viewed as structurally equivalent to the child identified patient in a nuclear family (Category 1) or to one of the spouses in a couple seeking couple therapy (Category 3). The only difference is that the cohabiting adult is both the identified and the organizing patient. The structural ideal includes as many of the appropriate key patients as possible in the initial interview regardless of whether the presenting problem is individual or interpersonal.

With Sharon Neuville, a married 47-year-old woman seeking therapy for depression, the therapist requests that her husband participate in the first session. Her husband's presence can be helpful in various ways. It permits the therapist to assess the marital relationship as well as the husband's investment in his wife's depression or recovery. It also permits the therapist to begin to establish an alliance with the husband to facilitate the treatment of his wife's depression or other problems that may emerge. Generally, including the partner in the first session with a cohabiting adult presenting primarily individual problems provides more information than excluding the partner.

The invitation to the partner to attend the first interview ideally should come from the identified patient. If the identified patient is unsuccessful in recruiting the partner, the therapist can attempt recruitment directly. In recruiting the partner, it is important to avoid communicating the presumption that there are relationship problems (unless they are presenting problems) or that the partner is implicated in the problem-maintenance structure. Rather, the partner is invited to the first session to help the therapist understand the identified patient's presenting problem.

There are at least three circumstances in which the cohabiting partner or system members (child or parent) should be excluded from the initial interview. They should not be included when their presence would hurt the development of the alliance with either the identified patient or the partner. The best indicator of potential alliance damage is tenacious resistance to the idea of including the partner from the identified patient or the partner. In the face of such resistance, the therapist should relent and see the identified patient alone.

The second circumstance occurs when it is clear that the presenting problem cannot be adequately or appropriately identified and explored in the presence of the partner. For instance, a husband engaged in an affair seeks therapy when his jealous mistress threatens to call his wife. To include the wife in the first session would preclude talking about the presenting problem and to include the mistress would probably jeopardize the possibility of building an alliance with the wife and including her in subsequent sessions.

The last circumstance for excluding system members from initial interviews with cohabiting adults is developmental inappropriateness. It is frequently useful to involve teenagers and older children and sometimes even younger children in initial interviews when one of their parents is the identified patient. Children are invariably affected by and knowledgeable about their parents' problems and may provide useful information. With some presenting problems, however, the presence of a child, particularly a younger child, is contraindicated. For instance, it would not be appropriate to include children in an initial interview with a father seeking treatment for a sexual perversion. The revelation of such problems could easily and unnecessarily traumatize his children.

INITIAL INTERVIEW: SUMMARY

The operating principle for the first session is to include as many key patients as possible. This principle is fairly straightforward with Mode of Presentation Categories 1 and 3: nuclear families with children and couples with relationship problems. It needs to be applied more selectively with binuclear families with child problems and with adults seeking individual therapy: Categories 2 and 4. Flexibility is the key with binuclear families, and cohabitation is the core distinction with individual adults. With all systems and modes of presentation, the structural ideal should be modified if it appears that it may damage emerging alliances.

THE EARLY SESSIONS

As well as helping the therapist build the alliance and "join" the patient system (Minuchin, 1974), the early sessions (Sessions 2–5) provide an opportunity to obtain crucial information from relevant system members in different intervention contexts. *The goal of the early sessions is to create a working plan for the middle phase of therapy.* This plan contains two primary components. The first, addressed in Chapter 6, is a working definition of the major presenting problems and a preliminary model of the problem cycle. The second component, a working structure, delineates which members of the patient system will be involved in what ways. The structure of the early sessions differs according to mode of presentation.

NUCLEAR FAMILY WITH A CHILD AS IDENTIFIED PATIENT

It is ideal with this mode of presentation to have the first session with the full family and the second session alone with the identified patient. As well as facilitating an alliance with the identified patient, an initial individual session (after the family session) accomplishes several objectives. It builds the alliance with the parents by structurally acknowledging their presentation of their child as the identified patient. It also may provide information from the identified patient that might not emerge in the family context. This is particularly crucial in cases of sexual or physical abuse.

It may also be useful to see a parent or parents within the same therapy interval (e.g., week) as the individual session with the child. This session may yield information that the parents were unwilling to share in the initial family session. This information might pertain to facts or feelings about the identified patient or to problems within other subsystems of the patient system (adult, marital, or sibling) that the parents or the therapist might consider inappropriate to share with the child.

The decision to conduct a session with the parents alone is complicated in this early phase of treatment. One of the major complications hinges on the distinction between report and action information. *Report information* is what people tell the therapist about themselves and others. *Action information* is what the therapist learns about an individual or interpersonal system from observing action or interaction sequences (Breunlin & Schwartz, 1986); it is information from sequential action: what people do with the therapist and each other over time.

Both report and action information are essential in understanding a system. However, action information tends to be more spontaneous, genuine, and unconscious. Action information increases with the addition of key patients to the direct system. Adding patients to the direct system expands the intervention context and provides more opportunities to test crucial hypotheses directly early in treatment.

For instance, in the first session with the Jensens, the therapist asked the mother, Marie, how she feels dealing with Danny most of the day alone at home. After hearing that she felt overwhelmed and frustrated, the therapist asked her if she shares those feelings with anyone. Marie began to cry and said "not really." At that point her husband, Dan, stated forcefully to Marie that he tries to talk to her but that she won't do what he says to do with Danny. She responded angrily that he does not understand and is seldom around anyway.

Up to this point in the interview, Danny had been playing appropriately with a toy truck. As his parents conversed, his behavior escalated to the point that, when his mother lamented her husband's lack of understanding and availability, he rammed the truck into the wall. This disruption was followed by Dan harshly reprimanding Danny and turning to the therapist to say, "See, he cannot even play for 5 minutes without causing a problem."

The action information in this vignette can be used to support or reject various hypotheses. With the Jensens, a primary hypothesis is that Danny's behavioral problems function in part to regulate the marital system. The action information described reflects a sequence in which Danny disrupts a conflictual interaction between his parents. This sequence supports the more specific hypothesis that Danny's disruptive behavior detours conflict (Minuchin, 1974) between his parents.

The therapist might have waited to ask Marie about her feelings concerning her son's problems until a second session with the parents only. The therapist would have learned about the marital conflict but would not have observed the relationship between the conflict and Danny's behavior. The therapist would have lost the opportunity to identify the sequence and help the parents consider the possible relationship between their behavior and their son's problem. Danny's presence was contextually essential to provide the most meaningful action information.

This example highlights the fact that the therapist needs to think through which questions should be asked in the presence of which subsystems. By asking critical questions when the identified patient and other key patients are not present, the therapist runs the risk of losing action information that may be crucial in understanding the problem-maintenance structure. Once the "cat is out of the bag," it cannot be put back. Once the therapist asks a crucial question with the parents alone, it cannot be asked again in the child's presence without jeopardizing the parents' alliance with the therapist. The parents will inevitably ask themselves why the therapist is asking this question again and may feel "set up" and manipulated.

Despite these reflections, there are two valid circumstances in which it is essential to see parents alone, without the identified patient. The first set of circumstances is clear evidence of marital or adult problems that might be inappropriate or destructive to discuss in front of children. For instance, overt parental comments about marital distress without much defensiveness during the initial family session constitute a strong indicator for sessions with the parents alone. Similarly, a single parent commenting nondefensively about serious problems in his or her life in the first session is a good indicator.

Another indicator is substantial evidence in the first session of feared family secrets. Typically, the parents allude to things that they do not want to discuss in front of the children or the identified patient. In this situation, if for no other reason than preserving the alliance, the therapist should meet alone with the parents to find out the secret. Sometimes private disclosure is appropriate, as in the case of an affair, plans for or serious discussions about divorce, or life-threatening illness. At other times, it is inappropriate: The children already know the secret (and just pretend not to) or would benefit by its disclosure.

By meeting alone with the parent or parents, the therapist not only honors their privacy and strengthens the alliance with them, but also discerns the nature of the secret and the degree of danger involved in its disclosure. The therapist usually concludes such a session by encouraging disclosure in a subsequent session or series of sessions or by recommending nondisclosure and judicious management of the secret, at least for the time being.

The general rule of thumb in the early phase is to conduct sessions alone with the parents only in the face of compelling evidence of the need to do so (as indicated previously) or after the critical hypothesis-testing questions have been asked in the appropriate action-information context. Once the questions have been uttered in the full family context, repeating them alone with the parents does not have the same alliance risk as reversing the sequence. The parents may even welcome the opportunity to respond openly to a question they felt they could not answer candidly in front of their children. It is a good idea, with most nuclear families, to conduct a session alone with the parents at some point in the early phase of therapy. The only question is when.

BINUCLEAR FAMILY WITH A CHILD AS IDENTIFIED PATIENT

In contrast to the procedure with nuclear families, during the early sessions with binuclear families presenting with child problems, it is necessary to conduct sessions with various subsystems. The child who is an identified patient should be seen alone at least once. Individual sessions permit the child to talk in an "apolitical" context. It is also valuable to see each of the major households alone. The child should be seen with both sets of parents (or single parents) and siblings at least once. It is frequently useful in terms of information gain and alliance building to meet separately with the parents from each household.

Early sessions with the whole divorced family are an option that is not usually necessary but is frequently useful. Typically, the initial session includes all the key members of the patient system. Depending on the coparental alliance between the divorced parents, another full family session may or may not be useful. Sessions with the identified patient and siblings without any parents can be informative during this phase as well.

With divorced systems during this early phase, the therapist must be particularly sensitive to balancing the sessions with the two households. With poorly allied divorced coparents, arranging more sessions with the "other system" may damage the therapeutic alliance. In contrast, some divorced subsystems may feel relieved to be relatively ignored by the therapist. Typically, these subsystems feel overly blamed or terrified of involvement with the ex-spouse and his or her family. The therapist should be sensitive to the alliance requirements of the system and its various subsystems. The critical task is to maximize information gain without jeopardizing the alliance.

Sessions with Nonfamilial Systems

In both binuclear and nuclear families with a child with school problems, the therapist should directly contact, at least by phone, key people in the school system during the early sessions. Ideally, at some point during the early sessions, the therapist has a staffing or consultation meeting with the parents and key school personnel. The identified patient may or may not be present.

This meeting has several purposes. The first is to ensure that all the key players have the same understanding of the child's behavior at school and the school's stance toward that behavior. This diminishes pathological triangulation among the family, school, and therapist. The second purpose is to deepen the therapeutic alliance among the family, the school, and the therapist and to help all three systems function as allies to help the child. This goal may require considerable preparatory contact, particularly when the family and the school are not allied.

Such a meeting permits the therapist to assess directly the family and school systems, focusing particularly on their potential to work together to help the child. If the link between the family and school is beyond repair, or if the school is not competent to deal with the child or the family, that information needs to be obtained early in treatment. Of course, alliance considerations may dictate that the therapist meet alone with the school personnel or that any meeting with school representatives be postponed until the middle phase of therapy.

The issues concerning schools also apply with most other nonfamilial systems that are part of the patient system. For instance, it is imperative that most encopretic children have a thorough pediatric examination. It is also likely that the pediatrician will be involved in helping to break the encopretic pattern. During the early sessions with a family with an encopretic child, the pediatrician must be contacted and perhaps engaged directly in the treatment process.

COUPLES WITH RELATIONSHIP PROBLEMS

In working with couples presenting with relationship problems, it may be useful to include an individual session with each partner during the early sessions. Individual sessions permit the therapist to obtain information that the partners were not willing to share in front of each other. They may also strengthen the individual alliances with each partner and help the therapist get a sense of each partner independent of the other.

Individual sessions with couples can be fraught with pitfalls, however, and should not be used with all couples. First, they can diminish access to action information early in treatment. Second, they can leave the therapist with secrets that may be explosive and potentially jeopardize the alliance with one or both partners.

In general, *individual sessions should not be used with couples unless certain indicators are present*. The first indicator is the impression that one or both of the partners are not completely forthcoming. In the second session with Roberto and Louise Gomez, the therapist sensed that Louise's complaints about Roberto did not warrant her severe withdrawal from him in the last 4 months. The therapist raised this issue with the couple to no avail. At that point, the therapist asked for individual sessions with each of them. In her individual session, Louise confessed that Roberto hit her in the face during a fight 4 months previously. He had sworn her to secrecy, but now she felt that she could not honor his wish. She has felt numb toward him since the assault.

Another indicator is the existence of a weak alliance with one or both partners. Jim Denton and Arnie Morris, a chronically conflicted homosexual couple, seemed remote and distrusting of their heterosexual male therapist. In the second session, the therapist asked if they were uncomfortable because he was heterosexual. They denied any misgivings. After their third session, the therapist recommended individual sessions.

In the individual sessions, the therapist made a concerted effort to get to know the partners' individual histories, with particular emphasis on the emergence and development of their homosexual identities. Once again, the therapist asked each of them if he was uncomfortable with him as a heterosexual male. They each vigorously denied any misgivings, but Arnie acknowledged that he felt more comfortable after meeting with the therapist individually and seeing his comfort in openly and knowledgeably pursuing Arnie's personal history and the emergence of his homosexuality. After these sessions, the therapist felt more bonded to Jim and Arnie, and they were much more open and trusting in their communication.

Confidentiality Risks

If the therapist uses individual sessions at any time during treatment, particularly when one or both partners seem to be withholding information, confidentiality presents a major risk. If a partner confides information that he or she does not want shared with the other partner, the therapist's alliance with the nonconfiding partner could be jeopardized. This problem can be avoided by clarifying the confidentiality arrangement in advance. *The operational rule is to establish an arrangement that both partners understand and accept.*

At the end of the first session with Art and Angie Doleman, Art asked for an individual session. The therapist postponed discussion of that option until the second session. At that time, the therapist acknowledged a willingness to see Art alone but wanted to know the confidentiality basis on which Art wanted to be seen: total, partial, or no confidentiality. Art said that he wanted his session to be totally confidential. When the therapist asked Angie if that was alright with her, she quickly said, "Of course." However, the therapist then commented, "Wait a minute. I know what I am going to say may sound farfetched, and it is based on no information whatsoever, but what if Art tells me that he is having an affair with a woman at work and that he doesn't want me to tell you?" Angie responded, "I wouldn't like it, but better you should know than no one, or anybody else for that matter."

If Angie had responded that she could not continue to trust and work effectively if the therapist knew about Art's affair but did not tell her, the therapist would have worked out a partial confidentiality arrangement that would be acceptable to Art and Angie. Such an arrangement might involve the therapist's agreeing to keep certain information confidential (information about Art's thoughts, feelings, or actions that would not hurt or significantly impact on Angie) and other information not confidential (information pertaining to actions that could hurt or significantly impact on Angie). Whatever the arrangement, it must be acceptable in advance to both patients. When a confidentiality arrangement has been agreed on and followed, the likelihood of individual sessions disrupting the therapeutic alliance diminishes significantly.

Adults Requesting Individual Treatment

The primary goal of early sessions with an adult seeking individual therapy is to evaluate the patient system and the problem-maintenance structure sufficiently to make a decision about the focus and structure of the therapy during the middle phase. This decision hinges on two primary factors. The first and most critical factor concerns the cohabitation structure of the identified patient. The second factor concerns the presenting problems and the extent to which other patients appear to play key roles in the problem-maintenance structures.

The first factor, cohabitation structure, focuses on whether the identified patient lives alone or with someone else. In the preceding discussion of the first interview, the recommendation was that noncohabiting adults be seen alone for the first session unless they clearly indicate a desire to be seen with a relevant-other. Unless there is no relevant-other in the patient system, interacting directly with certain members of the patient system during the early sessions can shed important light on the presenting problems and the problem-maintenance structures.

Malcolm Whitley is 34 years old, divorced, lonely, and depressed. He has a 6-year-old son, Max, who lives with his ex-wife, Gloria. Malcolm sees Max every weekend and has recently been having lengthy phone conversations with Gloria, who is about to remarry. Malcolm's depression has increased over the 2 months since Gloria told him of her plans to remarry. Seen alone in the first two sessions, Malcolm expressed intense anxiety about losing his connection with Max when Gloria remarried. It was also beginning to dawn on him that Gloria's remarriage represented the final death knell of his subconscious fantasies of repairing the marriage and putting the family back together. The therapist recommended that Gloria come in for one of the early sessions with Malcolm to clarify her thoughts about the impact of her new marriage on Malcolm's relationship with Max.

When she came in during the fourth session, Gloria clearly communicated her commitment to maintaining Max's relationship with Malcolm. She also talked openly and caringly with Malcolm and the therapist about her perception that Malcolm had never gotten over the divorce and built a new life for himself. The session with Gloria not only helped to clarify expectations vis-à-vis Malcolm and Max, it also defined Malcolm's difficulty in moving beyond the divorce as a presenting problem. Additionally, the therapist got to know the "reality" of Gloria beyond Malcolm's reports.

At the end of the session, Gloria suggested that Max come in for a session, and Malcolm concurred. Max came in for the fifth session with his father. The therapist sensed a strong bond between them and moved further toward defining Malcolm's failure to grieve his marriage as the primary presenting problem. These early sessions with key members of Malcolm's family focused the subsequent individual therapy on his need to grieve and build a new, more satisfying personal life.

It can be useful to involve key patients with whom the identified patient has problems. Frank Ebel, a 25-year-old law student, sought therapy because he could not decide whether or not to move in with Connie, his girlfriend, who was pressuring him to get an apartment with her. At the therapist's urging, Connie attended the third session, in which it became clear that the moving issue was the tip of an iceberg of relationship issues between them.

The therapist used the next three sessions with Frank to decide whether to define the therapy as his individual treatment or as conjoint treatment for himself and Connie to work on their relationship and individual issues. In these sessions, Frank doubted his commitment to Connie. He also realized he wanted to sort out a variety of troubling feelings that he had with Connie and had experienced with women in previous relationships. The therapist and Frank decided that the primary context for the middle sessions would be individual, although they did not preclude including Connie down the line if it made sense.

With cohabiting individuals presenting for individual therapy (Mode of Presentation Category 4b), it is standard to involve key members of their patient system in the early sessions, regardless of the presenting problem. Lenore Cobbs, a single 32-year-old mother of four, came into therapy because she felt she was "going crazy" and might kill someone if she did not get help. Her desperation poured out in the first three sessions. She complained of feeling exploited by her children as well as by her diabetic and obese mother, who had been living with her for the past 3 years since her father died. Lenore had recently broken up with her boyfriend of 5 years because of his repeated infidelities.

The therapist recommended early sessions with all of the children and the grandmother. Lenore feared that the sessions might be too stressful for her mother, but with the therapist's encouragement, invited her in for a session with the kids and a session with Lenore. The sessions revealed that Lenore's children and mother loved and respected her and were not as helpless as she perceived them to be. After Lenore expressed her feelings of anger, exploitation, loneliness, and exhaustion, her family responded adaptively. The older daughter volunteered to do the laundry, her mother offered to cook more meals and take over the bills, and the second child, a 13-year-old son, committed himself to taking the younger children to swim classes at the local YMCA. The middle sessions primarily involved Lenore, although her mother and several of the children came in occasionally to discuss specific issues.

With noncohabiting individuals, as with cohabiting adults presenting for individual therapy, a critical decision that should be made by the end of the early sessions is whether the middle sessions will be primarily individual or conjoint. As the preceding examples illustrate, that decision hinges on the living arrangements of the identified patient, the nature of the primary presenting problems, and the problem-maintenance structure. The decision to involve other members of the patient system directly and consistently in the middle sessions is more likely with cohabiting adults, but it is not inevitable.

In recommending individual versus conjoint treatment at the end of the early sessions, the problem-maintenance factor generally outweighs the presenting-problem and living-arrangement factors. If key patients appear to participate actively in problem maintenance, regardless of living arrangements or the interpersonal versus individual nature of the problems, the therapist should recommend that these patients participate in the middle sessions. If the evidence is unclear and the individual presents interpersonal problems, the therapist should recommend the involvement of appropriate key patients in the middle phase.

Recommending purely individual treatment in the middle phase is appropriate only when the presenting problems are genuinely and primarily individual and the patient system does not appear to be invested in maintaining the problems. It is hard to make effective decisions about the interpersonal structure of the middle sessions, however, if key patients have not been involved in some of the early sessions, regardless of the living structure or presenting problems of the individual patient. Of course, all of these recommendations about structuring the early sessions should be altered if they are likely to harm the emerging alliance.

EARLY SESSIONS: SUMMARY

The purpose of the early sessions is to build a viable therapeutic alliance with key members of the patient system and to develop a working plan for the middle sessions. That plan consists of a consensually shared definition of the major presenting problems as well as an agreed-on interpersonal structure for the middle sessions. In terms of interpersonal context, the early sessions are the most flexible and exploratory of the four phases of therapy. With the frequent use of subsystemic sessions, the sessions should be organized to maximize action information and to avoid alliance disruptions related to confidentiality triangles.

THE MIDDLE SESSIONS: THE STRUCTURE OF ONGOING THERAPY

The early sessions conclude with a treatment plan that specifies which patients will constitute the direct system during the middle sessions. In all but the briefest therapies, the middle sessions constitute the bulk of the therapy. The predominant treatment structure during the middle sessions depends on the presenting problem or problems, the problem-maintenance structures, and the alliance requirements of the case. Each of the four modes of presentation has a preferred structure during this phase.

NUCLEAR FAMILY WITH A CHILD AS IDENTIFIED PATIENT

The preferred structure for this mode of presentation is family sessions directly involving the parents and at least the identified patient. Siblings ideally should be included as well. The full nuclear family structure can be complemented with regular or episodic individual sessions with the identified patient or other individuals or subsystems within the patient system.

Three variables influence the use of individual sessions in this mode. The first is the degree of object and self pathology of key patients who are involved in the problem-maintenance structure. In general, the more disturbed the patient, the more likely that individual sessions will be necessary to modify the problem-maintenance structure sufficiently to permit problem resolution.

Sheila Monnett, 14 years old, became despondent and attempted suicide after breaking up with her boyfriend of a year and a half. Her medication overdose fortunately was not enough to kill or damage her, and she and her parents were referred to outpatient therapy after a brief hospitalization. Sheila's parents had a disengaged relationship, and her mother had turned to Sheila for the emotional support she sought from her husband. Enmeshed with her mother, Sheila frequently functioned as an advisor, friend, and surrogate spouse.

Sheila's boyfriend, Ben, was her anchor outside the home. He took care of her the way Sheila took care of her mother. He was her friend, father, and confidant. When Ben broke up with Sheila, she was devastated. Her father remained emotionally unavailable, and her mother displayed a shocking lack of empathy. In fact, her mother resented Sheila's becoming emotionally unavailable to her. Sheila felt alone, trapped in her family, and overwhelmed with sadness.

The parents responded positively in therapy. The father moved closer to Sheila, and for the first time in 15 years, the mother turned to her husband for support. After 10 sessions, the parents asked to see the therapist alone to work on their marriage. As the mother got more nurturance from her husband, she became less narcissistic and more empathic with Sheila. However, Sheila did not respond to the therapy as positively. As her mother moved closer to her father, she felt betrayed. She became bitter toward her mother and felt suspicious of her father's overtures. She lacked the skills to articulate her feelings and sunk deeper into despondency.

Sheila's parents and therapist became alarmed at her withdrawal. During the early sessions, the therapist had met alone with Sheila twice. Because Sheila had seemed able and willing at that time to open up in family sessions (primarily about her grief at losing Ben), the predominant middle-phase structure, up to the time of her recent withdrawal, was full-family sessions, including irregularly her two younger siblings, Mark, 11, and Ruby, 7.

The therapist read Sheila's withdrawal as evidence of powerful object and self constraints and recommended at least weekly individual sessions for Sheila. The parents agreed, and a new structure emerged: weekly individual sessions with Sheila and additional weekly sessions alternating between the parents alone (focusing primarily on the marriage) and the full family (focusing on Sheila, family communication, and affective involvement).

Individually, Sheila was slow to open up. She did not want to face her sadness and anger about feeling used by her mother and abandoned by her father. She said at one point, "I'd rather die than hurt them." The therapist responded, "You almost did." Their work progressed, and Sheila began to clarify and accept her feelings. After 15 individual sessions over a 4-month period, Sheila felt ready to express her feelings to her parents. She decreased her individual sessions to twice a month and had additional sessions with her parents. Although they were painful, these sessions cleared the air and changed the family's patterns of relating and communicating. Sheila's mood and behavior improved with each session.

In some moderately to extremely disturbed patient systems, the patients requiring individual sessions may not include the identified patient. In this mode-of-presentation category, key blocks to problem solving are frequently maintained by major object and self constraints from adult members. With such systems, individual therapy should focus on the blocked adult.

Charles Mallory is the 46-year-old father of Ron, a depressed high school senior whose grades had precipitously dropped off. Ron also showed signs of withdrawing from family and friends. In the early family sessions, Ron expressed fears that he would not be able to get into his father's alma mater: Notre Dame University. Ron felt despair about disappointing his father, who assumed Ron would go to Notre Dame. Ron was also angry at his father for pressuring him to follow his path, regardless of Ron's needs and interests.

The early sessions revealed that Charles was enmeshed with Ron and unable to tolerate Ron's differentiation or anger. In the third session, Ron expressed his fear and resentment to his father, who responded with guilt-inducing disappointment. At the end of the fourth session with the family, the therapist recommended that Charles and his wife, Monique, come in for supplementary sessions to discuss ways to help Ron. The primary goal of these sessions was to engage Charles in sufficient individually focused work to enable him to hear and respond to Ron. The recommendation to include Monique derived from the therapist's impression from the early sessions that she would facilitate Charles's change.

The second reason for individual sessions, particularly with the identified patient, involves the developmental status of the child. The older the child, the more likely that individual sessions will be a useful adjunct to full-family sessions. In a family with a 16-year-old boy with drug and school problems, it would be inappropriate for the boy to discuss private aspects of his life, such as sex, in full-family sessions. This and other private topics can be addressed in individual sessions. This mixed structure supports the family and the child's developmentally appropriate needs for privacy and increased autonomy.

The third variable concerning individual sessions is the nature of the therapeutic alliance. Some children do not open up consistently to the therapist, or to anyone, in the presence of their parents. Their alliance with the therapist is not sufficiently strong to overcome their parentally linked inhibition. Such children require individual sessions until they feel comfortable enough to open up in a family context. Frequently, with younger children, a home visit focusing on the child's room and toys strengthens the bond between the child and the therapist.

Conversely, some children open up only in the presence of their parents and possibly their siblings. Frequently, these children feel so scapegoated and ashamed of their status as "a psychiatric patient" that they resist any structure that reinforces that role. For them, individual sessions structurally acknowledge their problem status, and they will not open up alone with the therapist, even if individual sessions are developmentally appropriate. These children often open up quite dramatically in family sessions.

Behavioral Permission

Early family therapists commonly presumed that the primary determinant of child psychopathology was a dysfunctional marriage. This presumption led them to shift quickly from family to marital therapy. As soon as possible, the therapist would get the child out of the direct system and focus exclusively on the couple: the "real problem." Many families dropped out of therapy feeling blamed and manipulated. Typically, this premature termination was preceded by a period of progressive work on the marital system followed by a major regression in the symptomatic status of the identified patient.

Frequently, the presumption of marital pathology as the primary constraint in children's problems is accurate. In such situations, the critical decision is when to diminish the child's involvement in the direct system and focus primarily on the marital system. The most important factor in this decision is whether the child's regulation of the marital system can be openly acknowledged by the child and the parents. The primary vehicle for evaluating this factor is the concept of "behavioral permission." Do the child and other key patients have behavioral permission to acknowledge the child's systemic function?

There are two primary components to the concept of behavioral permission. The first pertains to the child's felt sense of permission and safety from the parents to open up with them and the therapist about his or her concerns about the marriage. The second concerns the therapist and parents' receiving permission from the child to focus primarily on the marital system.

Behavioral permission involves not just verbal permission to talk about the family and the marriage but the actual experience of observing the parents talking directly about their problems. The parents can say to the child, "It's okay to talk. Tell the therapist whatever you really think." If children are regulating the marriage, they seldom open up in the face of this verbal permission. If the parents open up about their marital issues in front of the children, however, and the children's attempts to defocus are empathically neutralized by the therapist or the parents, the children frequently open up with remarkable insight and candor. They need to see their parents open up before they can open up or let the therapist treat their parents.

In this type of system, observing the parents discussing their marital issues with the therapist is a corrective emotional experience for children. They learn that the "hot" issues can be addressed without catastrophic consequences and that the therapist is competent to handle the parents and their problems. Now the child can step out of the marital protector role and freely discuss genuine feelings and thoughts, letting the therapist take the lead in treating the parents. With behavioral permission, the child no longer needs to be the symptomatic regulator of the marriage.

Sometimes the parents give children behavioral permission to open up about the family and their function within it, but the child may not give the parents or the therapist permission to do so. Typically, this is the case with children who are more severely disturbed or are traumatized physically or sexually. Tina Green, 13 years old, was about to hang herself when her older brother, Lewis, walked into the basement and found her standing on a stepladder. Hospitalized for psychiatric care, Tina resisted any discussion about her family and their relationships. In family sessions, she refused to speak about anything substantial, focusing instead on when she could get out of the hospital. Tina's parents openly acknowledged their marital problems and that Dad was a recovering alcoholic. They even opened up the possibility that the father may have been physically or sexually abusive to Tina when he was drinking. Tina refused to pursue these issues, walking out and returning to her hospital room if they were brought up. After extensive inpatient individual therapy, Tina started to share her feelings and thoughts about her family and her father's abusiveness.

BINUCLEAR FAMILY WITH A CHILD AS IDENTIFIED PATIENT

Binuclear systems with a child as the identified patient are the most idiosyncratic and complex systems, involving at times up to four or more parents and multiple siblings. Frequently, hostile feelings predominate between ex-spouses as well as between other parent–parent dyads within the system. The key operating concept in working with these systems is flexibility.

The frequent use of subsystem sessions uniquely characterizes the middle-phase treatment of binuclear systems. Sessions with all of the parents (biological and step) are typically less frequent, even when biological parents communicate effectively. The three previously mentioned indicators for individual sessions—level of psychopathology, developmental status, and quality of alliance—apply also with binuclear systems.

Ideally, most of the sessions involve the identified patient and the custodial parents; some of the sessions involve the identified patient and the noncustodial parents; and fewer sessions involve all of the parents and the identified patient. Siblings may or may not be involved in any of these structures. If the parents have joint custody, the sessions with each system should be balanced, unless there is some compelling reason to focus primarily on one system. The sessions with all of the parents or parents from different households should be used only to address specific issues pertaining to the interaction between households and ex-spouses. Frequently, sessions with the identified patient and one parent are useful when they focus on problems within that parent–child dyad.

These guidelines should be modified depending on the interpersonal locus of the primary constraints. Typically, the therapy focuses on the subsystem that contains the principal constraints. For instance, if a primary constraint is the too-distant relationship between the identified patient and the noncustodial parent, the therapy should focus primarily on that subsystem.

School Sessions

With any system that includes a child with school problems, the school must be directly involved at some point. If the contacts in the early sessions established an adequate alliance with key school personnel and implemented the school-related aspects of the adaptive solution, only minimal contacts with the school may be necessary during the middle phase. Telephone calls may be sufficient. Because of the number of parents involved in binuclear systems, it is usually impossible during the early sessions to establish an alliance that is sufficient to conduct a school staffing to create an effective plan of action.

If the early contacts did not establish an adequate alliance or engage the school in solving the problem, additional middle-phase contacts are necessary. These contacts may require regular consultations with or supervising of teachers or guidance personnel concerning the design and implementation of special programs for the identified patient. If major problem-solving blocks emerge regarding the school's part of the adaptive solution, an assessment may have to be made about the capacity of the school to change and the feasibility of the child continuing in that school.

If the school personnel are willing and able to work on providing the necessary programmatic and supportive services, even if those efforts are somewhat problematic, it is usually worth the therapist's time and effort to work with the key representatives in some ongoing way. If the school is not willing or able to make the requisite effort, however, alternative school placement probably should be sought. A key concept to keep in mind when working with schools is that key school personnel are part of the patient system and may require the same amount of therapist skill, patience, and resourcefulness that other family members or even the identified patient requires.

Particularly with binuclear systems, it is important to involve all of the key parents (biological and step) in the school component of the adaptive solution. All of the parents in a binuclear system probably should be invited to any school staffing. Excluding a parent frequently jeopardizes that parent's alliance with the school and the therapist. The therapist may even help the school to work effectively with a conflictual binuclear system.

COUPLES WITH RELATIONSHIP PROBLEMS

The ideal middle-phase structure of therapy with couples who present their relationship as the primary problem is conjoint sessions, regardless of whether they have children or not. The presence of children in the sessions usually inhibits the parents and is developmentally inappropriate. Children do not need to be privy to the intimate details of their parents' relationship. A clear and relatively strong generational boundary is reinforced by this therapeutic structure. This conjoint structure can be modified by adding individual sessions with the partners or by including other key patients as guests.

Individual Sessions

Sessions with the individual members of a couple can be useful in several scenarios. When there is a weak therapeutic alliance with one or both partners, one or more individual sessions frequently strengthen the alliance. Sometimes sessions with one partner have to be balanced with sessions with the other one, although this is not always the case. The need for balanced sessions occurs when one partner feels threatened by the individual sessions with the other partner.

Individual sessions are useful and necessary for couples who are separated. With such couples, individual sessions can be regularly interwoven with conjoint meetings. Individual sessions permit work with each partner on his or her individual issues without gratuitously traumatizing the other partner. This is crucial when one or both partners are engaged in other intimate relationships. If the couple moves closer to reconciliation, the therapy structure should probably reflect that fact by an increase in the proportion of conjoint sessions and a decrease in the individual ones. Within this framework, the therapist functions like a bridge between the partners who also recognizes and facilitates their individual development.

Individual sessions are also useful to deal with current or past extramarital affairs with intact couples. Exploring the past affair with the unfaithful partner may be critical to resolving the presenting problem. Doing so in the presence of the faithful partner, however, usually is unnecessarily painful and inhibits the unfaithful partner from fully exploring the meaning of the affair. Once the affair has been affectively neutralized, it can be useful to continue exploration in a conjoint context.

On the other hand, it is usually essential for the unfaithful spouse to be present when the faithful spouse explores the meaning of the affair. Witnessing the reliving of the faithful partner's experience, hearing the pain the affair inflicted, and empathically understanding the faithful partner's experience are critical for the healing process in the treatment of such couples.

When one partner is actively and overtly engaged in an extramarital relationship, individual sessions are essential. The details and meanings of that relationship for the unfaithful spouse need to be explored, which can be done appropriately only in an individual context. Typically, these situations are not stable, and the affair ceases or the partners separate.

The last scenario for individual sessions involves problem-maintenance structures that include potent object and self constraints. As discussed in Chapter 3, the progressive bonding process with profoundly constrained patients requires individual sessions and may ultimately require separate individual therapies with other therapists for one or both partners.

Guest Sessions: Older Parents and Siblings

Besides including individual sessions, the couple context can be modified in the middle sessions by including other key patients as guests. Typically, these sessions occur as prearranged time-limited therapeutic episodes of three or more sessions over a fairly short time period. Ideally, a guest episode includes weekly sessions with the guests and at least one weekly session with the couple to debrief and prepare for the next guest session. The invited key patients are defined as guests because they attend the sessions as guests of the couple, not as patients who are themselves seeking help from the therapist. The goal of these sessions is to help the constrained spouse and partner to address constructively the relevant transgenerational constraints with the appropriate members of the indirect system.

The most common guest-session format involves the parents of one of the spouses participating in a therapeutic episode with their child and child-in-law. Consistent with the interpersonal premise, the child's spouse should be included in most, if not all, of the guest sessions. Less common variants involve siblings of a partner or the couple's children.

As mentioned in Chapter 2 in regard to the family-of-origin orientations, there are various specific reasons for inviting the parents of one spouse in couple therapy to participate in guest sessions. All of them involve problem-maintenance structures with significant transgenerational constraints. The first specific reason is to change maladaptive interaction patterns with the parents that constrain marital problem solving. Engaging the parents directly in a treatment episode can help the therapist to understand the couple better and to change the interaction pattern.

A second reason for inviting parents into treatment is to unblock a stuck marital therapy. Frank and Darlene Lundberg were in treatment for a year and a half. Their communication improved, their capacity for mutual empathy increased, but their sexual relationship remained problematic. Darlene still had "mysterious pain" during intercourse. Medical evaluation failed to reveal any biological determinants of the dyspareunia. Also, when she felt insecure, Darlene still depreciated Frank.

Darlene's father incessantly depreciated Darlene and her mother, calling them nitwits. Darlene invited her parents to a series of sessions in which she confronted her father's depreciating behavior toward her. She also confronted her mother's failure to confront and stop his devaluing behavior toward women in general and toward her and her mother in particular. For five painful sessions, her parents listened but failed to understand Darlene's message. They just did not get it. Eventually, the sessions with Darlene's parents ended with Darlene "releasing" them. Her father temporarily curbed his behavior, but the changes were to be short-lived.

The most interesting outcome of the sessions with Darlene's parents occurred in her relationship with Frank. The dyspareunia disappeared, and sex became totally pleasurable. Darlene also stopped depreciating Frank when she felt anxious. The explanation for change that emerged was that Darlene had for years displaced her anger at her father onto Frank and simultaneously identified with her father. By directing her anger where it belonged (at her father for depreciating and her mother for permitting it) and by facing her parents' and particularly her father's inability to understand her, she reorganized herself affectively and let go of the destructive identification with her father as a depreciator.

Important siblings with whom a spouse is destructively involved can be usefully invited into therapy. Sibling sessions can be helpful also when a sibling relationship has not been destructive but has been underused. Engaging a disengaged sibling can broaden the support network for the spouse, potentially diminishing the demands on the marriage and disengaging a pathologically enmeshed couple.

Guest Sessions: Children

Children may be invited into a therapy that focuses on their parents' marital relationship when the children need to learn "hot" news or when a problem exists with the children that blocks resolution of the presenting problem. Most commonly, adult children of older couples attend guest sessions.

Married for 35 years, Larry and Sara Darby entered marital therapy when Sara asked Larry to move out. Sara's request was precipitated by her discovery that Larry was having an affair with a colleague at his accounting firm. Sara and Larry had been private about their turmoil, and their children (aged 32, 29, and 25) sensed the problems but did not know the causes. After 4 months in therapy, the Darbys invited their children into therapy to inform them of the present circumstances of their marriage and open the possibility of dialogue, support, and involvement with their children on a more adult basis. Although they were offended by their father's infidelity, after several sessions the children were able to respond supportively to each parent on an individual basis.

Lew and Rosalie Tannenbaum, in their late 60s, had been married for over 40 years. Their two married children, a son and a daughter, had become reluctant to leave their children on overnight visits at Lew and Rosalie's home since Rosalie's moderately debilitating stroke the previous year. The children had communicated their concerns to Lew but were afraid to offend their mother.

Lew and Rosalie had entered therapy after her stroke. They were struggling with their feelings about and the realities of her disability. Eventually, in therapy, Lew told Rosalie about the children's concerns about leaving the grandchildren with them. Rosalie denied the problem. She thought Lew was making up stories and exaggerating her disability. In response to her incredulity, Lew suggested that they invite the children into therapy to discuss the issue.

To preclude a destructive confrontation and to better understand the children's concerns, the therapist had an initial session alone with them and their spouses. This session also helped the therapist to assess their feelings for their mother and their roles vis-à-vis their parents' marriage. This session revealed that the children and their spouses were empathically concerned with Rosalie and that the likelihood of a destructive confrontation was minimal.

The children and their spouses participated in three sessions with Rosalie and Lew. Rosalie was hurt and angry when confronted. The children told Rosalie that they wanted to find a way for her and Lew to be with their grandchildren that was not too stressful for Rosalie and in which the grand-children could be properly cared for. Lew volunteered to take over more child-care responsibilities with the grandchildren, and shortened, less taxing visits were planned. These sessions not only solved the grandchild visitation problem, but also facilitated the whole family's confrontation with the phys-ical and emotional consequences of Rosalie's stroke. The sorrowful and lov-ing feelings that emerged in the session strengthened the support system around Lew and Rosalie.

Frequently, problems with children are discussed at some length in marital therapy, particularly when they impinge on the marital relationship. An increasingly common scenario involves stepsystem sessions, with adult step-children as guests. These sessions are useful when problems with stepchil-dren arise in later life marriages resulting from divorce or the death of a spouse. Generally, the goal of these sessions is the clarification and strength-ening of boundaries regarding the stepparent as well the resolution of grief for the lost marriage or parent.

It is relatively rare within problem-centered therapy for younger children to be introduced into the direct system when the primary presenting prob-lem is the couple's relationship. Ideally, the children's problems are dealt with in the couple therapy without involving the children directly.

Ralph and Linda Fisk, each 35 years old, had been in treatment for 3 months for chronic marital conflict. A major conflict concerned their 6-year-old son and 4-year-old daughter. Ralph felt that Linda was inconsistent with the children and that they were disobedient and unhappy. During the 3 months of therapy, the therapist developed the hypothesis that Linda's expe-rience in her chaotic family of origin was being repeated with her children. She had tremendous difficulty sticking to any limits with the children and alternated between periods of rage and indulgence.

At the end of the third month, the therapist confronted Linda about her behavior with the children. Encouraging consistency, the therapist coached Linda, in Ralph's presence, in how to set and stick to limits. Initial targeted behaviors were bedtimes and talking back. Linda began to change her behavior with the children. As their behavior improved, Linda felt great relief and Ralph was extremely pleased. The house began to calm down, and the level of conflict in Ralph and Linda's relationship diminished.

The therapist's intervention with Linda could easily have been disastrous. It was successful for several reasons. First, by the time of the confrontation, the therapist had established a strong alliance with Linda. She did not feel betrayed or abandoned. Second, unlike Ralph, the therapist confronted

Linda without anger or depreciation. Third, Ralph was not invested in maintaining Linda's inconsistent behavior with the children. When she changed, he welcomed and supported her new behavior.

If the therapist's intervention with Linda and Ralph vis-à-vis the children had not been successful, the therapist would have faced a choice: bring the children into therapy for a child-focused episode or refer Ralph and Linda for family therapy with another therapist. The risk in bringing the children in, even for a relatively brief episode, is that it takes the focus away from the marital issues and jeopardizes the therapeutic momentum. The general operating principle is that if the couple are actively working on their issues and including the children would detract, the couple should engage in family therapy with another therapist. If the couple therapy has lost or never gained momentum, bringing the children in for a guest episode can be useful.

If a brief episode (3–6 sessions) of child-focused therapy does not ameliorate the children's problems, a choice has to be made about the ongoing focus of treatment. Should the therapy refocus on the couple and exclude the children, in which case another therapist may be brought in to work with the full family? Or should the therapy be redefined as family therapy with a dual and probably alternating focus on the children and the couple? That decision depends on many factors, primarily the likelihood of success of each alternative. Regardless of the decision, it is crucial that the couple and the therapist agree about the foci and structure of treatment.

In summary, guest sessions can be done with any members of the indirect patient system during the middle phase of therapy. The most crucial guideline in conducting guest sessions is to prepare adequately. The direct-system members should be as clear as possible about their goals for the sessions and the likely responses of the guests. The more that is thought through in advance, the more productive the guest sessions.

Involving Other Therapists in the Direct Therapist System

During the middle phase, when it becomes necessary to conduct individual sessions with key patients, it is usually better for the same therapist to conduct the conjoint and individual sessions with members of the same patient system. This increases coordination of efforts, minimizes redundancy and fragmentation, and tends to keep all of the "therapies" focused on the presenting problems.

There are times, however, when these individual sessions should be conducted by another therapist. The decision to bring in another therapist for the individual sessions (or for the conjoint sessions) hinges on the nature of the problem-maintenance structure and the alliance requirements of the patient system. Beyond overt patient requests, the primary sign that another therapist should be brought into the therapist system to conduct the individual or conjoint treatment of a key system member or members is failure to change. When the therapist has attempted to work with a system member individually and that treatment fails to modify the constraints, the therapist should encourage the patient to see another therapist. This step typically occurs after the therapist has intensified the individual treatment, and change still does not eventuate.

In some relatively rare situations it may be better for the original therapist to become the exclusive individual therapist of one system member, in which case another therapist should be brought in as the system's therapist. These situations usually occur when the patient has established a strong alliance with the original therapist and there is little chance that he or she will be able to do so with another therapist.

Maurice Lanier, a 55-year-old CEO of a large manufacturing company, was in couple therapy with his wife, Grace, for a year. After initial progress, the therapy stalled. Grace was unhappy and talked about leaving the marriage if Maurice did not cut back on his work schedule and start to devote more time to his marriage. Maurice expressed fears about cutting back on his job and about losing Grace. Conjoint family-of-origin work revealed that Maurice's mother's death when he was 9 constrained his ability to open up with and depend on another person. Also, his fear of poverty and insatiable desire for financial security, formed during his childhood spent in poverty, left him terrified to cut back his work.

After a year in couple therapy, Maurice was blocked. He seemed incapable of internalizing the therapist, forgot the sessions the minute they ended, and had developed hardly any observing ego. After some unproductive adjunctive individual sessions, their therapist, Roger, recommended ongoing individual therapy for Maurice with another therapist. Maurice responded that he would only get into individual therapy with Roger. He and Grace both felt it would take him too long to begin to trust another therapist.

Roger told Maurice and Grace that he felt the couple should not discontinue their conjoint therapy. He was sure that they would drift even further apart without a context and facilitator who could expand the communication channels that had begun to emerge between them. Roger also thought the intensity and exclusivity of treatment that Maurice needed would preclude his also functioning as the couple therapist. Roger recommended that a female colleague take over the couple therapy. After extensive discussion, the couple consented.

Again, the problem-centered ideal is for one therapist to conduct all of the individual and conjoint sessions with a patient system. However, some systems require multiple therapists, particularly to conduct exclusive and intensive individual therapies. To avoid pathological triangulation and the fragmentation of the direct treatment system, it is extremely important that the therapists are able to communicate directly and openly with each other. They need a good within-system alliance. Typically, the conjoint therapist functions as the coordinator of the direct therapist system, facilitating communication between the therapists and maximizing their allied operation.

Individuals Seeking Individual Therapy

With individual adults seeking individual therapy, the decision to work conjointly or individually is usually made during the early sessions. As stated previously, with a cohabiting individual, the middle phase relies primarily on a conjoint context, whereas with most noncohabiting individuals, the middle phase primarily involves individual work.

If the therapy was "interpersonalized" in the early phase, and the middle phase primarily involves conjoint work, the middle phase can best be conceptualized within the couple therapy framework. A shift to individual context work may or may not be necessary, but it is definitely not out of the question or dangerous. This is not the case with the reverse: shifting to a conjoint context during a primarily individual middle-phase therapy.

If the early-phase decision cast the middle phase within an individual context, it can be perilous to switch to a primarily conjoint context. Once a therapist conducts a significant number (10 or more) of uninterrupted individual sessions with a patient, the intensity of the alliance, particularly the transference aspect of the bonds dimension, is such that introducing other patients into the direct system disrupts that alliance. Most patients feel abandoned, and the therapist's efforts to create alliances with other patients injures patients who are more narcissistically vulnerable. The special link with the therapist is compromised, and the overall alliance is jeopardized.

This cautionary note is not meant to preclude introducing another patient into an individual direct system, but to identify a risk. If conjoint work becomes necessary, it is usually less disruptive for the key patients to get into conjoint treatment with another therapist. If that is impossible, other patients can be introduced into the direct system, but it must be done with considerable preparation.

Rhoda Blair, a 40-year-old divorced mother, was in individual therapy with Raoul, a psychiatrist, for over a year. Her major presenting problems were difficulty in developing relationships with men since her divorce 3

years previously and her continuing struggle to assert her needs constructively in important relationships. Rhoda lived in Chicago with her 16-year-
old son, Len. Len's father was remarried and lived in San Francisco.

Over the preceding 3 months, Rhoda spoke increasingly about the problems she was having with Len. He had become more and more withdrawn,
and his grades were falling off. Rhoda was worried and talked about bringing Len into therapy with her. Raoul did not dismiss the idea, but he raised
concerns about the impact of such a move on his alliance with Rhoda. They
decided that Rhoda would try to get Len to see a therapist who specialized
in treating adolescents and young adults.

When Rhoda broached this idea with Len, he said that there was nothing
wrong and he did not need a "shrink." After discussing Len's response,
Rhoda and Raoul decided that the next best alternative would be for Len to
come in with her for several sessions. These sessions would focus on Rhoda's
relationship with Len as well as his depression. They also decided not to offer
Len a choice but for Rhoda to insist that he come in with her for at least two
sessions.

Len reluctantly agreed to come in with Rhoda. In the first session, he was
defensive and withdrawn. He answered questions monosyllabically and
volunteered nothing. In the second session, Raoul asked to see Len alone for
the last half hour. When Rhoda left the room, Raoul asked Len about his life
since the divorce. Len confessed that he missed his father terribly but felt
that he could not express such thoughts without hurting his mother. He also
feared that his father was losing interest in him now that he had remarried
and might begin another family with his new wife.

Raoul asked if Len would be willing to talk about these thoughts and feelings with his mother, and Len said that he did not feel ready. Len asked if he
could see Raoul alone for several more sessions. Raoul invited Rhoda back
in for the last 5 minutes of the second session. He told her about Len's
request and asked her to think about it until they could discuss it at their
next individual session. At that session, Rhoda said she did not mind if
Raoul met with Len individually. She wanted to be sure that what she said
to Raoul was confidential and that her individual sessions with Raoul would
not be diminished. Raoul assured her of his confidentiality and said that he
would find a different time to see Len that would not interfere with his availability to her.

Raoul continued Rhoda's individual therapy and saw Len for eight individual sessions. In these sessions, a major issue was Len's perception of his
mother as not strong enough to handle his concerns and negative feelings.
Raoul reassured him repeatedly that Rhoda could handle whatever Len had

to say without falling apart. Finally, Len was ready. He and his mother had three sessions together in which Len opened up. Rhoda encouraged Len to reach out to his father with his concerns. Len's depression improved, and his withdrawal diminished. He continued to see Raoul individually twice a month for the next 5 months, during which he reconnected with his father and communicated more comfortably with his mother.

If Rhoda had resisted Len's involvement or gone along with it but "acted out" signs of resistance and discomfort, Raoul would have recommended that Len see someone else. That might have been possible once Len had the experience of opening up with Raoul during the second session. Raoul continually talked with Rhoda about her experience of bringing Len into the direct system, and each structural shift was negotiated in advance. There was never a question in Rhoda's mind concerning Raoul's commitment to her therapy; she knew that if Len's involvement jeopardized her alliance with Raoul, alternative strategies for dealing with Len's issues would be sought. Similarly, Len was not "seduced" or deceived by Raoul into thinking that Raoul was as committed to him as he was to his mother. Len clearly understood that Raoul was his mother's therapist first and his therapist second. The boundaries and commitments were clear, and changes in those boundaries were negotiated and approved by Rhoda first and Len second.

THE MIDDLE PHASE: SUMMARY

The middle sessions constitute the "working" phase of therapy. The interpersonal structures for most of the modes of presentation tend to be cast during the early sessions and remain relatively constant during the middle phase. Because of the need for so much subsystemic work, the binuclear family presenting with a child as identified patient tends to have the most fluid and varied structures. Guest sessions with couples and individual adults are common and can be immensely productive when patients are "stuck" in therapy. Most commonly, parents are invited in for these guest sessions, but siblings and children can also be included.

The middle phase concludes when the therapy system decides to stop therapy. That decision heralds the end of the middle and the beginning of the termination phase. Toward the end of the middle phase, before the decision to terminate, the therapist usually experiences an increasing sense of superfluousness. The patient system increasingly solves its problems without recourse to the therapist. The patient system has internalized the therapist and takes the therapy into its own hands. Toward the end of the middle phase and into the beginning of the termination phase, the key patients increasingly decide who will be seen in what context, and the therapist intervenes in that decision-making process only if the key patients appear to be making an unwise decision or acting out unconscious concerns destructively.

TERMINATION

Within an integrative therapy, the termination process is not an event or phase that occurs only at the end of therapy; it characterizes the entire course of therapy. Patients leave the direct system in the early and middle phases, some never to be seen in therapy again. This is the case with guests and with patients who engage in therapy episodically. These partial terminations require a minitermination process.

The *termination phase* entails terminating with the entire patient system. Its primary goal is to disconnect therapist and patient systems. Beyond that purpose, termination facilitates internalization of the therapist system and the development of the collective observing ego within the patient system, reinforces what key patients have learned, and psychosocially positions the patient system to minimize posttherapy regression. The following tasks accomplish these goals: reviewing the therapy, exploring potential future problems and their possible solutions, saying good-bye to the therapist, anticipatory grieving of the loss of the therapy and the therapist, and discussion of the conditions and terms of possible reengagement in therapy.

The termination phase lasts long enough to accomplish these goals and tasks. The shorter the therapy, the shorter the termination phase for both subsystem and full-system terminations. When patients leave the direct system during the early and middle phases, they require a termination experience that engages them in the tasks described. This can be done individually or conjointly depending on the nature of their involvement, their preferences, and the preferences of the remaining members.

During the termination phase, the interpersonal structure of the therapy resembles the predominant structure of the middle phase. *The primary guideline during termination, regardless of mode of presentation, is that the regular members of the direct system during the middle phase be involved directly in the termination.* Decision making during termination pertains to two issues: whether and how to include members of the direct system who were episodic patients at some previous point in treatment, but who are not now (at the onset of termination) actively engaged in the direct system, and which subsystems of the direct system should be seen in what way during termination.

NUCLEAR FAMILY WITH A CHILD AS IDENTIFIED PATIENT

The critical structural issue during termination with nuclear families with problems with children is whether and how to engage patients who left the direct system during the early or middle phases. It can be assumed that if the decision to terminate has been made, these members of the indirect system are relatively symptom-free or at least doing as well as can be expected in regard to the presenting problems. The reengagement question focuses on the quality of their prior minitermination process as well as their position in regard to potential regressions.

Larry and Ruth Goodman sought therapy for their 11-year-old son, Randy. Academically precocious, Randy was overweight, withdrawn, and socially isolated. He had few friends and spent most of his time reading or in front of his computer. Both parents, Randy, and his 9-year-old sister, Harriet, attended most of the first 12 sessions. During this time it became clear that the major problem was marital conflict, with Randy providing a legitimate alternative focus for both parents. They could fight over him, but they avoided directly addressing critical issues between them.

As the family approached the twelfth session, two things happened. Larry and Ruth requested marital therapy, and Randy's problems started to improve. He was less resistant to his parents' efforts to encourage him to socialize; he started a diet under his pediatrician's supervision; he talked more to his parents and sister; and he just seemed happier.

Sessions 12–30 primarily involved the parents alone and addressed marital issues. Randy and, to a lesser extent, Harriet were discussed at times, but they attended only two sessions (16 and 20). These were primarily checkup sessions and confirmed the parents' reports that Randy's improvement continued. The Goodmans' termination phase began after the thirtieth session, and the question came up whether the children should be brought into the direct system.

After consulting with Larry and Ruth, the therapist recommended that the children not be reengaged for several reasons. The children had already gone through minitermination processes when they left the direct system after session 12. The two sessions they attended after that were clearly defined as checkup or booster sessions as opposed to reengagement sessions. The children had stopped asking their parents about the therapy; for them, the therapy was over. The primary process to be terminated was the marital work.

This example illustrates various guidelines for deciding whether and how to engage indirect-system members during termination. The primary question is, Would anything be gained by including them? If they have already gone through their own minitermination process, and if they are well positioned to deal with potential future regressions, they do not need to be included. On the other hand, if they did not go through a minitermination and the relationship was left unresolved, they should be reengaged.

If the members of the direct system and the therapist think that the indirect-system members in question went through an adequate minitermination but are not well positioned to deal with future problems, they should be reengaged. This is typically the case when the work that has occurred within the direct system since the departure of the indirect-system members differs significantly from what was expected. For instance, if Larry and Ruth had decided to discontinue the marital therapy not because the marriage had improved so much, but because they felt stuck and wanted to take a respite, it might be appropriate to involve Randy and Harriet for at least a session during termination to fill them in on the status of their parents' relationship, to clarify their feelings and fears about it, and to discuss ways in which they might react if their parents regressed.

If the direct-system members and the therapist decide to include some members of the indirect system during termination, the primary question concerns how these members should be involved. With the Goodmans' "respite" scenario, the children might be involved for a session or two at the maximum, given that the whole termination phase may last only two to four sessions. Barring extraordinary circumstances, members of the indirect system are seldom involved during termination for more than a session or two. These should not be the last sessions, however, because temporarily reengaging and terminating with the indirect-system members interferes with saying good-bye to the direct-system members.

BINUCLEAR FAMILY WITH A CHILD AS IDENTIFIED PATIENT

The termination phase with binuclear systems with a child as identified patient does not differ fundamentally from this phase with nuclear systems. It is more complex because of the multiplicity of subsystems and alliances within most binuclear systems. A unique problem with binuclear systems occurs when most of the middle-phase work focused on one household.

In this unbalanced situation, it can be useful to reengage the other parent and his or her nuclear family for at least a session during termination. As well as maximizing the likelihood that everyone leaves therapy with a common understanding of what happened and what is expected in the future, including the noncustodial subsystem during termination maintains the alliance with that system and strengthens the framework for future treatment in case of major regressions or the emergence of new problems.

School Involvement During Termination

When terminating with both nuclear and binuclear families with children with school problems, it frequently is useful at least to "touch base" with the school during termination. This is particularly the case when school personnel have not been consistently involved during the middle sessions.

Touching base ranges from a phone call to the child's teacher or guidance counselor, to a meeting with the parents, the child, and key school personnel. The former, less intensive contact may entail only informing a teacher that therapy is about to stop and that all seems to be going well. The latter, more intensive involvement is typically required when a new school plan needs to be implemented posttherapy. In this situation, the guidance counselor or school social worker may be taking over therapy, or new academic and behavior policies may be in the offing.

The basic rule for school involvement during termination is that the greater the need for the school to be active posttherapy, the greater the involvement. This rule also applies to the involvement of other helping systems during termination, such as medical or social welfare programs. If the system needs to do something different, it needs to be involved in termination.

COUPLES WITH RELATIONSHIP PROBLEMS

Couples with relationship problems should be seen together if that has been the basic structure during the middle sessions. If individual sessions have been used extensively during the middle phase, they should be phased out during termination. As discussed in the section on progressive bonding in Chapter 3, termination gives the relational partners back to each other. By phasing out individual sessions, the therapist relinquishes responsibility for the partners and their relationship and turns the problem-solving process over to the couple. Clearly, the last session or sessions should be conjoint with both partners present.

INDIVIDUALS SEEKING INDIVIDUAL THERAPY

With adults who were seen conjointly with partners or friends, these friends or partners should be involved in termination commensurate with their involvement during the middle phase. If they were involved in every session, they should be present in most if not all of the termination sessions. If they were only episodically involved in the middle sessions, they might attend one or two of the termination interviews.

If members of the indirect system were not involved during the middle phase but were involved initially or during the early sessions, the guiding principle is to involve them during termination only if there is some compelling reason to do so. This is particularly true when the individual's middle phase was of significant duration and intensity. Bringing indirect-system members into the therapy at termination is likely to disrupt the bonds component of the alliance with the direct-system member. In the context of the intense feelings frequently associated with termination, the patient may feel violated and demeaned by the change in the therapist's mode of relating if another person enters the therapy at this point. To join with the other person, the therapist may have to sacrifice the patient's sense of connection, thereby damaging the alliance and jeopardizing the therapy at this final stage: not a risk worth taking.

Clearly, if an indirect-system member was never involved or was involved only for the initial session, he or she should not be involved during termination. The intimacy and intensity of a totally or primarily individual psychotherapy generally precludes involving indirect-system members in the termination sessions. Although they can be involved, it is risky and seldom necessary.

CONCLUSION

This chapter has presented a comprehensive framework for decision making about who should participate in therapy. Patient systems were broken down into four major modes of presentation: nuclear family with children, binuclear family with children, couples, and adults seeking individual therapy. The last category was subdivided into cohabiting and noncohabiting adults. The process of therapy was divided into four major phases: initial, early, middle, and termination. Guidelines were presented for each mode of presentation in each phase of therapy.

Nature does not come cleaved as neatly as this chapter. The phases described do not really exist "out there," nor do the modes of presentation. Both are useful constructs for presenting ideas about the structure of therapy. A patient system in one mode of presentation may present other problems later in therapy. A nuclear system presenting with a child's problem later may present as a couple with a relationship problem. This kind of change can lead to recycling of the phases of therapy. A new problem can lead to a new beginning.

An integrative therapist continually makes decisions about whom to include at what point in therapy. The dual criteria for this ongoing decision making pertain to who needs to be present to accomplish particular tasks and the nature of the alliance with key patients. Ultimately, these decisions must be guided by feeling and intuition as much as by theoretical guidelines and careful thinking.

CHAPTER 6

Identifying the Problem Cycle

EVERY SIGNIFICANT AND ENDURING presenting problem has its own problem cycle. Problems ebb and flow; they increase and diminish. Couples do not fight all the time. They have alternating periods of relative calm and conflict. A depressed man has moments of feeling better and worse. A delinquent daughter is not always in trouble. The periodicity of a problem defines its problem cycle.

Problem cycles embody two primary components. The first is the *problem sequence:* the sequence of events that precedes, includes, and follows the emergence of the problem behavior. The second is the *alternative, adaptive sequence:* the sequence of events that initially resembles the problem sequence but does not include the emergence of the problem behavior. Different cycles have different periodicities (Breunlin & Schwartz, 1986; Breunlin et al., 1992); some repeat as frequently as every few days, and others, as infrequently as every few years. Parts of one problem cycle may be parts of other cycles. Problems exist within a network of cycles, with different periodicities at different levels of activity.

The twin tasks of pattern identification and modification can be operationalized further: *The two primary tasks of the problem-centered therapist are identifying and modifying the problems cycles of the major presenting problems.* Like assessment and intervention, these tasks are inseparable. Problem-cycle identification shapes and transforms the problem cycle. For the sake of clarity, however, this chapter focuses on problem-cycle identification, primarily emphasizing the problem sequence of the cycle. Chapter 7 completes the discussion of the identification of the alternative, adaptive sequence of the cycle and moves into cycle modification. Chapter 8 focuses on modifying the constraints that prevent cycle modification and adaptive problem solving.

A problem cycle can be conceptualized as a circle that lies horizontally on top of the cylindrical problem-maintenance structure that ultimately shapes and drives the cycle, as depicted in Figure 6.1. Different parts of the problem-maintenance structure connect to different parts of the problem cycle. The periodicity of the presenting problem reflected in the problem cycle reveals important features of the underlying problem-maintenance structure. In fact, this periodicity constitutes the primary vehicle for exploring and modifying the problem-maintenance structure.

This chapter presents six steps for delineating the problem cycle. The first identifies the presenting problems: their onset, vicissitudes, and contexts. The second identifies solutions that key patients have brought to bear on the presenting problems. These two steps identify the behavioral or surface features of the problem cycle, focusing primarily on the organizational constraints in the problem sequence. The third step targets the biological system that underlies the problem cycle, attending particularly to biological constraints that impair problem solving. The fourth and fifth steps address the two primary components of the meaning metaframework: the emotional and cognitive systems that underlie the problem cycle. The sixth step, integrating the first five, begins to complete the cycle by identifying an alternative, adaptive sequence.

The therapist questions and probes the problem cycle to construct a clear model of the cycle as well as its problem-maintenance structure. These questions and probes focus initially on the contemporary metaframeworks: the behavioral, biological, affective, and cognitive aspects of the cycle. Initially, therapy targets these aspects of the cycle in the most direct way. These efforts are discussed in Chapter 7. If necessary, the therapist moves down the problem-maintenance structure, with the problem cycle as the ultimate reference point, until the cycle shifts and the problem improves. Chapter 8 details this process.

The sequence for exploring the problem cycle can be conceptualized as a series of steps with particular tasks and goals. Although presented in a relatively linear fashion for heuristic purposes, these steps do not have to be conducted in this sequence. Furthermore, just as decision making about the interpersonal structure of therapy continues over the course of therapy, these problem-cycle exploration steps do not begin and end at definitive points in therapy but continue throughout therapy. A particular step and its tasks are more focal in the tapestry of interventions at a particular point, but the step does not end when it recedes temporarily into the background.

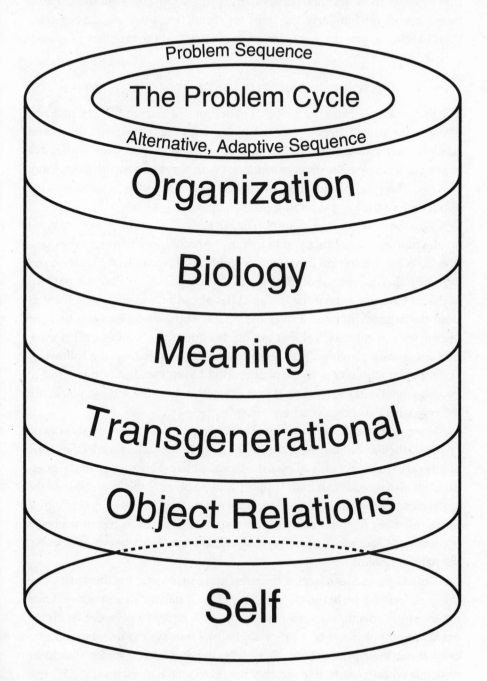

Figure 6.1
The Problem Cycle and the Problem-Maintenance Structure

Problem Sequence

The Problem Cycle

Alternative, Adaptive Sequence

Organization

Biology

Meaning

Transgenerational

Object Relations

Self

Consistent with interactive constructivism, a particular problem cycle links to a problem process "in reality," but it is also an evolving construction that becomes more accurate (closer to the problem process "out there") with new information. Similarly, the steps for identifying the cycle are constructions of what in practice is a seamless exploration of the problem process.

STEP 1: IDENTIFYING THE PRESENTING PROBLEMS

The first task delineates the problem definitions of each of the key patients. This process usually begins over the phone with the organizing patient and continues fairly intensively during the early sessions. As problems evolve, disappear, and emerge, the process continues with varying intensity throughout therapy. The guiding question in the therapist's mind is who says what about each of the key presenting problems.

A valuable and standard question to ask early in the first session is, What are the problems that bring you to therapy? Another way to phrase the question is, What are the problems you would like help with in this therapy? Typically, this question should be asked nonspecifically to all of the patients at the first session, even if the therapist has already received partial answers from the organizing patient over the phone. If the therapist fears that the organizing patient may feel that asking this question devalues the information previously provided, the question can be prefaced by the following: "I've spoken with you over the phone, and I haven't spoken with the rest of you, so what I'd like to do is start from scratch at this time and ask you about the problems that bring you here today."

Asking nonspecifically means that the therapist directs the question to no one in particular but throws it out to the group. The lack of a specific target at this early point not only allows the therapist to get an answer to the question, but also provides an initial opportunity to observe the interaction of the key patients. Who answers first? How do others react? Do they nod in agreement, frown, or feign boredom? Who responds next? Their responses begin to illuminate leadership, power, agreement, and involvement patterns within the patient system.

As the key patients describe the presenting problems, the therapist accurately reflects his or her understanding of each patient's perspective. Once the therapist adequately understands the first patient's perspective on the presenting problems, it is appropriate to ask other system members specifically about their perspectives. Generally, the second responder should be someone whose perspective sensibly would follow. For instance, in an initial session with a family, if the mother responds first, to support the natural hierarchy, the therapist might solicit the father's understanding of the presenting problems before moving on to the children. Particularly when the father may be poorly allied with the therapist, soliciting his opinion directly may be experienced as reaching out and expressing interest.

Soliciting and accurately reflecting patients' perspectives are two ways to build therapeutic alliances with key patients early in treatment. Empathically reflecting problem statements contributes particularly to the goals component of the alliance. Expressing concern and interest in each person's unique perspective builds bonds. If possible, the therapist should understand each of the key patients' perspectives on the presenting problems before the end of the first session.

THE NATURAL HISTORY OF THE PRESENTING PROBLEMS

Understanding the presenting problem and its problem-maintenance structure entails identifying not only who says what about the presenting problem, but also the problem's natural history. Delineating a problem's natural history involves focusing on three event clusters: (1) the onset or emergence of the problem and the psychosocial context temporally associated with onset; (2) the ongoing vicissitudes of the problem and their psychosocial contexts; and (3) the precipitating circumstances that led to the current referral.

Onset

Frequently, questions about onset reveal more about the problem-maintenance structure than any other questions. Two questions—When did it begin? What was going on at that time?—provide the dual focus for exploring problem onset. It is crucial to pin down, as closely as possible, the exact time when the problem first emerged and what was going on in the lives of the key patient-system members at that time. With the Brand family, the 16-year-old son, Taylor, began having school problems 4 years ago. Taylor's parents separated for the first time 4 years ago and divorced 2 years ago. Two years ago, Taylor's school problems got so bad that his school recommended special placement. This scenario of problem onset and exacerbation suggests hypotheses linking Taylor's school problems with his parents' relationship. A top interpersonal hypothesis is that his problems link his parents and maintain some semblance of their predivorce relationship. This hypothesis is further supported by the fact that Taylor's behavior recently deteriorated even further, prompting the parents to seek therapy a month before his mother was planning to remarry.

Frequently, patients are not clear about when the problem emerged and may have difficulty recalling the time of onset. Similarly, they may not easily remember what was going on in their lives beyond the emergence of the problem at that time. Despite this resistance, the therapist should probe as specifically and tenaciously as possible to determine the time of onset as well as significant contextual events. Of course, persistence and tenacity should not jeopardize the therapeutic alliance.

The Elias family entered therapy when their youngest child dropped out of his last year of college and came home. Sean, 24, had been in and out of college since the age of 18. He complained that he felt depressed and lost and did not know what he wanted to do with his life. The family also complained that their 26-year-old daughter, Sandra, was living at home and doing nothing. She had been involved with drugs and had gotten pregnant several times since dropping out of college after her freshman year; each pregnancy was aborted. Currently, she was not working.

After eight sessions in which there was little progress, the therapist requested a "live" consultation with a colleague with whom she regularly consulted. The consultant's primary intent was to identify the onset of the presenting problems. Midway into the interview, the consultant explored the extent to which the parents, Frank and Shelly, share their concerns and worries. Although both children were invited to the session, only Sean decided to attend.

CONSULTANT: Mrs. Elias, when your husband is worried about something or someone, does he let you know?

SHELLY: I don't think so. Frank keeps most of his worries to himself. So do I.

FRANK: You see, we're already under enough pressure with all of the problems with the kids. Shelly and I don't want to add to the burdens we're each already carrying.

CONSULTANT: Has it always been this way between the two of you: Each of you keeping your worries to yourself, protecting the other person?

SHELLY: No, it didn't used to be this way. We used to share everything.

CONSULTANT: When did things change? When did you stop sharing?

SHELLY: When we went into mourning for Sandra.

CONSULTANT: What do you mean "went into mourning"? Sandra's very alive.

SHELLY: I mean she changed. She was fine and then got onto the wrong track.

FRANK: It's like we lost her—lost the girl we knew.

CONSULTANT: When did that happen? When did you lose her?

SHELLY: I'm not sure. Maybe 6 or 7 years ago, when all the trouble started.

SEAN: That's also about the time I started to have trouble. Senior year in high school after I broke up with Linda. I could hardly get out of bed to get to school.

CONSULTANT: So you were 17 or 18 at the time, and Sandra's 2 years older, right?

SEAN: It was just after Thanksgiving. I was 17.

CONSULTANT: What was going on at that time in other aspects of your lives, outside of the kids?

FRANK: My mother died somewhere in there. I can't remember exactly when. She had a heart attack and died 2 days later. It came out of the blue.

CONSULTANT: Do you remember exactly when she died?

SHELLY: It was before Thanksgiving, because I remember she wasn't at your brother's that year. We always go to Frank's brother's house for Thanksgiving. We were all down that year, almost in shock.

CONSULTANT: Were you close with your mother-in-law?

SHELLY: Yes, she was like a mother to me since my own mother died 15 years ago. She was good to all of us.

CONSULTANT: Do you still miss her?

FRANK: I used to, but with all of the problems with the children, who has time to think?

CONSULTANT: It must have been very hard mourning for your daughter at the same time you were all mourning your mother. A lot of loss and sadness all at once.

SHELLY: It was awful. [She starts to cry.]

CONSULTANT: I don't think you've gotten over the loss and the pain to this day. It's still fresh for all of you.

In this vignette, the consultant identifies the time of onset as well as a major contextual event associated with symptom onset in both children. Shelly's comment about going into mourning for her daughter clearly links her daughter's problems with the death of her mother-in-law. Sandra did not die; the grandmother did, suddenly and unexpectedly. Shelly's mourning comment suggests the following meaning constraint hypothesis. Perhaps the mother and father's grief about his mother's death was displaced and attenuated by the emergence of psychological symptoms in both children. Frank's comment further supports this hypothesis: "With all of the problems with the children, who has time to think?"

This grief-management hypothesis leads to more extensive and general hypotheses about the patient system. It suggests that the Elias family may have unconscious rules about experiencing and expressing grief and sadness. The children's symptoms may help the parents, and perhaps the children, avoid their grief and sadness about the paternal grandmother's death. That both of the children have not been able to leave home suggests that their failure to separate may help the entire family, and in particular the parents, avoid the grief work attendant on leaving home for all of the family members.

Vicissitudes

The second task in identifying the natural history of the presenting problem delineates the vicissitudes of the problem. When does the problem get better, and when does it get worse? When does it recur, and when does it disappear? As with onset, it is critical to identify the contextual events associated with these changes. A clear picture of the problem's process and the contextual events associated with its ebbs and flows helps in the formulation and refinement of the major hypotheses.

Questions for the Elias family would be as follows: When did Sean become symptomatic? When did his depressions emerge? What events link to their emergence and recurrence? In the preceding vignette, Sean ties his initial depression to the loss of his girlfriend, Linda. He could hardly get out of bed after they broke up. Were his multiple departures from college associated with similar losses and depressive episodes? If the answers to these questions are affirmative, they support the hypothesis that Sean has internalized the family's difficulty with grief work. His depressions and school failures may be reactions to romantic losses as well as attempts to avoid the intense sadness and pain associated with these losses. Such questions generate data that facilitate understanding possible individual as well as interpersonal constraints that block effective problem solving.

The Schultz family presented with their 14-year-old son, Lawrence, as the identified patient. He was verbally abusive to both of his parents and was having academic and behavioral problems at school. During the first session, the therapist focused on *when* Lawrence was abusive with his parents.

THERAPIST: When does Lawrence get most abusive? When is he at his worst?

MRS. SCHULTZ: He's pretty bad all the time. It seems like he yells at my husband and me constantly.

MR. SCHULTZ: When Lawrence and I were away fishing for 5 days in August, he was wonderful. When we're all home, he's difficult and argues with my wife about everything.

THERAPIST: What about when you're not home? How is he then?

MR. SCHULTZ: What was he like when I was out of town 10 days ago?

MRS. SCHULTZ: He was pretty good. He had some friends over and didn't give me much of a hard time.

THERAPIST: Is that the way Lawrence usually behaves when your husband is out of town?

MRS. SCHULTZ: Yes, come to think of it. He's a little better when Larry's out of town. Maybe it heightens his lagging sense of responsibility.

THERAPIST: When both of you are around, are there particular circumstances or times when Lawrence is better or worse?

MRS. SCHULTZ: He's pretty bad all the time, but he seems to be even more irritating when Larry and I are trying to talk with each other.

LAWRENCE: You call that *talking*?

THERAPIST: Lawrence, what do you mean?

LAWRENCE: They don't talk. They shout.

THERAPIST: So you get more irritating to your parents when they're fighting or not getting along with each other?

LAWRENCE: Yeah, I guess. I can't stand it when they fight.

That Lawrence is less symptomatic when his father is not around suggests that his symptoms might have something to do with a triangular process that involves him, his mother, and his father. Specifically, Lawrence's symptomatic behavior may regulate a process between his parents. Because that process does not occur when his parents are not together, he needs to be symptomatic only when they are together.

The vignette also reveals that Lawrence's symptoms covary not only with structural changes in his family, but also according to the nature of the interaction between his parents. He gets worse when they conflict. Thus, the emerging hypothesis about the interpersonal function of his symptoms becomes even more specific: they regulate or interrupt conflict.

Referral Precipitants

It is essential to understand the specific circumstances that have led the patient system to seek help at this time. Particularly with chronic problems, "Why now?" becomes a crucial question. Generally, systems seek help in response to two precipitating scenarios. In the internal scenario, something important has shifted within or around the patient system that makes the chronic situation intolerable to one or more key patients. In the external scenario, the problems have exceeded the permissible deviation limits of a larger system in which the patient system is embedded.

The Brand family, discussed previously, illustrates both scenarios. Taylor's behavior deteriorated when his parents separated 4 years ago, worsened when they divorced 2 years ago, and is deteriorating even further as his mother approaches remarriage. The primary locus for his deterioration was school, from which the referral was initiated. The current deterioration in the face of his mother's plans to remarry coupled with the fact that the stages of his academic deterioration coincided almost perfectly with the stages of his parent's disengagement buttress the emerging hypothesis that his problems reconnect his parents and reestablish some semblance of his predivorce family system.

Frequently, internal precipitant scenarios relate to developmental changes in system members. A common scenario is the "empty nest" middle-aged couple who present for marital therapy when their youngest child leaves home. They can no longer organize themselves so completely around the children and must confront the deficits in their marriage that child rearing permitted them to avoid. Without the children as an alternative focus, one or both parents now find their marital homeostasis intolerable. Stewart and Joanne Christman illustrate this scenario. Stewart's rigid control and refusal to share leadership became intolerable to Joanne after their youngest child left home. These precipitant scenarios tell the therapist about the driving concerns of key patients (Taylor Brand's concern for his parents' relationship); the deficits in particular systems (the Christmans' marriage); and new, emerging strengths within key subsystems (Joanne Christman). Delineating precipitant scenarios clarifies the emerging picture of the patient system and the problem-maintenance structure, helping to focus the early stages of therapy.

Natural History Summary and Guidelines

The hypotheses that come out of the initial exploration of the nature, onset, and vicissitudes of the presenting problem as well as the referral precipitants, are preliminary formulations about the constraints that prevent problem resolution. If these hypotheses were to be located spatially within the problem-maintenance structure, the contemporary interpersonal and biological hypotheses would be located toward the top of the structure and should be explored initially. The historical and individual hypotheses would be located toward the bottom of the structure and should be explored only after the interpersonal hypotheses have been investigated and found insufficient. *The more a presenting problem's onset and vicissitudes directly relate to specific contextual events, the greater the likelihood of interpersonal determination. In contrast, the more a presenting problem's onset is not linked with specific contextual events and, even more important, the more the problem does not vary consistently with any interpersonal contextual events, the greater the likelihood of historical, individual, or biological determination (or a combination of these).* For instance, if Lawrence Schultz's problems did not vary according to the presence of his father, and if his problems did not vary significantly with the behaviors (conflict versus affiliation) of his parents, such a scenario would suggest greater intrapsychic or biological determination.

As indicated previously, a primarily biological scenario appears superficially similar to a primarily intrapsychic scenario, in that the problems do not covary as much with contextual determinants as they do in primarily interpersonal scenarios. When biological constraints play a major role in the problem-maintenance structure with a disorder like clinical depression or attention deficit hyperactivity disorder (ADHD), the symptoms may improve or deteriorate under certain circumstances, but they are almost always present to some degree. Furthermore, late-adolescent onset of some major psychiatric disorders such as schizophrenia is consistent with a primarily biological scenario.

These assertions are not variant guidelines or prescriptions but suggestions about what kind of evidence leads to particular types of problem-maintenance hypotheses and where assessment and intervention efforts might be focused within the problem-maintenance structure. Generally, the more a problem varies consistently with contextual events, the more likely that its primary constraints are contemporary and interpersonal; the less it varies with such events, the greater the likelihood of historical, intrapsychic, or biological constraints.

MULTIPLE PRESENTING PROBLEMS: THE PROBLEM LISTS

Systems typically have multiple presenting problems. Identifying and organizing multiple problems is a key task in the initial and early sessions as well as throughout the course of therapy. During initial contact with the referral source and the organizing patient, the therapist begins to develop a mental list of the patient system's presenting problems. This list also includes nonidentified problems that relate to the presenting problem. This *therapist problem list* exists over the entire course of therapy. A fluid list, it involves an evolving rank ordering of the problems in regard to work priority: which problems should be addressed now and which later.

This prioritized problem list also links to the therapist's evolving formulation of the problem-maintenance structures for the presenting problems. For instance, seeking couple therapy, the Olsens presented problems dealing with money, in-laws, and their sexual–intimate relationship. In organizing and prioritizing these problems, the therapist intuitively placed the sexual–intimate issues at the top of the list. This decision flowed from an emerging hypothesis that the Olsens' money and in-law problems derived primarily from their failure to work out their intimate, sexual relationship and that if the latter improved, the former problems would resolve themselves or be easily remediated. In other words, the sexual–intimacy problems played a more powerful role as constraints in the problem-maintenance structures of the money and in-law problems than those problems played within the problem-maintenance structure of the sexual–intimacy problems.

Presenting-Problem Consensus

Seldom is there perfect agreement among the key patients about the nature and importance of the presenting problems. However, when there is sufficient agreement—when the key players basically agree about the major problems—the therapist needs to help the patient system decide which problems to focus on first. This involves the creation of a *consensual problem list* between the patient and therapist systems. In contrast to the therapist's list, which may be partially shared with the patient system, this is an explicit list, constructed and shared with the key patients. The therapist's problem list informs but is seldom identical to the consensual problem list.

Like the therapist's problem list, the consensual list rank orders the presenting problems. This rank order reflects an evolving understanding between the therapist and key patients about which problems will be addressed first. Naturally, if any of the presenting problems are urgent or pose an imminent danger to any of the patients, they go to the top of the consensual list. For instance, if a divorce or separation is imminent, it should be addressed immediately, taking precedence over communication or intimacy problems. Similarly, if physical or sexual abuse is occurring, even if it is not a presenting problem, it should go to the top of the problem list. If none of the problems is urgent or dangerous, it is appropriate for the therapist to focus the therapy by asking the key patients what they want to work on first and, later in therapy, what they want to work on now.

Letting the key patients decide which problems to focus on is generally a sound operating principle at first and throughout therapy. As mentioned previously, urgent and dangerous problems justify overriding this principle. Additionally, situations may emerge later in therapy when the therapist should insist that particular problems be addressed. The most common nonurgent override scenario occurs at points in therapy when patient-system members avoid what they should be talking about and use other problems in the service of that avoidance. For instance, during the middle phase of therapy, the Olsens may be more comfortable fighting about their in-law problems than addressing their sexual relationship.

Agreement–Disagreement Patterns

One of the most difficult problems in regard to multiple presenting problems occurs when key patients disagree about what constitutes a presenting problem or the severity of a presenting problem: its rank on the consensual priority list. Patterns of agreement and disagreement reveal patient-system dynamics and facilitate hypothesis construction.

Prematurely focusing on patterns of agreement and disagreement can skew patients' responses and limit the therapist's accurate understanding of each member's perspective. For instance, the question, Do you agree with your wife about Jimmy's problems? should be preceded by asking Jimmy's father how he sees the problems. Typically, as key patients share their perspectives on the presenting problems, patterns of agreement and disagreement emerge spontaneously. To confirm emerging impressions or to clarify disagreements, it is valuable for the therapist to query agreement specifically. However, the explicit exploration of agreement and disagreement patterns can jeopardize the alliance with highly defensive systems in which the members do not want to reveal their interpersonal dynamics. Such systems require the indirect and implicit exploration of such patterns.

If there is serious disagreement about what constitute the presenting problems, the therapist needs to address the disagreement directly. For instance, Eileen Johnson complains that Jimmy, her 11-year-old son, does not work hard enough in school. George, Jimmy's father, states that the problem is that Eileen won't get off Jimmy's back. This type of discrepancy must be explored. George needs to be asked if he agrees at all with his wife about Jimmy's underachievement, and similarly, Eileen needs to be asked whether she agrees with her husband about oversupervising Jimmy. If there is some mutual agreement about either of the problems, that problem becomes a presenting problem and a target for therapy.

If a consensus cannot be established among key patients about any major problems, a relatively rare circumstance, the therapist can identify the metaproblem: the patient-system members' inability to agree and work together. That disagreement may become the first presenting problem to be addressed. Early in therapy, it is particularly critical not to take sides with either party in a problem-identification dispute. Identifying the metaproblem of the disagreement lets the therapist avoid taking sides and jeopardizing the alliance with any patient. As the therapist accurately empathizes with each key patient's view of the presenting problems as well as with the patients' disagreement with each other, the bonds component of the alliance is built. The patients feel individually heard and respected without being coerced to agree or abandon their unique perspectives.

Once the metaproblem of disagreement is broached, patient-system members frequently find a problem they agree about, and therapy proceeds. It is almost as if they agree on a problem to short-circuit the therapist's exploration of their emotional system, which their disagreement reveals. Additionally, the empathic and respectful exploration of patient-system members' individual perspectives seems to soften the hard edges of their disagreement and facilitates identification of some common presenting problems.

PROBLEM IDENTIFICATION WITH INVOLUNTARY SYSTEMS

As legal and social service systems become increasingly integrated, more patient systems are involuntarily referred by the legal system for psychotherapy. These systems present in one of two ways. In one type, key patients "own" the problems for which they have been referred and sometimes even present additional problems. These systems take at least some degree of responsibility for their problems and genuinely engage in therapy. Within these "responsible" involuntary systems, the process of problem identification is similar to the process in voluntary cases. These systems fit the external-referral scenario discussed previously.

In contrast, the second group of involuntary cases does not "own" the problems for which the members have been referred. Typically, these systems feel forced into therapy by the legal or social service systems and have difficulty genuinely engaging in therapy. In regard to problem identification, the difficulty is that they do not present any problems for which they are seeking help. They do not want to be in therapy and resent the fact that they have to submit to the intrusions of the therapist system.

The primary risk with these "irresponsible" involuntary systems is pseudotherapy, in which the members pretend to engage in therapy sufficiently to satisfy the coercive referral source. In the worst case scenario, the patient system plays the patient and the therapist plays the therapist, but no genuine work occurs. The alliance, particularly the bonds component, never develops.

To avoid creating a pseudotherapy system, the therapist must openly confront the dilemma facing the patient system. As illustrated in the following vignette, this entails acknowledging the feelings of the key patients about the involuntary referral and directly raising the pseudotherapy dilemma. It also involves asking the key patients if there are problems that they would like to pursue with the therapist. Ultimately, the only problem they may wish to pursue is the problem with the referral source that sent them to therapy. Getting that source to let them discontinue therapy may be the first goal of the genuine therapy system.

The Singers were referred by the Department of Child and Family Services (DCFS) because the parents, Leon and Arlene, had physically abused their 7-year-old son, George, beating him with an electric cord. In the first interview, the therapist asks about their feelings concerning the involuntary referral.

MR. SINGER: Arlene and I don't think we need to be here. We understand what that DCFS worker told us and we won't do it again. We're gonna use time out instead of getting physical. We've learned our lesson.

THERAPIST: So you and your wife feel that this therapy is not necessary. You've both decided to try punishing him without violence and you think you can do that. So you feel like you learned your lesson and don't need anything more at this time.

MRS. SINGER: That's right. We just got carried away that once and it's not gonna happen again.

THERAPIST: How do both of you feel about being forced to come see me?

MR. SINGER: I don't like it. Just because we made a mistake, now we got you and DC whatever breathing down our necks. We can raise our boy without you looking over our shoulders.

THERAPIST: I'm glad that you can be so direct and honest with me. The only problem is that the judge and DCFS have stated that both of you and George need to be in weekly therapy for at least 3 months.

MRS. SINGER: But can't you tell the judge and the DCFS worker that we know what we did wrong and won't do it again? If you tell them that we don't need therapy, they'll believe you.

THERAPIST: I could tell them that you both feel what you just said. At this point, after just one session, I can't honestly say whether you need therapy or you don't. I need to get to know all of you and how you work as a family better.

MR. SINGER: So how long is it gonna take to figure this out?

THERAPIST: I don't know. I think meeting with both of you as a couple three or four times, meeting with George alone several times, and with all of you several times should give me some sense of what you're like and what you might need, if you need anything.

MR. SINGER: So what are we talking about here? Six to eight sessions?

THERAPIST: Yes, that should be enough for me to be able to make a recommendation to you, DCFS, and the Court.

MR. SINGER: Does today's session count in the six?

THERAPIST: Yes it does, but I'd like to plan on eight sessions and count this as one of the eight.

MR. SINGER: You're the boss.

THERAPIST: Well, I guess I'm the boss in a certain sense and not the boss in a certain sense.

MRS. SINGER: What do you mean, you're not the boss?

THERAPIST: I mean I'm the boss of how many sessions we're gonna have, but you two are the bosses of whether this is gonna be bullshit therapy, a waste of all of our time, or whether we're gonna really talk straight to each other and use our time together productively.

MR. SINGER: What do you mean "bullshit therapy"?

THERAPIST: I mean the two of you coming in here, dragging George in, bringing your bodies and pretending to talk about stuff, but really not opening up about anything that's important to you and that you care about. Not letting me know anything about who you really are, what problems you have, and how you truly feel and what you actually think about the things I have to say.

MRS. SINGER: How are we supposed to open up to you, to trust you, when everything we say is going straight to the judge and DCFS? We don't want to lose George.

THERAPIST: I know that you don't want to lose George. Let me tell you the kinds of things I can end up telling the judge after we've done some work for a while. If it's been bullshit therapy, I can tell her that you never opened up; I don't really know whether you'll abuse George again; and we never did any real, honest work. But if we make this a real therapy, I can tell her that you both really opened up, worked hard, and are struggling seriously with your problems and how they link up to managing and helping George. I don't expect you to be perfect or even anywhere close to perfect. What I'm looking for is, Are we really struggling with the problems that got you into trouble and are we making any progress?

MRS. SINGER: So what's gonna happen if we talk about some things that aren't so nice, that might make the judge worry about us and George?

THERAPIST: I can't say for sure, but what I will say is that if you open up in this therapy and we get into what's really going on, I'm gonna be a hell of a lot more impressed than if you never let me in. And I'm far more likely to fight for you with DCFS and the judge if I feel like we're really working as partners than if I feel that you're just putting in your time trying to get me and everybody else off your back. The choice is up to you. I'd like to try to help.

MR. SINGER: Well, let's try it for a couple of sessions and see how things go.

THERAPIST: Do you agree with your husband, Mrs. Singer?

MRS. SINGER: I'm not sure we really have much of a choice, but I'm willing to give it a try.

THERAPIST: Okay, let's get started and see how it goes. What are some of the problems I might be able to help you with?

MRS. SINGER: Well, I've had trouble controlling George since he went into day care when he was 4. I just don't know what to do with him.

In this vignette, the therapist directly confronts the dilemma. If the Singers want the therapist on their side, they must open up in the therapy. By remaining closed, they will not help and may even hurt themselves. The open exploration of the pseudotherapy dilemma with irresponsible involuntarily referred systems increases the probability of developing a genuine therapeutic alliance based on a real consensus about presenting problems. With some closed or dysfunctional patient systems, however, no amount of confrontation and exploration will lead to genuine therapy. If the physical and mental health risks are great enough with such highly resistant systems, alternative placement of the at-risk patients may be necessary.

THE EVOLUTION OF PRESENTING PROBLEMS

Presenting problems evolve. Frequently, the initial presenting problems resolve or transform relatively quickly. When they resolve, the therapy may terminate or move on to other problems. When they transform, they usually link to other problems that were not on the original consensual problem list. This transformation relates to the evolution of the therapeutic alliance, particularly the bonds component of the alliance. As key patients bond to the therapist, as their levels of trust and comfort grow, they present "deeper" problems they have been reluctant to discuss.

This reluctance has at least two sources. The first is fear of the catastrophic consequences of discussing *conscious* nonpresenting problems that could disrupt the patient system's homeostasis. In these cases, one or more key patients are aware of the problem. For instance, Mrs. Schultz can talk about her coparental problems with Mr. Schultz in regard to Lawrence, but she fears that talking about her marital problems will enrage her husband and further disrupt her marriage, her family, and herself.

The second source of the reluctance is fears about *unconscious* problems. In these cases, the key patients are not consciously aware of the problems. For instance, Sally Delaney consciously experienced her primary problems as

Joe's impotence and the sense of distance in their marriage. As their therapy progressed, she increasingly allowed herself to acknowledge her sense that Joe had been and was being unfaithful. She had not wanted to "see" the overwhelming evidence of his infidelity because it was so fundamentally discrepant with her image of Joe and his commitment to the marriage. To acknowledge consciously what she had unconsciously sensed was to shatter the foundation of their marriage. To face this reality filled her with rage at her husband, with dread and terror about the future of the marriage and the family, and with fears about her own future.

Frequently, unconscious problems have historical and, particularly, psychodynamic components. For example, a 17-year-old girl with anorexia may be unaware of her rage at her parents for communicating to her over the course of her life that she was acceptable only as "a perfect girl." As therapy progresses, she increasingly experiences her problems not as a struggle over food and eating but as a struggle within herself about facing her anger and disappointment about her parents' shallow and conditional commitment to her. Integrating this sense of herself as an angry and disappointed young woman into her "perfect girl" self becomes a new challenge. In addition, how to deal with these new feelings toward her parents poses another conscious problem.

The emergence of new presenting problems and the reduction or disappearance of older ones is normal in any but the most short-term and single-problem-focused therapies. The therapist needs to integrate the new problems flexibly into the consensual problem list. Frequently, the therapist may lead the way in moving a problem from the therapist's list to the consensual list: in making a nonpresenting problem a presenting problem. Typically, in these situations, the therapist sees obvious problems that key patients either do not see or are not ready to deal with.

Making a nonpresenting problem a presenting problem clearly involves patience and timing. The key patients need to be ready to define the nonpresenting problem as a presenting problem or the process will not work. However, the therapist can increase the readiness of the patient system in two ways. The growth of the bonds component of the alliance can strengthen patients' self structures sufficiently to allow them to confront frightening and painful problems they would rather not address. Second, the therapist can desensitize key patients to a critical nonpresenting problem by exposing them to the problem increasingly as therapy progresses. By bringing the problem up and then backing off, the therapist not only exposes key patients to the problem without catastrophic consequences, but also tests the patients' readiness to confront the problem.

In the following vignette, the therapist is in the middle of the eighth session with Leon and Roz Goldberg, a couple in their late 50s who have sought therapy because their 23-year-old son, Ray, refuses to leave their house. Prior to therapy, Ray, the youngest of three boys, withdrew to his room, coming out only occasionally for a meal when his parents were out or asleep. Ray had been peculiar for a number of years, but recently he had begun hoarding newspapers and talking animatedly to himself. Ray refused to be evaluated at a hospital or to see a psychiatrist.

Working with the Goldbergs, the therapist saw that there were major marital problems that neither partner wanted to address. During the fourth session, when the parents were exploring the strategy of forcing Ray either to get help, to get a job, or to get out of the house, a deep marital rift emerged. Roz talked about how she did not trust Leon and doubted that she could work with him as an ally to help Ray. When the therapist tried to explore her distrust, she said that neither she nor her husband was interested in "marriage counseling." The therapist backed off and focused exclusively on their coparental management of Ray. Now, in the eighth session, their difficulty working together resurfaces.

ROZ: There you go again. You're impossible. Why did I ever think you could handle Ray with sensitivity or compassion? You've always had a stone for a heart.

LEON: Don't start on that. You've never forgiven me. Is that my fault? You're the one with a stone for a heart.

THERAPIST: Wait a minute. You're both tearing into each other with the same accusations. You're just jabbing at each other. Stop it. If it's not hitting you yet, it's smashing me in the face. The two of you have some serious marriage problems that we should begin addressing, because they cause you both a lot of pain and, even more critically, they interfere with your ability to help Ray.

ROZ: Okay, I'm ready to put my cards on the table. I'll never trust him. Not after what he did. He betrayed me and the whole family. He's shameless.

THERAPIST: Is it okay with you, Leon, if Roz tells me about what happened?

LEON: Sure, be my guest. Just remember that there are two sides to every story.

THERAPIST: Roz, tell me what happened.

ROZ: It's very hard to talk about it. [She starts to cry.] I don't know if I want to get into it now. It's just too painful.

THERAPIST: We don't have to get into it now if you aren't ready, but the more

I work with you, I don't think we can avoid dealing with your marriage. You both try to keep a lid on your pain and your problems with each other, but the problems with Ray are increasingly putting you in a position where you can't go on without facing each other. We're gonna have to put our feet in these waters eventually.

ROZ: I know it, but I'm not ready.

LEON: Roz, we've got to face these problems. I haven't betrayed you in 14 years, and you still act as if it was yesterday. It's enough penance already. I've paid.

ROZ: You've paid. Yeah. You've paid. Nothing like the hurt I had. I don't know if I can ever get over it.

THERAPIST: How do you want to proceed with this? We keep stepping into it and then backing out.

LEON: Let's talk about this next session. It's too hot for us to talk about alone at home.

THERAPIST: Is that okay with you Roz?

ROZ: I think so. Maybe I'll feel stronger then. I definitely don't want to talk about it at home with Leon. I'd rather have the explosion here if there's gonna be one.

THERAPIST: So we'll get into this next time. And the two of you won't talk about it until then.

In the following session, the Goldbergs began to explore their marital problems, which included an affair that Leon had had with a family friend that ended 14 years before when Roz caught them. Over the next series of sessions, the marital problems, particularly the distrust in the marriage, became more focal than the problems with Ray. In fact, the therapist stopped linking the marital problems to the problems with Ray. Not surprisingly, the parents began to deal with Ray more cohesively, eventually getting him into treatment with a psychiatrist. Subsequently, the Goldbergs continued their therapy, focusing primarily on improving their marriage.

PRESENTING PROBLEMS AND MANAGED CARE

When therapy occurs under managed care, the care manager needs to be privy to both the therapist's list and the consensual problem list. Ideally, an *approved problem list* should be established with the care manager and the key patients during the early phase of therapy. This list usually includes some formulation of the problems within the categories of the current *Diagnostic and Statistical Manual of Mental Disorders* (American Psychiatric Association,

1994), as well as a formulation using the language of the key patients. The approved list comprises the problems for which the therapy is being funded at that point.

The more the care manager understands the presenting and nonpresenting problems on the therapist's list, the greater the likelihood of a strong alliance with the care manager and appropriate treatment for the patient system. In other words, the therapist contracts with the care manager to address particular problems. The more the care manager understands the therapist's thinking about the problems on the approved list and those that fall outside of that list, the more the care manager becomes a partner in the treatment process. Changes in the approved list do not come as surprises to the care manager and are more likely to be approved.

STEP 2: IDENTIFYING THE ATTEMPTED SOLUTIONS

The second step in delineating the problem cycle identifies the patients' attempted solutions to the presenting problems. Two basic questions drive this step. The first concerns the problem-solving process: Who has attempted what solutions to the presenting problem? The second targets the outcome of the solutions: Did they work, and if not, why not?

THE ATTEMPTED-SOLUTION PROCESS

The therapist needs to identify and understand the role and sequence of each key patient's participation in the efforts to solve the presenting problem. This process requires specific questioning of each of the key patients about what they have attempted and when and how they attempted it. It is also critical to understand the reactions of each of the other key patients, including the identified patient if there is one, to the efforts to solve the problem. Were they cooperative and facilitative? Were they passively helpful or aggressive? Did any of them attempt actively to sabotage efforts to solve the problem?

Key patients may give vague answers to the therapist's questions and even act irritated when the therapist pushes for clarification. Despite this resistance, it is critical for the therapist to develop a specific picture of the patient system's problem-solving process in regard to the presenting problem. The more specific the picture, the more data available for constructing problem-maintenance hypotheses. Essentially, "truth" is in the sequential details. Once again, although specificity is critical, the therapist should not push so hard as to jeopardize the therapeutic alliance. Following is a portion of dialogue with the Schultz family, toward the end of the first session, when the therapist begins to explore their problem-solving process.

THERAPIST: How have the two of you attempted to deal with the problems with Lawrence? Specifically, I'd be interested first in how you've tried to handle his abusive behavior at home.

MR. SCHULTZ: I tell him I won't put up with it. I try to be very firm and clear with him.

THERAPIST: Mr. Schultz, what do you do specifically when he's abusive? Is there a recent example you could tell me about?

MR. SCHULTZ: Yes. Last week when I came home from my trip to California, he and Marjorie were yelling when I came in the door. I always try to support Marjorie as much as I can, so I told Lawrence to shut up and go to his room. He started to argue with me, and I tried to explain to him that he should not talk to his mother that way. Finally he went to his room.

MRS. SCHULTZ: Yeah, finally, after another 15 minutes of argument. He's definitely on his way to being a great lawyer. He'll argue till he and you are blue in the face. Larry and Lawrence argue, argue, argue, but it doesn't seem to change anything.

THERAPIST: What do you mean it doesn't seem to change anything?

MRS. SCHULTZ: Well, Lawrence maybe goes to his room, but the next time he'll argue and shout at both of us as if this last incident never happened. He doesn't ever seem to learn he can't talk to us that way. Maybe he's got some kind of learning disability.

THERAPIST: Let me back up a little bit. Mrs. Schultz, how did you feel about the way your husband handled Lawrence last week when he came back from his trip and you and Lawrence were fighting?

MRS. SCHULTZ: Well, it was business as usual. God comes home and tries to make everything okay. Larry tries to be tough and definite, but Lawrence just doesn't take him or me seriously.

THERAPIST: Lawrence, what were your thoughts about that incident?

LAWRENCE: What incident?

THERAPIST: The incident last week when your dad came home and you were arguing with your mom.

LAWRENCE: Yeah, so what about it?

THERAPIST: What do you think about the way your parents handled it: your dad coming in and telling you to shut up and go to your room?

LAWRENCE: He always does that. He doesn't try to find out what's going on. What we're arguing about. He comes in like some kind of king or something and tries to lay down the law.

THERAPIST: What does your mom do when he does that?

LAWRENCE: She usually shuts up. She let's him handle me.

THERAPIST: Do you think she supports what he's doing with you? Was she one hundred percent behind his telling you to shut up and go to your room the other night?

LAWRENCE: How am I supposed to know? Why don't you ask her?

THERAPIST: Okay, I will. Mrs. Schultz, did you agree with the way your husband dealt with Lawrence the other night?

MRS. SCHULTZ: Well, kind of.

THERAPIST: What do you mean "kind of"?

MRS. SCHULTZ: Sometimes I think Larry shoots first and asks questions later.

THERAPIST: How do you mean?

MRS. SCHULTZ: Well, he comes in and jumps on Lawrence without finding out what's going on. I may be in the middle of working something out with Lawrence and our voices may be raised, but I may feel that we're getting somewhere. It may look like a stupid fight if you don't look carefully at what's going on. But like the other night, I thought I was getting somewhere, and Larry barges in and lays down the law.

THERAPIST: So you felt he should have slowed down and gotten the lay of the land before jumping in.

MRS. SCHULTZ: Exactly. I feel like he doesn't respect my ability to deal with Lawrence. He's got to jump in and take over without even asking me if I need his help or why we're arguing.

THERAPIST: Why don't you tell him to back off? Why don't you let him know you want him to stay out of it, at least for now?

MRS. SCHULTZ: Well, I don't want to undermine him in front of Lawrence. It makes Larry furious when he feels I'm undermining him or not fully supportive of what he's doing with Lawrence.

THERAPIST: So Larry would feel undermined if you asked him to back off or stay out of it? Why don't you check that out with Larry right now? Ask him if he'd feel undermined.

MRS. SCHULTZ: Well, would you? Wouldn't you feel like I was undermining your authority with Lawrence if I did that.

MR. SCHULTZ: I'm not sure. I guess it depends on how you did it and what was going on at the time.

This interaction reveals numerous important details about the Schultz's problem-solving process. First of all, Mr. and Mrs. Schultz do not synchronize with each other; their leadership styles are not coordinated. Mr. Schultz intrudes into conflictual interactions between his son and his wife without finding out what the conflict is about or the status of the conflict (e.g., productive, unproductive, or hurtful). Even more important, he does not stand behind his wife and support her but relegates her to the sidelines and steps onto the field himself. He acts as if he does not trust her or respect her ability to deal with Lawrence.

Second, this interaction reveals that Mrs. Schultz does not confront her husband directly but allows him to intercede and undermine her authority. Her reluctance allegedly derives from her fear that he will feel undermined if she stands up to him when he interferes. The end of the vignette also shows that Mr. Schultz can accept his wife's confrontation if it is done in a yet-to-be-specified way under certain yet-to-be-specified circumstances.

The analysis of the Schultz's problem-solving pattern clearly reveals the process of their ineffectiveness and some of the reasons behind their inability to work as coleaders. The specificity of the pattern lays the groundwork for formulating a more adaptive solution. From this short interaction, it is possible to begin to formulate what needs to change.

THE IMPACT OF ATTEMPTED SOLUTIONS

Once the therapist delineates the problem-solving process (who does what, when), the outcome of the attempted solutions needs to be identified. With the Schultz family, the therapist continues as follows:

THERAPIST: Mr. Schultz, I'd like to come back to what we've just been talking about. Do you think this pattern of you coming in and rescuing the situation is working? Is Lawrence getting the message and shaping up?

MR. SCHULTZ: Well, I think he knows I mean business. It's another story with my wife. I think Lawrence knows he can push her around if I'm not there.

THERAPIST: But the problem is that you can't be there all the time. Sometimes, in fact more often than not, your wife has to deal with him alone. Is your strategy helping her do that?

MR. SCHULTZ: Well, if she'd just listen to me, it would work.

THERAPIST: So your strategy is just to tell her what to do.

MRS. SCHULTZ: He wants me to be a female Larry. I can't and won't.

THERAPIST: So Mr. Schultz, what is your wife telling you about your efforts to tell her what to do with Lawrence?

MR. SCHULTZ: I guess they're not working.

LAWRENCE: You don't listen to her or me, and you just think you can tell everybody what to do. It doesn't work with me or with Mom. Do you get it?

MR. SCHULTZ: So what am I supposed to do? If all of you are so smart, what am I supposed to do?

This interaction clearly defines Mr. Schultz's problem-solving strategy as ineffective. As much as he tries, it just does not work; in fact, it backfires. His son and his wife are so mad at him about his style and tactics that they passively resist and undermine his efforts to help. The three of them have created a destructive cross-generational coalition. The critical piece of the interaction is Mr. Schultz's dawning awareness that even though his approach makes sense to him, it does not and will not work. An essential component of this step is helping the key patients see that what they have been doing to solve the presenting problem is not working and is unlikely to work in the future. This clarity about the ineffectiveness of the current problem-solving patterns augments the search for more adaptive solutions.

IDENTIFYING SYSTEM STRENGTHS

Delineating attempted solutions also helps identify system strengths. In the following dialogue, the therapist explores Fred Wilson's attempts to deal with his wife's depression.

THERAPIST: Mr. Wilson, how have you attempted to deal with your wife's depressive episodes?

MR. WILSON: Generally, I can see them coming. She starts to pull away and get more withdrawn. I used to ignore these early signs and hoped they'd go away. Well, that just seemed to make matters worse. Now I start talking to her right away. I ask her what she's thinking. When I can get her to tell me, she usually says she's thinking a bunch of awful things about herself. I used to try to argue with her about these thoughts, but that never worked. I'd try to tell her a lot of good things about herself, but it was like water off a duck's back. Now I just try to be with her: to listen and let her know that I love her. But it's like she's under a black cloud, and I just can't get her out from under.

THERAPIST: You've really worked on this—trying to help her—but you don't feel that you've been very successful.

MRS. WILSON: But he has. He can't cure my depressions, but knowing he's there and he loves me helps. I'm not so alone.

This vignette reveals Mr. Wilson's desire to help his wife, his sensitivity to and empathy for her plight, his capacity to try strategies and modify or abandon them if they do not work, and his love for her. It also shows that his wife appreciates his efforts and experiences them as helpful. The vignette illustrates the strengths of the marriage and the maturity and sensitivity of the partners. It also argues against interpersonal–organizational problem-maintenance hypotheses and provides data in support of biological constraints.

IDENTIFYING ATTEMPTED SOLUTIONS OVER THE COURSE OF THERAPY

Like problem identification, identifying attempted solutions occurs throughout therapy. During therapy, exploring how key patients attempt to resolve their presenting problems provides a progress report, a sense of how the system is doing. By continually monitoring the system's efforts to address the presenting problems, the therapist stays in touch with the changing problem cycle and the system's evolving problem-solving process. Even when the focus of the therapy shifts down the problem-maintenance structure, identifying the status of the attempted solutions keeps the therapeutic process connected to the problem cycle at the top of the structure. It keeps the therapy problem-centered and lets the patients know that even though their focus may be more historical, the process still links to the problems for which they seek help.

STEP 3: IDENTIFYING THE BIOLOGICAL SYSTEM

Identifying presenting problems and attempted solutions details the problem cycle. These first two steps are fundamentally behavioral: they are concerned with the sequential behaviors of the key system members in regard to the presenting problems. These steps help to define the behavioral focus of the therapy: what is wrong and what has been done to try to fix it.

With the third assessment–intervention step, the therapy moves into the second layer of the problem-maintenance structure and explores the biological system that underlies the problem cycle. Of particular concern are the biological processes that link to critical points in the problem cycle. Specifically, this step explores biological processes that are part of the presenting problem or that constrain the patient system's ability to solve the presenting problem. As mentioned previously, the best indicator of major biological constraints is the failure of presenting problems to vary consistently with contextual events.

Biological processes are most likely to play an explicit role in the following presenting problems: substance abuse, major mental illnesses, and failures in normal functioning with a clear organic base. A fourth category pertains to sexual dysfunctions with a clear organic component.

Many systems present substance-abuse problems. These include eating disorders and drug and alcohol addictions. Generally, biological processes play a significant role in these disorders and need to be considered, particularly in analyzing the attempted solutions. A critical question is, Did the attempted solution entail a biobehavioral component? Second, Was that component implemented appropriately? The third question is, What was the outcome of the biobehavioral attempted solution? The answers to these questions reveal important aspects of the problem-maintenance structure.

When mental illnesses such as schizophrenia, major depression, and manic depressive disorder are presented, biological processes play a significant role in the problem-maintenance structure. Attempted solutions that do not involve medication are seldom effective and usually reflect patient-system ignorance, denial, or bias. The relative contribution of these three factors should be evaluated as early as possible.

Organic disorders that impair normal functioning include mental retardation, learning disabilities, developmental disorders like autism, and degenerative disorders such as Alzheimer's and Parkinson's diseases. In their undiagnosed early phases, the system may present the identified patient as a behavioral problem, not understanding the biological basis of the disorder. Once again, the failure of the major symptoms to vary consistently with contextual events indicates biological determination. Alternatively, these disorders may present after they have been diagnosed, when the patient system finds they cannot manage them effectively.

All of the previously mentioned disorders as well as many other medical disorders can constrain the patient system's ability to resolve its presenting problems. A schizophrenic or drug-addicted father will have difficulty providing the leadership his delinquent son needs. A learning-disabled daughter may not be able to learn particular material no matter how well her parents structure her studying. The narcissistic self-preoccupation of early Alzheimer's disease may render the wife in a distressed couple even less able to empathize with her husband's concerns.

The guiding question concerning Step 3 is, To what extent do biological constraints block resolution of the presenting problems? Whenever biological constraints appear to penetrate the problem cycle, they should be pursued. In such situations, a thorough medical or psychiatric evaluation, or both, facilitates understanding of the problem cycle and, most important, helps construct alternative, adaptive solutions.

STEP 4: IDENTIFYING MEANING: THE EMOTIONAL SYSTEM

With the fourth assessment–intervention step, the therapeutic process moves into the domain of affect, a primary component of the meaning layer of the problem-maintenance structure. Every problem cycle has a system of emotions that underlie and penetrate the cycle. This affective system embodies the emotions of the key patients that link to critical points in the problem cycle.

THE ROLE OF EMOTIONS IN PROBLEM-CENTERED THERAPY

Emotion plays a key role in problem-centered therapy. Building on the theories of Ekman (Ekman & Friesen, 1975), Greenberg (1993; Johnson & Greenberg, 1994), and Izard (1977, 1993), problem-centered therapy posits an *action facilitation theory of emotion* (Pinsof, 1983). This theory asserts that emotions play a central and indispensable role in human motivation and problem solving. Emotions facilitate action or behavior. Specifically, emotions either facilitate or inhibit effective problem solving. They also add genuineness, intensity, vitality, and spontaneity to problem solving. Without emotion, problem solving becomes an empty, primarily cognitive endeavor that is seldom integrated or enduring.

That emotions facilitate action does not mean that emotions cause action or that actions do not facilitate emotion. The relationship between action and emotion and, for that matter, among emotion, action, and cognition (which will be addressed in the next section) is mutual, not linear. There may be linear phases in the emotion, action, and meaning cycle in which one component "drives" or plays a more primary motivational role. Nevertheless, their fundamental relationship is recursive, or mutual. Affect plays a facilitative role in this process.

Most contemporary theories of emotion posit the existence of a number of universal and discrete emotions, including anger, sadness–grief, joy–happiness, fear, disgust, and shame. Some theorists add surprise (Ekman & Friesen, 1975) and contempt (Gottman, 1993). Each emotion accomplishes multiple functions, ranging from regulating mental and motor activities to the communication of internal response predispositions and action tendencies. The general consensus is that the face is the predominant organ of emotional expression, although voice and body posture contribute.

Problem-centered therapy targets each of the previously mentioned emotions. Frequently, they are addressed with the previously mentioned labels. More often, they are tapped in the vernacular of the patient system. Anger may be irritation, resentment, being "pissed off," or rage; sadness–grief may be hurt, emotional pain, loss, or loneliness. The terms *anxious*, *uptight*, and *tense* usually refer to a general emotional and psychophysiological arousal related to fear.

Problem-centered therapy is not primarily concerned with emotion per se. It is not based on a model of affective health toward which it moves patients. Emotions are important insofar as they facilitate or impede adaptive problem solving. Therefore, the model does not assert that it is "good" to express anger rather than internalizing it. Anger is important because it motivates problem solving. It is far less important to help patients vent anger than to help them learn to use their angry feelings to address the problems that make them angry.

In general, problem-centered therapy is not predicated on a catharsis theory of emotion; however, exceptions concern sadness–grief, love, and joy–happiness. Sadness–grief is not as linked to external action and problem solving as are the other specific emotions. Sadness–grief functions primarily to help the psychological self deal with the loss of important self objects. Sadness–grief is an emotional process whereby the self heals itself. The "work" of sadness–grief is primarily internal and occurs as the emotion is experienced and expressed. This is not to diminish the role of rituals (symbolic external action) in grieving or the value of social grief work, but to assert the special valuing of sadness–grief within problem-centered therapy. With most other emotions, the emphasis is not on expressing them per se but on using them to engage in adaptive action leading toward resolution of the presenting problems.

Frequently, therapists confuse sadness–grief with depression. Depression is not an emotion but a complex of emotions and cognitions that inhibits adaptive problem solving and jeopardizes mental and physical health. Unlike sadness–grief, depression does not need to be experienced and expressed. It is difficult to distinguish sadness–grief from depression, because depression frequently contains sadness–grief and links to loss. Distinguishing features are that depression typically involves self-depreciating (and sometimes other-depreciating) cognitions or a suppression of psychological and sometimes even physical functions that feels hollow or empty of emotion.

Two other exceptions within problem-centered therapy are love and joy–happiness. Unlike joy–happiness, love is not viewed by researchers as a specific emotion. From the perspective of a clinical theory like the problem-centered model, love is a discrete and critical emotion in social life. As in sadness–grief, experiencing joy–happiness and love is more important than any problem-solving activity that flows from these emotions. Both usually lead to affiliative and constructive activities, but experiencing and communicating love and joy–happiness at times constitute ends in their own right, particularly with conflicted and alienated systems.

Beyond the scientific limits of emotion research, the problem-centered model also concerns itself with emotions like jealousy, envy, pride, guilt, and emptiness. Whether any or all of these should be thought of as discrete emotions or blends of more primary emotions is not of great concern in a clinical theory. Each of these emotions is important insofar as it constrains and facilitates adaptive and maladaptive behaviors.

Emotion work in problem-centered therapy is complex. Sometimes one emotion masks another "truer," or more primary, emotion (Greenberg, 1993); for example, anger may be a defense against hurt, or sadness may be a defense against anger and the actions that might flow from anger. The model does not take an invariant stance toward any emotion. Each emotion or set of emotions must be evaluated contextually and sequentially to understand which is more primary and which is secondary and defensive. The extent to which an emotion needs to be expressed rather than used to facilitate some other kind of activity derives from an analysis of the context in which it emerges and the role it might play in adaptive problem solving.

In understanding the emotion system underlying the problem cycle, the critical issues are identifying which emotions are present and which emotions are missing and the extent to which what is present or what is missing facilitates or hinders problem solving. Sometimes, a system needs to learn to inhibit a particular emotion and to experience and express another. For instance, in a divorcing couple, one or both partners may need to inhibit their feelings of affection for each other. In fact, for one or both, anger may be far more adaptive in going through the divorce process. In problem-centered therapy, the therapist needs to explore and understand the emotional system contextually, in terms of the sequences in which particular emotions occur, in terms of the presenting problems and attempted solutions, and in terms of what is missing or present in too great a degree for effective and genuine problem solving.

Although this fourth step, identifying the emotions that underlie and impact the problem cycle, comes after the first three, it usually occurs as part of each of the previous steps. Seldom if ever does it or should it constitute a discrete step in its own right. For instance, in identifying the presenting problems, the therapist asks key patients how they feel about the presenting problem as well as each other's problem definitions. Similarly, the therapist asks key patients how they feel about their own and each other's attempts to solve the presenting problems.

KEY EMOTIONAL TURNING POINTS IN THE PROBLEM CYCLE

In identifying the emotional system, the therapist does not catalogue all of the emotions that flow through the entire cycle. Affect identification is more problem-centered. Primary attention is paid to identifying the particular emotions associated with critical points in the cycle. These points occur when an alternative, more adaptive behavior would break up the problem cycle and lead to problem resolution. At these turning (or option) points, different emotions and actions could lead to different outcomes.

Rose Goodman, the custodial parent in a divorced family, complained that she could not control her 5-year-old son, Ryan. During the second session, Ryan was playing noisily, and the therapist commented that he could not hear what Rose was saying. Rose turned to Ryan and nicely asked him to be quiet. Ryan ignored her. She turned to the therapist and, with a helpless look, shrugged her shoulders. The therapist suggested she try to quiet Ryan again. Rose tried, but Ryan ignored her. At this point, Rose turned to the therapist with tears in her eyes and said, "I can't do anything."

Rose's tears emerged from what looked like a blend of frustration and sadness. What was clearly missing and would have been far more adaptive in this situation was anger. Rose's anger at Ryan's not listening could have been a basis for Rose to escalate, not only instrumentally, but affectively. If she had stood up and said in a firm voice, "Ryan, stop that right now. Come over here and draw something for me with these crayons and paper," he would have listened. Her tears were inappropriate in this situation; her missing anger could have led to constructive action.

Turning points in problem cycles typically precede the emergence of the problem sequence or related problem behaviors. These are the points at which an informed observer would note that the system was "losing it" or falling into old, destructive patterns. An example is the moment in a conflictual marital interaction when the husband becomes verbally abusive and the wife counters with a personal attack. Typically, such an exchange escalates the conflict, loses the focus on the problem that led to the conflict, and physiologically arouses both spouses to the point that they cannot process complex information and listen.

In the following dialogue, the therapist affectively unravels the turning point. This vignette concerns Lionel and Enid Stratton, a conflictual couple in marital therapy.

MRS. STRATTON: Something happened I want to talk about.
THERAPIST: Is that okay with you, Lionel?

MR. STRATTON: Yeah, I know what she wants to talk about. It's a disagreement we got into over the weekend.

MRS. STRATTON: That's right. We were over at a friend's house, partying and all, and it was getting late. I thought we should be heading home, but Lionel refused. I kept asking him to leave, and he acted as if I wasn't even talking to him.

THERAPIST: What happened then?

MRS. STRATTON: I decided to leave on my own and he could come home in a cab when he was ready. So I got up, said good night to our friends, and left. I didn't even look to see if he was getting up or noticed that I was leaving. So I went home and went to bed. We didn't talk for the rest of the weekend.

MR. STRATTON: I was in the midst of telling this guy about some of my experiences in Vietnam, and we were really talking. He had been there, in the Army. I was a Marine.

MRS. STRATTON: I don't care what he was or you were. I was exhausted and wanted to go home and you didn't give a shit.

MR. STRATTON: All you think about is yourself—are you having a good time or are you tired or whatever. You're so goddamn selfish that it's unbelievable. Everything has to be the way you want it or I'm being a pig.

MRS. STRATTON: That's not true. I work hard all week, I do almost all the housework and taking care of the kids, and you sit on your fat ass and drink beer and watch TV. I am sick of it. You don't do shit for me or anybody else.

THERAPIST: Wait a minute. Stop! I want to go back to something. Lionel, how do you think Enid felt when she was asking you to go home and you didn't respond?

MR. STRATTON: As usual, she was pissed off. She was jerking my chain, and the dog wasn't jumping fast enough.

THERAPIST: Ask her how she was feeling. See if you're right. Try to do it without sarcasm.

MR. STRATTON: You were pissed off, right?

MRS. STRATTON: Right. You bet. I was exhausted and you didn't seem to notice or care.

THERAPIST: Hold it. I think you were feeling more than just pissed off, and I'm not sure your perception that Lionel didn't care or notice you is accurate. I think you were also feeling hurt that Lionel was not attentive to your needs at that moment. You felt he didn't care about you.

MRS. STRATTON: That's right, I felt he didn't care. I was hurt and then I got angry.

THERAPIST: Yes, I think that's the way it may go a lot with the two of you. Enid, you feel hurt and get angry, and Lionel, you shut down and get passive. By the way, Lionel, is Enid accurate that you did not care how she was feeling at that time—that she was exhausted?

MR. STRATTON: I do care about how she feels, but I was talking to someone who seemed to have some understanding of what Vietnam was about. He understood. I knew she wanted to go, but I didn't want to stop what was happening at that moment.

THERAPIST: Have you let Enid know how hard it has been for you to not have someone to talk to who really can understand what it was like for you in Vietnam? How lonely it's been to have no one to share it with?

MR. STRATTON: No, I haven't wanted to talk about it until recently. I guess she didn't know.

In this vignette, the therapist penetrates below the surface of Lionel and Enid's actions to their feelings and experience. Enid was hurt by Lionel's lack of attention when she was exhausted and wanted to go home. Lionel was so engrossed in talking with a fellow veteran that he did not want to leave. Talking with this new friend was a long-awaited, gratifying experience. Unfortunately, neither Enid nor Lionel stopped to problem-solve. She could have told him how much she needed to go home and how she felt hurt that he was not attending to her; he could have explained the importance of his discussion; and they could have negotiated. They might have stayed a little longer; Lionel could have arranged to get together later with his new friend; or Enid could have gone home alone without bitterness.

Instead, Enid's hurt came out as anger. Lionel's reaction was to ignore her, which further infuriated her. Similarly, in their interaction in therapy, when Enid accuses Lionel of "not giving a shit," he immediately escalates and calls her "selfish." From that point, the conflict escalates until the therapist interrupts. Their moving to anger instead of expressing hurt and their blaming attacks instead of expressing concerns and needs constitute critical affective components of the Strattons' problem cycle.

The therapist, in the Stratton vignette, asked about and labeled emotion. Additionally, the therapist should ask about the communication of emotion. The therapist began to do this at the end. However, as in the general exploration of emotion, the examination of affective communication should be problem-centered. The emotions that are explored should be clearly identified as relating to the presenting problems and the problem cycle. In working with the Schultz family, the problem-centered therapist would not ask, simply, "Do you get angry at your husband?" He or she more likely would ask, early in therapy, "Do you get angry at your husband when he interferes with your attempts to work things out with Lawrence?" Linking the exploration of the affective system to the presenting problems and the problem cycle minimizes patient resistance and helps to build the alliance.

STEP 5: IDENTIFYING MEANING: THE COGNITIVE SYSTEM

In addition to understanding the affective system, the therapist needs to understand the system of cognitions that underlie the cycle. The cognitive system embodies the thoughts and intentions patients attribute to their own and each other's behaviors within the problem cycle. In the Stratton vignette, Enid attributed Lionel's lack of response to a lack of caring. In contrast, Lionel attributed his lack of response to being engrossed in conversation with his new friend, an important experience from which he did not want to be diverted. Because Lionel had not shared with Enid his longing for this kind of experience and relationship, she did not understand what this experience meant to him.

In the case of Rose and Ryan Goodman, Rose's tears in the face of Ryan's ignoring her were based at least in part on the meaning Rose attached to Ryan's behavior as well as her own behavior in their confrontation. For Rose, Ryan's behavior meant that he was damaged and incapable of responding. It was as if her son were deaf. He was not being defiant; he was handicapped and could not help it. Rose's sense of herself was that she was "nice," incapable of "being mean." Rose had been physically and emotionally abused by her mother and had made an early and unconscious commitment never to act like her. Thus, being tough with Ryan was tantamount to becoming her abusive mother: an odious prospect.

The therapist explores the cognitive system by asking key patients what they think about critical aspects of the problem cycle. This task is best accomplished through meaning queries: What does this behavior or event mean to you? It can also be informative to ask key patients what they think particular events or actions mean to other key patients. With the Strattons, Lionel could be asked: What do you think it meant to Enid that you were ignoring her when she wanted to leave? Such a question helps evaluate the *empathic capacity* of the patient system: the capacity of key patients to understand each other independently of their own concerns and interests. Assessing empathic capacity is particularly crucial with conflicted systems in which key patients' inability to see each other's behavior from any perspective other than their own constitutes a core constraint of the problem cycle.

Exploring the cognitive system, like exploring emotion, focuses around turning points in the problem cycle. Unraveling the meaning of turning points is a critical task in problem-centered therapy. It is more accurate to say the "meanings" of turning points, because in troubled systems the meaning system is at best fractured, if not fragmented. There are multiple, antagonistic, and even mutually exclusive meanings attributed to particular events by different patients that inhibit problem solving and promote unproductive conflict. The therapist initially needs to get some sense of the capacities of the key patients to identify the meanings they attribute to the components of the turning points, how much they can grasp the meanings others attribute to those components, and the extent to which these meanings can be changed.

As in exploring affect, exploring the cognitive system seldom occurs independently of the problem-identification, attempted solution, biological, and emotional-system steps. Behaviorally, it is not a step in its own right but a crucial accompaniment to the others. At the beginning of treatment, the exploration of the cognitive system can only be relatively superficial. The degree to which it has to become more extensive over the course of therapy depends on the ease and rapidity with which the patient system embraces the next step: identifying and implementing a more adaptive solution to their presenting problems.

STEP 6: COMPLETING THE CYCLE: IDENTIFYING THE ALTERNATIVE, ADAPTIVE SEQUENCE

Building on the notion that patient systems actively maintain their problems, earlier work viewed the problem cycle as a circular *problem-maintenance cycle* (Feldman & Pinsof, 1982). Problem behaviors or symptoms were located at the bottom (6 o'clock) of the circle, and the alternative, adaptive behavior at the top (12 o'clock). Drawing on systems theory, the alternative, adaptive behavior and the problem behavior homeostatically regulated each other. When the problem behavior exceeded the system's permissible deviation limits, the corrective sequence of alternative, adaptive behaviors kicked in; when the alternative, adaptive behavior exceeded permissible deviation limits, the corrective sequence of the problem behaviors kicked in.

The classical conflictual couple exemplified this cyclical model as they oscillated between intimacy and conflict. As intimacy became too frightening, they escalated conflict; as conflict became too frightening, they escalated intimacy. Intimacy and conflict regulated each other as the couple moved around their problem-maintenance cycle.

This circular problem-maintenance formulation was too simplistic and reductionistic. It assumed that every problem behavior regulates some kind of alternative, adaptive behavior, and vice versa. The problem-centered model now views that as a possible but not necessary scenario. Sometimes problem behavior regulates other behaviors or activities, and sometimes it does not. Problems or symptoms may regulate nothing, an interpersonal process, a biological process, a psychodynamic process, or some combination. With couples, conflict may regulate nothing, interpersonal distance patterns, intrapsychic anxieties about intimacy, or some combination of these and other factors.

Similarly, systems are not always somewhere on the circle. The couple presenting with conflict is not always either escalating conflict or escalating intimacy. They engage in conflictual interactions part of the time. The rest of the time they spend involved in the myriad activities that people engage in, including but not solely escalating intimacy. The circular model bound the problem and adaptive sequences too tightly to each other and presumed a continuous knowledge of the system's life at all times that is epistemologically impossible.

The sixth step in the assessment–intervention sequence concludes with the preliminary identification of a sequence of behaviors that represents a practical and viable alternative to the problem sequence. The problem-cycle model does not presume that this alternative, adaptive sequence regulates the problem sequence or vice versa. The sequences may regulate each other or they may not. In the life of the patient system, other important sequences generally occur between the problem and alternative, adaptive sequences.

The identification of an alternative, adaptive sequence relates to the quest for system strengths. Like the solution-focused therapist, the problem-centered therapist searches for exceptions to the problem rule. This search is predicated on the assumption that there are times in the patient system's life when the problem sequence gets launched but does not escalate destructively. With the Schultz family, at times Lawrence begins to act provocatively, but the sequence does not escalate, and his behavior remains within normal limits. Similarly, at times his parents begin to conflict, but stop it without Lawrence's involvement.

As troubled systems evolve over time, the alternative, adaptive sequence may occur less and less frequently, and the problem sequence more and more often. With such evolved and troubled systems, the present scenario may be so bleak that the therapist may have to look in the past for examples of alternative, adaptive behaviors. For example, the Elias family was better able to deal with losses and separations before the death of the paternal grandmother. Additionally, the parents shared their worries and concerns with each other. After the grandmother's death, alternative, adaptive sequences of sharing concerns and dealing with loss diminished, replaced by a system in which the marital partners were isolated, and feelings were not shared. Everything became internalized, even with the children.

The therapist needs to delineate the natural history of the adaptive sequence. One might ask the Elias family how the sharing pattern evolved over time and how it became increasingly less frequent to the point that currently it looks nonexistent. The therapist also explores the contemporary context: the onset conditions, vicissitudes, and consequences (outcomes) of the adaptive sequence. With the Schultz family, it means understanding what precedes a nonescalating parental conflict or a sequence in which Lawrence begins to provoke but does not follow through. The critical task in beginning to identify an alternative, adaptive sequence is developing an understanding of what is different. Why can the patient system deal effectively with the potential problem situation in one context and not in another? In other words, what are the contextual determinants of successful as opposed to unsuccessful problem resolution?

In the following vignette with the Schultz family, the therapist explores an alternative, adaptive sequence:

THERAPIST [to Mrs. Schultz]: So, last Monday night, Lawrence started to argue with you about watching a TV show before he'd finished his homework. How did you handle that?

MRS. SCHULTZ: I told him *no*. He started to argue with me, and I told him that if he argued he wouldn't be allowed to watch TV when he finished his homework.

THERAPIST: How did he react?

MRS. SCHULTZ: He stopped arguing and went in and started his homework.

THERAPIST: What was the difference? Why on Monday night did he do what you requested, whereas a couple of weeks ago he wouldn't stop and just kept on and on?

MR. SCHULTZ: Well, I was out of town again on Monday night. I guess we're starting to see that he's better when I'm not around. Maybe I should just move out.

THERAPIST: Well, maybe your not being around had something to do with it. But I wonder what else may have been a factor. I think there's more to it than just your not being around. Lawrence, do you have any sense of what made the difference, other than your dad was not around?

LAWRENCE: No, I don't know why it was different.

MRS. SCHULTZ: The difference was that he knew I meant business. I was ready for him to fight me, and I would have taken TV away in a flash. I was resolved.

THERAPIST: So you think he sensed you really were not going to back down on Monday night. Why didn't he think you meant business a couple of weeks ago?

MRS. SCHULTZ: I think I didn't really mean business a couple of weeks ago. I'm feeling stronger now and more hopeful.

THERAPIST: Lawrence, did you sense that about your mom, that she's feeling stronger?

LAWRENCE: I guess. Everybody was feeling better Monday night.

In this vignette, the adaptive sequence is preceded by a positive change in the mother's mood. Her shift from depression to positive affect and a sense of confidence was recognized by Lawrence and Mr. Schultz. The shift may have recontextualized the problem sequence and permitted it to have a constructive outcome. As well as sensing his mother's greater resolve, Lawrence sensed that she was psychologically stronger and less in need of him as a distraction from her marital frustrations.

In some systems, the alternative, adaptive sequence does not occur with the critical subsystems but in other domains. For instance, Loretta Butler is unable to assert herself in the context of her family, but she can be an assertive leader at the hospital. The critical questions in such situations are, What is different about the adaptive and the problem contexts? Why can Loretta Butler assert herself in one context and not in the other?

Similarly, key members in some systems may engage in alternative, adaptive behaviors that could ameliorate or resolve the presenting problem, but they do it exclusively in regard to other, nonpresenting problems. For example, the parents of an acting-out developmentally delayed 14-year-old girl may have great difficulty setting and enforcing consistent limits with her, but they may be able to set and enforce limits effectively with their 16-year-old son. The critical question here is, What has prevented the parents from using their limit-setting and enforcing skills with their daughter?

The scenarios envisioned here are predicated on the assumption that at some other time, or in some other context, or in regard to some other problem, the key patients have engaged in some form of alternative, adaptive behavior that could be used at least to improve if not to resolve the presenting problem. Some systems may never have engaged in such alternative, adaptive behaviors, however, or their capacities to do so may have deteriorated so dramatically that they are now disabled.

With systems that have never engaged in relevant alternative, adaptive behaviors, the therapist has to identify, encourage, and ultimately teach the patient system to try them. With disabled or "burned-out" systems that currently lack the resources to engage in any behavior that might begin to interrupt the problem sequence, the therapist may have to engage other systems that might be able at least temporarily to provide the resources and skills necessary to modify the problem sequence. This action may involve placing a symptomatic patient in another residential system or introducing new helpers into the system, such as homemakers or in-home social service providers.

PRELIMINARY AND ONGOING CYCLE MODELS

At the conclusion of the sixth assessment–intervention step, the therapist should have a fairly clear picture of the problem sequence and its context as well as an emerging picture of an alternative, adaptive sequence and its context. This picture lays the groundwork for the next step in the assessment–intervention process: identifying and implementing an adaptive solution, the topic of the next chapter.

Before concluding, it bears reiterating that the construction and elaboration of a model of the problem cycle in the minds of the therapist and key patients is an ongoing and never-ending task. Time and experience refine the model, providing a clearer and more detailed picture of the problem sequence; the alternative, adaptive sequence; and the temporal and functional relationship between them. The elaboration of the problem cycle stops when the patient system resolves or ameliorates the presenting problem.

CHAPTER 7

Modifying the Problem Cycle—I: Implementing an Adaptive Solution

I N PROBLEM-CENTERED THERAPY, the therapist and the patient systems engage in an active and focused change process. This active and focused quality becomes most apparent in the sixth and seventh steps of the assessment–intervention sequence, in which the therapist helps the patient system to identify and implement an adaptive solution to the presenting problem. After the therapist has identified the problem cycle; its problem and alternative, adaptive sequences; and their affective and semantic systems, the therapist moves out of the exploratory role and actively, if not aggressively, intervenes to change the problem cycle. Modifying the problem cycle entails four basic tasks: (1) identifying an alternative, adaptive solution to the presenting problem; (2) establishing a solution consensus with the key patient-system members about the suitability of the adaptive solution; (3) implementing the adaptive solution; and (4) evaluating the outcome of the implementation process and making a decision about the appropriate next steps.

IDENTIFYING AN ADAPTIVE SOLUTION

The first task, begun in step 6 at the end of the last chapter, delineates *the adaptive solution: the simplest, most direct, and most cost-effective intervention that key patients can perform to solve their presenting problem.* This task identifies what needs to happen to solve the presenting problem: the process goal of therapy. The identification of an adaptive solution derives from at least five sources: (1) the therapist's knowledge of the problem cycle; (2) the emerging picture of the patient system, particularly its gross structure, its human and economic resources, the developmental levels of the system and the key patients, and the patient system's "culture"; (3) the therapist's understanding of the problem-maintenance structure; (4) the therapist's knowledge of the accumulated professional and scientific wisdom about the presenting problem and effective solutions; and (5) the key patients' understanding of what needs to change to solve the presenting problem. For clarity, this section discusses these sources separately; in practice, they are inseparable.

THE PROBLEM CYCLE

The first source for identifying an adaptive solution is the therapist's understanding of the problem cycle: the presenting problem; the attempted solutions; the biological, affective, and cognitive systems that underlie the cycle; and the alternative, adaptive behavior sequence. By understanding the ways in which the patient system has attempted and failed to solve the presenting problem, the therapist can begin to formulate alternative, adaptive solutions. This emerging formulation also derives from an understanding of the alternative, adaptive sequence in the problem cycle. Knowing under what conditions the system has been able to avoid or ameliorate the presenting problem provides valuable leads as to what needs to be done to remedy the presenting problem now.

Sometimes analyzing the problem cycle reveals a fairly simple, straightforward, and obvious solution. For instance, the Elias family needs to learn to grieve and come to terms with loss, on both collective and individual levels. In another system, an adolescent boy presents mild conduct-disorder problems. The problem-cycle analysis reveals that the parents do not consistently establish or maintain behavioral limits. All the parents may need to do is to set and enforce appropriate behavioral limits. In fact, the problem-cycle analysis may reveal that they are already doing this as their alternative, adaptive solution but do not do it consistently.

With most systems, however, and particularly with patient systems in which the path to the presenting problem is blocked by various nonpresenting problems, the adaptive solution consists of related activities that need to occur within various subsystems to resolve the presenting problem. These activities can be thought of as micro tasks or micro adaptive solutions. These micro tasks are not necessarily directly or sequentially linked to the presenting problems.

For example, Mr. and Mrs. Schultz need to address and resolve their coparental conflict and possibly their marital conflict insofar as these problems impede their ability to deal effectively and appropriately with Lawrence. Specifically, Mr. Schultz needs to learn to respect the boundary around the parental subsystem of Mrs. Schultz and Lawrence. As part of that process, he needs to support his wife in her dealings with Lawrence rather than usurping her role in the problem-solving process. He needs to learn to wait, hold back, and let his wife and son work out their conflict. Concomitantly, Mrs. Schultz needs to learn to be firmer with Lawrence as well as with her husband. With her husband, that entails blocking him from interfering when she deals with Lawrence and letting him know what kind of help she wants from him with Lawrence. These micro tasks modify how each of the key patients participates in the problem cycle.

Typically, the problem-cycle analyses also reveal various affective and cognitive tasks that necessarily accompany and facilitate implementation of the adaptive solution. For instance, as part of learning to grieve and come to terms with loss, the Elias family must learn to experience and express sadness. Mrs. Schultz needs to see herself, cognitively, as a more competent and powerful person with both Lawrence and her husband.

THE PATIENT SYSTEM: STRUCTURE, RESOURCES, DEVELOPMENT, AND CULTURE

The therapist's understanding of the patient system is the second source for identifying adaptive solutions. Although the initial exploration of the problem cycle is problem-centered, the therapist inevitably develops some understanding of various aspects of the patient system, with particular emphasis on four domains or metaframeworks (Breunlin et al., 1992): (1) the organizational structure of the system, (2) the resources available to the system, (3) the developmental levels of the key systems and subsystems, and (4) the culture of the patient system.

Structural Organization of the System

In formulating adaptive solutions, the therapist considers two structural dimensions. The first, the *gross organizational structure* of the patient system, specifies who is living with whom and their relative degrees of actual or potential involvement in the problem-maintenance structure. For instance, if the presenting problem of an 11-year-old conduct-disordered girl occurs within a nuclear family embedded within a large and involved extended-family system, the potential adaptive solutions typically differ from those available to an isolated single-parent family. Similarly, the potential adaptive solutions for a binuclear family with a conduct-disordered 11-year-old daughter differ depending on the coparental relationship between the divorced parents as well as their degrees of involvement in their daughter's life.

The second aspect of structure that influences identification of an adaptive solution concerns the nature and location of the current *psychosocial boundaries* within the patient system. Building on Minuchin's (1974) classical definition, psychosocial boundaries are rules that specify who can do what with whom, when, and where. Based on a boundary analysis, the adaptive solution should create or reinforce adaptive boundaries and weaken maladaptive boundaries. For instance, if the therapist's analysis of the patient system's boundaries reveals a weak generational boundary, as with the Schultz family, the therapist and key patients should seek adaptive solutions that strengthen the generational boundary and the coparental system. The therapist would not recommend any adaptive solution that encourages Mr. Schultz to override his wife's problem-solving efforts with Lawrence. Rather, the adaptive solution should strengthen her parental position as well as the coparental alliance between the parents.

Patient-System Resources

The identification of an adaptive solution must also take into account the human and economic resources available to the system. A system with a large and attentive extended family typically has more human resources to deal with a troubled child than a single-parent system that is geographically isolated from its extended-family support network. Similarly, a wealthy family has a wider array of potential adaptive solutions than a poor family. To some extent, financial resources can make up for deficient human resources in that facsimiles of those human resources can be purchased. For instance, a well-to-do but isolated single parent with an underachieving 9-year-old son can hire tutors instead of engaging a nonexistent or unavailable coparent or extended family.

Development

A normative understanding of the biopsychosocial stages that families and individuals pass through and the collective and individual tasks associated with those stages provides a crucial framework for crafting an adaptive solution. Developmental frameworks delineate what needs to be done at a particular individual or collective developmental level and what needs to be done next, in the subsequent stage or level. This prescriptive aspect of developmental frameworks provides a type of generic guidance for systems that are stuck in certain stages. For instance, the Warrens presented for therapy with their youngest child and only son, 19-year-old Jamie, as the identified patient. Jamie had refused to go to college when he graduated from high school and promised to get a job to help support himself and contribute to the family. A year later, Jamie had not gotten a steady job. Sleeping until noon, staying out until the early morning with his friends, he had pushed his parents to the point that they sought therapy.

The Warrens were at the tail end of the launching stage of family development. Similarly, Jamie was struggling with identity problems relating to the choice of a blue- versus white-collar career path. In this context, the therapist identified a number of adaptive solutions. The first involved the parents encouraging if not forcing Jamie to move out of the house and get his own apartment. If he were not living at home, Jamie would have to get a job to support himself. Second, the therapist recommended a series of individual therapy sessions for Jamie to help him more directly confront and work through his concerns about blue- and white-collar career paths. Finally, the therapist recommended a series of family sessions in which Jamie and his parents could explore issues pertaining to work, including blue- and white-collar identities, and concerns about the looming empty nest. All of these solutions were designed to help the system solve their presenting problem and move on to the next set of developmental issues.

Sometimes, when an individual or subsystem is performing at an inappropriately advanced level in certain areas, it is appropriate to facilitate a developmental regression to a prior level. For instance, a parentified 13-year-old girl who is responsible for the care of her younger siblings and her drug-addicted mother is referred to therapy by a physician because of stress-related gastrointestinal problems and headaches. Part of the adaptive solution may entail finding contexts for her where she can be nurtured and less responsible.

In providing guidelines, developmental frameworks should not be taken as invariant prescriptions about what to do and not do. Rather, they should be viewed as part of the ground from which the figure of the adaptive solution emerges. They contribute; they do not dictate. For instance, if Jamie Warren were developmentally disabled or mentally ill, a much more protracted adolescence living at home or in a protective setting might be more appropriate than some chronologically derived sense of what is appropriate.

Patient-System Culture

The patient system's culture critically influences the identification of adaptive solutions. As specified in Chapter 1, culture refers to the beliefs and practices that derive from a particular system's location in a set of biosocio-cultural contexts that define proper behavior and experience. A system's culture provides a set of opportunities as well as constraints concerning what constitutes an acceptable adaptive solution (Breunlin et al., 1992). The Tanakas came into therapy after Mr. Tanaka and his eldest son, Ted, got into a confrontation the night of Ted's high school graduation. Ted, an excellent college-bound student, asked his parents to allow him to stay out with his friends all night after his graduation. His father refused to bend Ted's standard weekend curfew of 1:00 A.M. Without telling his father, and in flagrant disregard of his father's wishes and rules, Ted stayed out all night.

Infuriated, Mr. Tanaka refused to speak with Ted but informed his wife that he would not permit Ted to purchase the car Ted had been saving for and needed for his summer job. He also said that he was no longer sure that he would pay for Ted to go to Princeton and that maybe Ted should stay home and attend a local university in Chicago. Hearing this news from his mother, Ted moved in with a friend's family and refused to come home or communicate with his father. His friend's parents convinced him to seek family therapy, and Ted became the organizing patient. He said that he would talk with his father or consider coming home only if he and his parents entered family therapy.

In working with the Tanakas, it quickly became clear to the therapist that Mr. Tanaka's view of himself as the unchallenged family leader and patriarch was being challenged by Ted, who viewed his father as a rigid "old-timer" who "thinks he's still in Japan 50 years ago." The obvious adaptive solution of encouraging the father to behave in a more flexible fashion consistent with late twentieth-century North American culture would not work with Mr. Tanaka. Any adaptive solution that challenged his authority or involved giving in would never be accepted by Mr. Tanaka, who even seemed to experience therapy as a challenge to his authority.

In the initial meeting with the whole family, the therapist sensed the tenuous alliance with Mr. Tanaka and decided it could be best preserved by not insisting the Mr. Tanaka attend the next set of sessions. In that session, the therapist also perceived that although he could be as stubborn and proud as his father, Ted loved his father and intensely desired to repair their relationship. Meeting with Mrs. Tanaka and Ted, the therapist began to explore the possibility of Ted engaging in some form of ritual or symbolic behavior that would constitute a peace offering to his father without Ted having to acknowledge overtly that he was wrong, a behavior Ted's pride would not permit.

After a series of sessions without his father, in which Ted ventilated about his father's rigidity and the injustice of his father's stance, Ted came up with an unusual and somewhat paradoxical plan. He decided to send his father the money he had saved for his car with a respectful note stating that, since Ted's goal was to bring honor to his family through his work and his studies, as the head of the family, his father should have the money Ted earned to buy a car to get him to his summer job. Ted concluded the note by saying he was sure his father would know how to use the money.

On receiving the note and money, Ted's father communicated through his wife that Ted should come home and they would buy his car together. When Ted came home, no mention was made about the graduation events or his father's threatened punishments. The note and money clearly restored the father's sense of his leadership role within the family and his son's commitment to honor the family and his father. Mr. Tanaka was then able to repair the relationship and actively support his son's plans.

THE PROBLEM-MAINTENANCE STRUCTURE

In addition to understanding the patient system—its structure, resources, developmental levels, and culture—it is important to use the therapist's growing knowledge of the problem-maintenance structure in delineating an adaptive solution. Early contacts with the patient system inevitably reveal data about the problem-maintenance structure that lead to the formulation of preliminary hypotheses. After two or three sessions, the therapist should have a fairly clear idea about some of the organizational and interpersonal constraints that prevent resolution of the presenting problem. With the Schultz family, the therapist's problem-cycle analysis in the early sessions suggests that Lawrence's symptoms may regulate conflict between his parents. A related but more remote interpersonal hypothesis suggested by the problem-cycle analysis is that Lawrence's symptoms may also function to regulate his mother's frustration and depression in regard to her relationship with Larry, her husband.

These problem-maintenance hypotheses should not inordinately influence the process of identifying an adaptive solution early in therapy, because they may lead the therapist to overestimate the pathology of a patient system and overlook system strengths that may not be readily apparent. For instance, the therapist might conclude on the basis of the aforementioned problem-maintenance hypotheses that Mr. and Mrs. Schultz will be unable to set and enforce firm and consistent limits with Lawrence, because to do so would remove him as a regulator of their conflict and Mrs. Schultz's marital frustration and depression. To come to this conclusion before directly testing their ability to set and enforce appropriate limits sells the couple short.

Early in treatment, incipient problem-maintenance hypotheses should influence the formulation of an adaptive solution primarily in the delineation of subtasks that constitute part of the overall solution. For instance, the therapist might share with the parents that it appears that Lawrence is most argumentative and disobedient when both his parents are around and there is actual or potential marital conflict; therefore, the parents should be particularly on guard for his testing their limits at those times. Similarly, the therapist might comment that when Mr. Schultz is out of town, Lawrence seems most responsive to Mrs. Schultz when she is not depressed and seems firm and definite; therefore, she might try to avoid communicating her marital frustration and sense of depression to Lawrence, particularly when she is structuring him. In other words, early, emerging problem-maintenance hypotheses should inform, but not inordinately constrain, the choice of the healthiest, most direct, simplest, and most efficient adaptive solution.

ACCUMULATED PROFESSIONAL AND SCIENTIFIC WISDOM

The fourth source for deriving an alternative, adaptive solution to the presenting problem is the therapist's knowledge of the literature on human problem solving, particularly the literature on family and marital functioning, sex therapy, interpersonal communication, child psychology, behavioral psychology, and depth psychology. The psychological and psychiatric literature is replete with strategies and methods for dealing with virtually every problem that a patient can present for treatment. This is not to say that there is a well-validated single solution for every presenting problem, but that the literature is full of ideas, strategies, and specific methods, some of which have been at least partially successful in dealing with most of the problems that patients bring to therapy.

For example, systematic desensitization, or progressive exposure techniques, have a long and reasonably well-validated history in the treatment of phobic disorders (Barlow, 1988). In regard to schizophrenia, the literature on psychoeducational approaches (Goldstein & Miklowitz, 1995; Hogarty et al., 1991) suggests that adults with schizophrenia do best (1) when they are medicated appropriately; (2) when their families are supportive, structuring, and not hostile to them; and (3) when their families have a basic knowledge of the state-of-the-art theory and research on schizophrenia, which takes the blame away from the family and emphasizes the biological underpinning of the illness.

Similarly, the literature on depression consistently identifies the need for depressed individuals to be more assertive, to learn to feel and express anger appropriately, and to diminish negative and increase positive thoughts (Beck, Rush, Shaw, & Emery, 1979). When a depressed individual cannot engage in these micro tasks, antidepressant medication may be indicated as a first step in addressing the block.

The literatures on phobias, schizophrenia, and depression can be helpful in formulating adaptive solutions for patient systems. With a family presenting with a young adult agoraphobic son who refuses to leave the house, the phobia literature suggests that the phobia will not improve with time alone. An active progressive or implosive exposure treatment is required. The adaptive solution necessarily involves the parents in actively requiring their son to leave the house, if only to see a therapist.

For a family presenting with a young adult schizophrenic daughter, the adaptive solution would involve at least the following components: that the parents require their daughter to take medication; that the parents learn to structure her life firmly but without hostility in regard to daily activities; and that the family members learn as much as possible about the biopsychosocial nature of schizophrenia. With a depressed father, the adaptive solution might involve helping him learn to use the anger he feels toward his last employer, who unfairly fired him, as a basis for more assertively seeking a new job and getting on with his life. It might also entail helping him and his family positively reframe his job loss as an opportunity for a better job in the future.

The accumulated professional and scientific wisdom in regard to particular problems and disorders changes over time. This source does not provide the perfect and definitive adaptive solution but allows the use of existing knowledge to formulate appropriate and reasonable courses of action to solve the presenting problems.

PATIENT-SYSTEM MEMBERS' SELF-KNOWLEDGE

A fifth source of adaptive solutions is the patient system. Frequently, key members of the patient system know what they need to do to solve or ameliorate the presenting problem. They may tell the therapist in the early stages of therapy, "I know what we have to do, we just haven't been able to do it." Asking key patients what they think they need to do to solve their problem frequently elicits constructive ideas that can be fashioned into a viable adaptive solution.

For instance, with the therapist's support, Mrs. Schultz may be able to say, "I know what needs to happen here. Larry needs to stop rescuing me and let me fight it out with Lawrence. He needs to trust, and I need to as well, that I can handle him." It is valuable to ask key patients what they think has to happen within their system to resolve the presenting problem not only early in therapy, but throughout the course of therapy as well. Seeking their expertise and knowledge on an ongoing basis emphasizes the healthy aspects of the system, reinforces the shared experience of the therapist and key patients as allies, and allows the therapist to assess the extent to which the patient system possesses the cognitive and behavioral skills to solve their problem.

SOLUTION-IDENTIFICATION SUMMARY

Delineating an adaptive solution typically uses all five of the aforementioned sources. To craft an effective adaptive solution, the therapist has to know what has been tried at various points in the problem cycle and what has and has not worked. The therapist draws on the emerging picture of the patient system and the problem-maintenance structure, as well as on his or her knowledge of human development and psychosocial problem solving. Ideally, key members of the patient system contribute their intimate knowledge of their problems, their system, and what might work. Crafting an adaptive solution creatively and collaboratively links patient and therapist systems.

This task concludes with the identification of an adaptive solution to the presenting problem. A minimal criterion for this solution is that it point out a relatively clear and appropriate course for the therapy to pursue. Ideally, it also delineates a set of fairly specific activities that key patients can pursue to solve the presenting problem. Identifying an adaptive solution is like finding a lighthouse for a lost ship. It establishes location, but more important, it establishes a sense of direction.

ESTABLISHING A SOLUTION CONSENSUS

Implementing an adaptive solution requires the establishment of a consensus within the therapy system about the appropriateness and relevance of the adaptive solution. This task is seldom accomplished as a separate endeavor but coincides closely with the first task of identifying an adaptive solution. Establishing a solution consensus relates particularly to the task and goal dimensions of the therapeutic alliance. The adaptive solution is a patient-system task, directed toward the goal of resolving the presenting problem.

A solution consensus is reached when the key members of the therapist and patient systems agree about the suitability of the adaptive solution that will be implemented to solve the presenting problem. As with the alliance, the key members not only need to agree about the suitability of the adaptive solution but also need a sufficient degree of mutual commitment to and psychological comfort with its planned implementation.

CONSENSUS LOCI AND DISSENSUS RESOLUTION

A solution consensus needs to emerge at three loci: within the patient and therapist systems and between the two systems. Strategies for resolving solution dissensus (lack of consensus) at each of these three loci are discussed in the following sections.

Within-System Consensus

The key members of the therapist system need to agree about and commit to the adaptive solution. For therapists working outside of managed care, institutional, or group practice contexts, this is seldom a problem. However, for therapists in such settings who are part of a clinical team or under some form of clinical or managed care supervision, solution consensus can be critical.

To the extent that key members of the therapist system disagree about the adaptive solution, the potential for fragmentation and polarization increases. The therapist system can fragment vertically, across hierarchical levels, or horizontally, within a level. In a common vertical dissensus, when a supervisor and therapist disagree about an adaptive solution, various negative scenarios can emerge. The therapist can try to use the therapy to demonstrate his or her "correctness," showing the supervisor the error of his or her ways. This situation can result in the therapist's overinvesting in a particular solution and being insensitive to feedback from the patients that the solution is not working. More commonly, it results in a breakdown of the alliance between the supervisor and the therapist, depriving the patients of the synergistic expertise of the professionals. In a worst case, vertical managed care dissensus, disagreement between the therapist and care manager about what needs to happen in a patient system can result in the discontinuation of third-party financial support for the therapy, possibly forcing the patient system to terminate prematurely.

The most common and potentially problematic horizontal dissensus in the therapist system occurs with therapists working on clinical teams. If the team splits concerning the suitability of an adaptive solution, various negative scenarios can emerge. The split may impair the capacity of the team to function effectively as a unit. It can become a fragmented system, engaging in various forms of pathological functioning, such as destructive triangulation and scapegoating. Alternatively, if a consulting team disagrees with the therapist, the therapist may become isolated and stop using the team as a consultation resource.

With both horizontal and vertical within-system dissensus, the primary problem is not that members of the system dissent but that they polarize. Dissent is not inherently destructive; it becomes so only when the disagreeing members of the system disengage, stop communicating effectively, exaggerate the extent to which they disagree, and attribute various extreme positions to each other.

Key strategies for resolving disagreements within the therapist system about adaptive solutions include facilitation of communication, boundary clarification, and as a last resort, constructive triangulation of a third party. In many polarized situations, the two sides have stopped listening to each other. Facilitating communication can restore dialogue and permit the parties to realize that their disagreement is not so fundamental and that compromise solutions can be worked out. For instance, the parties may agree to try one solution first and, if that does not work, to try another. Or they might come up with a compromise solution that embodies both sides' concerns and goals.

Boundary clarification is particularly, but not exclusively, useful in vertical dissensus, when one party has authority over the other. For instance, if the student understands from the beginning that the supervisor is in charge of the therapy and represents the final authority about what will happen with a case, it will be clear that in conflict situations the supervisor's preference prevails. Similarly, in managed care situations, if the therapist understands from the beginning that the care manager is the final authority, the care manager must at least accept if not support the solution or the therapy is not viable. Polarized and stuck vertical dissensus situations frequently result from unclear boundaries and rules about who is really in charge and has the final authority. Clarifying hierarchical boundaries and power relationships can ameliorate vertical within-system dissensus.

Constructive triangulation can also be thought of as mediation or, under certain circumstances, arbitration. In both situations, the dissenting parties bring in a mutually agreed-on or institutionally determined third party to help them. In mediation, the third party's goal is to help the dissenting parties work out a mutually acceptable solution. In arbitration, the third party is empowered by the dissenting parties or the institutional context to determine the adaptive solution. Beyond mediating and arbitrating, the third party ideally should facilitate clear communication and effective problem solving. Although it is important in all scenarios, this facilitator role is particularly critical with horizontal dissensus. When a team of equals fragments and polarizes, a facilitator can resolve disagreement, establish cohesion, and help find an adaptive solution with which the key players can live.

Far more common and typically more pernicious than therapist-system dissensus is the failure of the key members of the patient system to agree about an adaptive solution. The patient system can split and polarize horizontally or vertically and within or across generations. The divorce–stay together dissensus typifies a painful horizontal split. In this scenario, the overall adaptive solution for one partner of a couple seeking therapy is to improve and strengthen the marriage, but the solution for the other partner is to separate or divorce. The couple in this situation cannot agree about the general or the specific directions of the therapy. What needs to happen for each of the partners differs radically.

The divorce–stay together dissensus typifies a class of adaptive-solution disagreements in which one party's adaptive solution "naturally predominates" over the other's. Usually, in the divorce–stay together dissensus, if the prodivorce partner is adamant, his or her agenda predominates. The reason for this, simply put, is that it takes two to make a marriage and one to make a divorce. The prodivorce partner can proceed with his or her agenda regardless of the attitudes, feelings, or behavior of the partner. The promarriage partner cannot: The cooperation and participation of the partner are essential to work on the marriage. If this type of couple continues in some form of conjoint therapy, the major adaptive solution is to help the members separate with as little pain and suffering as possible for themselves and other key members of their system. Helping the "losing" partner accept the inevitability of the adaptive solution and encouraging the "winning" partner to implement the adaptive solution in as sensitive and nondestructive a way as possible constitute the best therapist strategy in most such disagreements.

Vertical dissensus pertains primarily to patient systems who present with one or more children as the identified patients. In vertical dissensus scenarios, the parents and children do not agree about the appropriateness of the adaptive solution. When the parental and child subsystems cannot work out some appropriate compromise through communication and problem solving, the adaptive solution of the more powerful subsystem typically predominates. The more powerful subsystem in this situation is the subsystem with the greater power to keep the patient system in therapy as well as the subsystem with greater skills, knowledge, access to resources, and natural authority. In most patient-system vertical dissensus situations, the most powerful and naturally authoritative subsystem is the older, parental subsystem; however, in patient systems with older and possibly even adult–child subsystems, the latter may predominate. Ideally, the predominance of the more powerful subsystem's solution is to the benefit, not the detriment, of the child or less powerful subsystem.

The dissensus resolution strategy in such vertical conflict situations depends on the determination not only of which subsystem is most powerful, but also of which subsystem's solution is the most likely to resolve the presenting problem effectively. If the more powerful subsystem's solution seems most appropriate in regard to the criteria mentioned in the section on identifying an adaptive solution, the therapist should support the implementation of its preferred solution. This type of appropriate side taking potentially damages the therapist's alliance with the weaker subsystem, however. To diminish these deleterious effects, the therapist should attend to and represent the interests of the weaker system as much as possible without jeopardizing the adaptive solution.

For instance, a 14-year-old boy who is failing in school may adamantly argue that his parents should not clamp down on him by removing his TV privileges and insisting that he do his homework every night before talking on the phone with his friends. In this situation, as the therapist sides with the parents and encourages the "clamp down" solution, the therapist should also encourage the parents to integrate as much of their son's wishes and concerns as possible without rendering their adaptive solution ineffective. Thus, the therapist might support the son's argument for restoring some TV privileges if he gets adequate grades during the first quarter after implementation of the new structure.

In vertical dissensus situations in which the adaptive solution proposed by the more powerful subsystem is less likely to succeed than the weaker subsystem's solution, the therapist confronts a dilemma. The resolution of this dilemma depends primarily on the nature of the therapeutic alliance, particularly the bonds component, with the stronger subsystem. If the therapist has a sufficiently strong bond with the stronger subsystem and the weaker subsystem's preferred solution is clearly superior, the therapist should support the weaker subsystem's adaptive solution.

Betty Linden, a recently divorced custodial parent, had been working in therapy with her three children for 8 months. She presented initially saying the children were uncontrollable at home and having problems at school. The therapist worked with the system in various configurations: sessions with Mom and children all together, individual sessions with Mom, occasional individual sessions with one of the children, and occasional sessions with Dad and Mom and with Dad and the children. Recently, the therapist had been primarily seeing Mom alone, focusing on her loneliness and minor child-management problems. The children's behavior had improved over the 8 months: all of them were doing well at home and at school.

Terry, the middle child, a 13-year-old daughter, requested a session with the therapist and Betty. During that session, Terry and her mom discussed their fights about her bedtime and curfew. Betty felt that she needed to be firm with Terry, sticking religiously to a weekday bedtime, whereas Terry argued vociferously for no set bedtime. She felt that a set bedtime was demeaning and that she could regulate her own sleep schedule. After listening to both sides, to Mom's surprise, the therapist recommended that Mom go with Terry's idea, that she could be in charge of her own bedtime. The caveats were that the new policy should be discontinued if Terry did not get herself up and off to school on time, if her behavior deteriorated at home, or if her grades dropped off.

Betty was initially shocked by the therapist's recommendation; Terry was thrilled. However, Betty's shock did not disrupt her strong alliance with the therapist, because she trusted the therapist's wisdom and commitment to her and her family. She also saw that enough conditions were built into the solution's implementation that if it had any deleterious effects, it could be discontinued. She also saw that if it worked, it would have the added benefit of her not having to wake Terry in the morning, a historically unpleasant task.

Allying with the weaker patient subsystem against the stronger one disrupts the alliance less when the therapist and patient system have been working together for some time and the bonds component (particularly trust and confidence) has had a chance to develop. This is seldom if ever the case at the beginning of therapy. Early in treatment, when the bonds are just forming, the therapist should make every effort to support the preferred solution of the more powerful subsystem unless it endangers mental or physical health or exacerbates the presenting problem.

Another within-system form of patient disagreement concerns *nonpredominance dissensus,* in which neither party's preferred solution naturally predominates. More often than not these nonpredominance situations involve horizontal dissensus between equal parties. For instance, a husband and wife might disagree about whether they should take a direct or an indirect approach to a sexual problem. If the therapist does not see any obvious advantage to a direct or an indirect approach, this situation would typify a horizontal nonpredominance dissensus.

Occasionally, nonpredominance disagreements involve vertical dissensus in which neither party needs to or should predominate, and the quality of their solutions is roughly equivalent. To illustrate, after 2 months in weekly individual and family therapy, Eileen Parker, an increasingly responsible, conduct-disordered 15-year-old, argues with her parents that she should not have to continue in individual therapy. Now that her behavior has improved, she feels that the individual therapy is no longer necessary and that family therapy is a more appropriate and sufficient format to address the issues she wants to tackle.

Her parents disagree with her, arguing that she is still "troubled" and needs treatment specifically for herself. They cite her recent blowup at home when her mother asked her to baby-sit for Sam, her 7-year-old brother. Eileen responds that maybe she is blowing up more at home because of the problems in the family that nobody has been willing to really talk about. She adds that it is far better for her to blow up at home than to get into the kind of trouble she was getting into outside of the home before.

If the therapist does not have a strong preference for either solution, the disagreement between Eileen and her parents should be defined as a temporary presenting problem that needs to be resolved within the family. The therapist takes the role of facilitator in this situation, helping Eileen and her parents struggle together to find a mutually acceptable solution.

With both vertical and horizontal nonpredominance solution dissensus, the therapist's basic strategy defines the dissensus as a metaproblem. This situation resembles that discussed in Chapter 6, in which key patients cannot agree about a presenting problem. Their disagreement becomes the metaproblem: the problem about their problems. The fight about solutions, from the perspective of the alliance, is a fight about tasks, whereas the conflict about presenting problems is a fight about goals. In both nonpredominance situations, the therapist does not side with either party but helps them, through their interaction, to find a mutually acceptable path toward a mutually acceptable goal.

Between-Systems Consensus

Of the three loci of consensus, the most critical locus exists between the key members of the patient and therapist systems. These two systems must establish consensus about and commitment to the adaptive solution. When they do not, the alliance and the therapy are in jeopardy. For instance, if the Warrens are fundamentally committed to Jamie's staying at home, the therapist's efforts to facilitate Jamie's departure will undermine the alliance and possibly destroy the therapy.

In general, if the key members of the therapist and patient systems cannot establish a solution consensus early in therapy, the therapist should accept the patient system's preferred solution as long as it does not jeopardize physical or mental health. For instance, the Warrens assert that they are just not ready to force the issue of leaving home with Jamie. The following excerpt comes from a session that the therapist had with Mr. and Mrs. Warren, without Jamie.

MRS. WARREN: I just don't feel that now is the time to force this issue with him. If we just keep encouraging him to get a job, maybe he'll finally do it. I'm worried he'll move in with his druggie friends and get in trouble with the police. We still have a little influence with him living at home.

THERAPIST: Mr. Warren, what are your thoughts about what your wife just said?

MR. WARREN: I pretty much agree with Jean. Maybe we should give him some more time, just keep the job pressure up without forcing a major confrontation.

THERAPIST: What are each of your thoughts about how to keep the pressure up without a major confrontation?

MRS. WARREN: We should just ask him regularly, like every couple of days, what progress he's made in looking for a job. We can also tell him about any leads we hear about and encourage him to follow up.

THERAPIST [to husband]: What about your thoughts?

MR. WARREN: I want to encourage him to apply at some employment agencies as well. We just need to stay on him and let him know that we mean business.

THERAPIST: This sounds good. Both of you agree that you want to up the pressure and keep it up without forcing some kind of showdown. I think it's definitely worth a try. My question is, what if it doesn't work? What then?

MR. WARREN: Well, if this doesn't work, maybe then we'll be desperate enough to try what you've been recommending, getting him out of the house.

MRS. WARREN: I guess we'll cross that bridge when we get there. Let's just hope that this works.

In this vignette, the therapist ends up supporting the parents' preferred adaptive solution, although he remains skeptical about its likelihood of success. At the most basic level, even though it may increase the duration of the therapy, allowing if not encouraging the key patients to attempt to implement an adaptive solution in the face of resistance from the therapist permits the therapy to continue. It avoids a premature rupture of the alliance and the possible demise of the treatment. In such situations, patients experience the therapist's commitment to help, even if they are not willing to accept the therapist's guidance at this point. The support also communicates respect to key patients: The therapist, at this point, defers to their judgment. Experiencing the therapist's commitment and respect intensifies the bond and strengthens the alliance.

As discussed in Chapter 3 concerning the alliance, it is appropriate to force a confrontation concerning an adaptive-solution dissensus only as a last resort. This situation usually arises after the key patients have tried it their way several times and found their adaptive solutions to be impossible to implement or not effective when successfully implemented. At this point it should be clear, at least to the therapist, that the adaptive solution advocated by the therapist system is the only viable way to go and that anything else would be a waste of time, money, and effort.

After the Warrens tried various solutions with Jamie short of an ultimatum that did not work, the therapist and the Warrens both felt that the therapy had come to a standstill. Jamie had not progressed at all and, in fact, seemed more involved with drugs than he was before. He also discontinued his individual therapy and stopped even making a pretense of looking for a job.

THERAPIST: What do you think we should do at this point?

MR. WARREN: I don't know. Nothing we've tried seems to have worked. He's as bad if not worse than ever.

MRS. WARREN: Maybe a little more time and he'll see the light.

THERAPIST: Jean, I don't think so. The evidence from your valiant efforts over the last 3 months says he's worse. Short of a "get a job or get out" confrontation, I think you've tried everything two reasonable and responsible parents could try. He needs stronger medicine. I think the time has arrived for the ultimatum: Get a job or get out of the house within the next 4 weeks.

MRS. WARREN: No, I just can't face doing that. I'm afraid it will push him over the edge.

THERAPIST: He's slowly going over the edge anyway. The only thing that might turn him around is if he finally has to take care of himself. Yes, he might have to get busted for drugs or ripped off by his druggie friends, but you can't go on enabling him not to be a responsible young adult.

MRS. WARREN: What do you think, Bill?

MR. WARREN: I think he's [the therapist] right, but I still don't want to push it to that point.

THERAPIST: I can understand that both of you are scared and don't feel ready at this point to force the issue with Jamie. However, I don't feel that I can go on in good conscience, taking your money and all of our time and efforts in therapy unless I feel we're heading in a direction that's likely to be productive. And I truly believe at this point that heading in the direction of an ultimatum is the only thing that stands a chance of working. I am convinced that more pressure without teeth in it, without an ultimatum, won't work. If the two of you just don't feel like you can do that now, I understand. Maybe we should stop for a while and see what happens. Maybe what you've been trying will work, or maybe you'll get to the point where the ultimatum strategy is something you could seriously consider.

MRS. WARREN: I know you're right. I don't want to stop our therapy at this point. You've been a great support to us, and you're the only one who really knows us and who we can be totally frank with. Maybe we just need more time to think about an ultimatum: how and when to do it.

MR. WARREN: Yes, if we could approach an ultimatum gradually, maybe we could get to the point where we could do it.

THERAPIST: That's fine with me. This, I firmly believe, is the direction we've got to head in now. We don't have to get to our destination of an ultimatum tomorrow. We just have to know what we're working toward, where we're going.

MR. WARREN: How and when might you see us giving Jamie this ultimatum?

THERAPIST: For starters, let me turn that question around. How would each of you answer when and how?

The therapist's goal in this interaction is not to get the key patients to agree to implementing the adaptive solution immediately. The goal is two-fold: (1) to confront and provide an ultimatum to the key patients about the necessity to try the adaptive solution advocated by the therapist, and (2) to identify and establish consensus about the direction of the therapy toward the implementation of that adaptive solution. Movement in the direction of an appropriate adaptive solution is almost as significant as implementing it.

If in a reasonable period of time the key patients have not begun to implement the adaptive solution, another confrontation may be required. By then, the bond between the therapist and the patients may be strong enough that the patients will be able to tolerate the fear and anxiety associated with the therapist's adaptive solution and implement it.

ADDICTION SOLUTIONS

A difficult adaptive solution dissensus that occurs mostly within the patient system or between the patient and therapist systems involves disagreements about pursuing additional, specialized treatment for a disorder for which the disorder bearer (usually, but not always, the identified patient) refuses the recommended treatment. This may occur with mental illnesses like schizophrenia and mood disorders, for which the patient refuses inpatient or psychopharmacological treatment.

The most common and pernicious variant of this solution dissensus concerns drug and alcohol addiction. In these situations, the addiction may be either a presenting problem or a nonpresenting problem that clearly interferes with patient-system efforts to resolve the presenting problem. In either case, the addicted member refuses to pursue appropriate specialized treatment, such as attendance at Alcoholics Anonymous meetings or inpatient or outpatient treatment.

Carlos Sanchez, a very successful Mexican-American corporate executive, was abusing alcohol for 15 years. Recently, his alcohol abuse started to affect his work performance; it had affected his marriage and children for many years. His American wife, Ellen, insisted that Carlos and she either get into marital therapy or separate. They were in treatment for three sessions when Ellen brought up the subject of his drinking.

MRS. SANCHEZ: Carlos, I know that you don't want to talk about this, but we must. If Linda [the therapist] does not know about it, she can't play with a full deck.

MR. SANCHEZ: It's not a problem and I don't want to discuss it.

THERAPIST: Fill me in on what you're talking about. I'm not saying we've got to talk about it at this time, but I'd like to know what it is you're talking about.

MRS. SANCHEZ: Carlos, I want to tell Linda.

MR. SANCHEZ: What she's talking about is that she thinks I have a drinking problem, which is nonsense. I have a few cocktails at night to relax, but that's about it.

THERAPIST: So you feel like Ellen is making too big a deal out of this. You like to drink, but you don't feel that you have a drinking problem.

MR. SANCHEZ: That's it exactly.

THERAPIST: Ellen, tell me how you see this issue.

MRS. SANCHEZ: Carlos has a serious drinking problem and it's getting worse. He drinks every night to the point where you cannot even have a sane conversation with him. The kids have learned to not even bother relating to him after dinner, if he makes it home for dinner. Two months ago he was arrested for drunk driving, and he currently is driving illegally on a suspended license. Last week he couldn't get up for work in the middle of the week. I called in to cover for him, but I told him I would not do it again.

THERAPIST: Carlos, what do you think about what Ellen said?

MR. SANCHEZ: It's full of exaggeration. I was sick with a terrible cold last week, that's why I couldn't get up. Yes, I was caught driving after a few drinks, and I was barely over the limit for being intoxicated on that machine. I have been under tremendous pressure, and a few drinks help me relax.

MRS. SANCHEZ: Carlos, "a few drinks" is a euphemism for a half bottle of Absolut, maybe with a half a bottle of wine thrown in as well. You've got a problem and it's getting worse. It's interfering with our family and our marriage.

MR. SANCHEZ: If it's such a problem for you, I'll cut down. That's not a problem. I can do it.

MRS. SANCHEZ: You've said that before. You cut down for a week or two and then it's back the way it was, even worse.

MR. SANCHEZ: I'm sick of you beating me up for this. Just because you had an alcoholic father doesn't mean that I'm an alcoholic too. Get off my case about this. I've had enough.

MRS. SANCHEZ: I'll get off your case about it alright. Maybe I'll even get out of this marriage. I'm sick of your denial and accusations. My father has nothing to do with this, other than putting me in a position where I can see denial and alcoholism pretty clearly.

THERAPIST: Ellen, is this a problem that you want to address in this therapy? I ask that question because you haven't brought it up in the first two sessions.

MRS. SANCHEZ: To be honest, I was afraid if I brought it up, Carlos would walk out of the therapy. But yes, this is definitely a major problem for him and for us and we've got to address it, here and elsewhere if necessary.

THERAPIST: What do you mean "and elsewhere if necessary"?

MRS. SANCHEZ: I mean that maybe Carlos should go into one of those inpatient alcohol treatment programs for a while—to dry out and get himself together.

MR. SANCHEZ: You're crazy. I don't need anything like that.

THERAPIST: Carlos, is there any truth for you in what Ellen is saying about your drinking?

MR. SANCHEZ: Well, sometimes I do drink a little too much, and recently I have been under a lot of stress at work. Maybe I should cut down a little.

THERAPIST: So for you there is a problem with drinking, but it's not as big as Ellen thinks it is.

MR. SANCHEZ: Yeah, I guess so.

THERAPIST: How about if we start tracking this and see how it goes. I realize that both of you are pretty polarized around this, so I'd recommend, if each of you can live with it, that for now we just track it. If it comes up as a problem between sessions, let's discuss it.

MRS. SANCHEZ: You mean let's do nothing. He wins Round 1.

THERAPIST: No, that's not what I'm saying. I think we should pay attention to Carlos's drinking. If it seems to be interfering with his health or your life as a couple and family, then we'll have to give it more attention. Let's keep our eyes open and see how this issue unfolds over time.

MRS. SANCHEZ: Okay, but I'll bet you right now that you'll see I'm right about this.

THERAPIST: Maybe as things unfold I will see that you're right. I'm open to that. Carlos, is it okay with you if you proceed as I've outlined?

MR. SANCHEZ: Yes, I can live with this plan for now.

The therapist in this vignette avoids siding with either party but attempts to create a context for further exploration of the drinking issue. Carlos's drinking gets defined as a potential presenting problem. At some point it may be necessary to confront Carlos with the necessity of his seeking some additional treatment for his drinking. To do so now would jeopardize the emerging alliance and ruin the therapy. This intervention permits the alliance, particularly the bonds aspect, to continue to grow. If a confrontation becomes necessary, the strength of the bond may be sufficient at that time to help Carlos face his addiction and do something about it.

There is little if anything to be gained by a premature confrontation concerning the necessity of seeking additional treatment for a mental illness or addiction. If the key individual or interpersonal systems are not ready to face the problem, forcing the issue will just rupture the therapy. When this happens, the patient system not only is out of therapy, but also may be traumatized in regard to future treatment. The growth of the alliance is the key in these situations, at times requiring the therapist to wait patiently as the therapeutic process unfolds.

IMPLEMENTING THE ADAPTIVE SOLUTION

The third task in modifying the problem cycle implements the adaptive solution identified and agreed on in the two preceding tasks. This is the point in therapy when the key patients need to do what they and the therapist know must be done to solve the presenting problem. Implementing the adaptive solution is a process, not a single, discrete event. This process can be broken down into two phases: planning and implementation.

PLANNING

The first phase maximizes the likelihood of successful implementation by planning who will do what at each point in the implementation process, predicting when problems are likely to arise, and planning potential reactions to those problems. The therapist should elicit as much of the plan as possible from the key patients, making it more likely that they will "own" the plan and the implementation process. The therapist at this point should be just "good enough"; he or she should not overplan or overplay the expert role. However, the therapist is not just a neutral facilitator. As needed, the therapist should provide guidance and recommendations for effective implementation.

At this point in therapy, the Warrens have decided to confront Jamie with a "get a real job or get out of the house" ultimatum. The therapist initiates the planning process with Jean and Bill.

THERAPIST: What are your thoughts about when and how you should deliver the ultimatum?

MR. WARREN: I think we should just go home tonight and tell him. I don't like beating around the bush.

THERAPIST: Jean, what are your thoughts about that?

MRS. WARREN: I think we need to think this through before we do it. Jamie is usually out at night, and he's also frequently not in the best shape when he gets home. I think we should talk to him before he goes out, like around dinnertime.

THERAPIST: Who should do the confronting? Both or one of you?

MRS. WARREN: We should definitely do it together. I think we'll have more power, and he'll know that we're both behind it. It gives him less room to manipulate.

THERAPIST: Bill, do you agree with what Jean's been saying?

MR. WARREN: Yes, I think we should do it together. And dinnertime is okay, although it might ruin a nice meal. I'd vote for doing it after dinner, before he's about to take off.

MRS. WARREN: That's fine with me. How about we leave a note for him tonight if he's not home saying we'd like to have dinner with him tomorrow. If he's there, we can just tell him.

THERAPIST: If you ask him, will he be there tomorrow night?

MRS. WARREN: When it comes to food, Jamie is Mr. Reliable.

THERAPIST: I think you need to decide who is going to tell him and what you're going to say. It's really critical that you're both on the same wavelength when you do this.

MRS. WARREN: Bill, I'd like you to take the lead. He listens to you more than he does me. But I think it's important that you're not too harsh with him.

MR. WARREN: I don't mind taking the lead, but I don't buy this stuff about being too harsh with him. This is the time to be tough and not to give him the benefit of the doubt.

MRS. WARREN: Yes, but you don't have to call him names or tell him he'll never amount to anything, like you've done at other times when you're mad at him.

THERAPIST: There's an important distinction here. Bill, you and Jean should be tough and firm but not attacking or demeaning. If you can do the confrontation calmly, it might even be more effective. It's also important for both of you to be clear about what you're going to tell Jamie.

MR. WARREN: I'm going to tell him he has to get a job or he can't live at home anymore.

THERAPIST: What's the time frame? By when must he have a job?

MR. WARREN: I'm not sure, what about a month?

MRS. WARREN: That's too long. He's had too much time already. Also, I don't want him hanging around all day and partying at night for another month. I can't stand much more of this.

MR. WARREN: Okay, what about 2 weeks?

MRS. WARREN: Yes, that's enough time for him to get something.

THERAPIST: You also need to agree about what constitutes a job. Would a 20-hour-a-week job qualify?

MRS. WARREN: No, he's got to get a full-time job, a real job.

THERAPIST: Bill, do you agree?

MR. WARREN: Yes. He's got to have real job. I don't want to have to go through this again. He's got to get a real job, and if he's going to live at home with us, he's going to have to contribute something to his room and board.

THERAPIST: Jean, are you with Bill on that?

MRS. WARREN: Yes, he should pay at least a quarter of his take-home pay.

THERAPIST: Good. Without overplanning this, I think there's one more thing you've got to think through and that is, what if he doesn't get a job within 2 weeks?

MR. WARREN: We'll tell him he's got to leave. He'll have to get out.

THERAPIST: What if he says he's not going to leave?

MR. WARREN: We'll cross that bridge when and if we get there.

THERAPIST: I don't think that's the best way to proceed. If the two of you have thought this through and agree on what you'll do at that point, your confrontation will be more convincing and your resolve will be more apparent.

MRS. WARREN: Bill, he's right. We've got to decide what we'll do if it comes to that. I think we should pack his bags and put them outside on the front porch. If necessary, we can even change the locks so his key won't work. If he tries to get in, even though it's horrible, I'd call the police.

THERAPIST: Wow! She really means business. Bill, are you with her on this?

MR. WARREN: I guess so. It sounds extreme, but the time has come for extreme measures.

In this vignette, the therapist asks questions that force the parents to think through how they will implement the adaptive solution. The therapist facilitates and supports their joint planning process; he avoids taking it over and telling the parents what to do. In certain situations, it may be necessary for the therapist to take a more directive role, telling key patients what to do and laying out the process; however, such a directive stance should be taken only when the facilitative stance has proved insufficient.

IMPLEMENTATION

In the second phase of this task, key patients (and at times, key members of the therapist system) implement the adaptive solution. This phase is also a process. With certain adaptive solutions in certain patient systems, implementing the adaptive solution may be a simple and straightforward event.

At first glance, the adaptive solution for the Warrens primarily involves a temporally and spatially discrete event: confronting Jamie.

Implementing adaptive solutions in other patient systems may play out over time and different contexts. For example, if Jamie's initial response to his parents' ultimatum is not positive, the adaptive solution will involve additional steps. With a couple presenting with a sexual problem, the adaptive solution may engage them in a course of sex therapy that might take several months.

The therapist works with the key patients during solution implementation to maximize the likelihood of success as well as opportunities for teaching the patients more effective problem-solving skills. When problem-centered therapy is most effective, it fulfills not only its problem-solving function but also its educational function. Patients not only learn solutions to their problems, they also learn a process of problem solving.

Problem solving involves a feedback loop that consists of at least three steps. In the first, *task implementation*, key patients perform a task that is a component in the solution-implementation process. *Impact evaluation*, the second step, assesses the impact of the task on the relevant members of the patient system. In the third step, *proximal task planning*, the key system (patient and possibly therapist) members plan the next step in the process, incorporating the feedback from the second step. This feedback loop repeats continually throughout the solution-implementation process. It is an extension of the basic clinical–experimental methodology that underlies the problem-centered model. Problem-centered therapy teaches the key patients to be "clinical experimenters" in solving their psychosocial problems.

In response to his parents' ultimatum, Jamie Warren readily agreed to get a job within the next 2 weeks. During the first week, he made various noticeable efforts at job seeking and reported that he had a job lined up at a local dry cleaning business that would start in 2 weeks. At the next therapy session, Mrs. Warren happily reported this news.

MRS. WARREN: We're thrilled. It's gone more painlessly than we ever anticipated. It looks like he's got a job at the local cleaners.
THERAPIST: Bill, you don't look as thrilled as Jean.
MR. WARREN: I'm not. I feel like Jamie is still pushing it. We told him he had to have a job within 2 weeks. After 6 days he tells us he's got a job that's going to start in 2 weeks. That's 3 weeks from when we told him. I think he's pushing it. Like he always does. We draw the line here. He pushes it 3 inches and says okay.

THERAPIST: You sound pretty irritated. You feel like he's pushing you around again?

MR. WARREN: Absolutely. He's not going to be able to get away with this kind of shit at a job. What are we teaching him if we let him get away with it now?

MRS. WARREN: Bill, why don't we give him the benefit of the doubt? The important thing is that he gets a job. What's a week or two?

MR. WARREN: It's a lot. Particularly with a kid like Jamie. I think he's testing us. We said 2 weeks; he says 3.

THERAPIST: Bill, what do you think you and Jean should do at this point?

MR. WARREN: I think we should tell him we said 2 weeks and we meant 2 weeks. He should start the new job a week sooner or get some in-between job for a week.

THERAPIST: So you really want to hold his feet to the fire around the 2-week deadline. Jean, how do you feel about that?

MRS. WARREN: What if he can't get the people he's gonna work for to start him sooner?

MR. WARREN: Then he'll just have to find something else.

MRS. WARREN: Who's going to want to hire someone for a week?

MR. WARREN: I don't know. But we should make that his problem. Not ours. Jean, we've got to let him know we won't put up with more of his crap, we really mean business, or else he'll just keep pushing.

MRS. WARREN: I'm afraid we'll push him too far.

MR. WARREN: What's too far? So far that he'll leave home? That wouldn't be so bad. He'd have to get a job then.

THERAPIST: Jean, are you worried pushing him too far could have other consequences?

MRS. WARREN: Well, I worry he might kill himself.

THERAPIST: With everything you know about Jamie, how likely do you think that is?

MR. WARREN: Real slim. He's manipulative and selfish. Maybe he's even scared. But I don't think he's suicidal.

MRS. WARREN: I agree. I don't think he'll kill himself. Okay, let's tell him he's got to be working within 2 weeks of when we talked to him. That was a week ago, so he's got a week to get going. What if he can't work sooner at the cleaners and can't find anything in between?

MR. WARREN: Let's not tell him this until he's tried everything else, but I think there's enough work around the house to keep him busy for a good week. If all else fails, he can work for us for that week. But he'll have to really work.

THERAPIST: So who is going to give him the news?
MRS. WARREN: Since Bill took the lead last week, how about if I tell Jamie?
MR. WARREN: Fine. Just be firm. Don't take his bullshit.

In this vignette, the Warrens discuss the potential meanings of the feedback from Jamie after their opening move and plan their next move. This process of intervene, evaluate, and plan continues until the adaptive solution is successfully implemented or it is clear that it is not working and has little likelihood of working with small, task-by-task adjustments.

EVALUATION AND DECISION MAKING

The last task in implementing an adaptive solution involves two integrated components. The first component evaluates the results of the previous task: solution implementation. The second determines the next major step in the overall process of therapy. Figure 7.1 illustrates the major steps in the therapy process up to this point and the three major potential outcomes of the implementation process.

In evaluating the results of the previous implementation step, the key members of the patient and therapist systems need to decide into which of the three outcome categories shown in Figure 7.1 the results fall: successful implementation, inappropriate adaptive solution, or blocked implementation. In regard to the successful resolution of the presenting problem, only the first category represents a clearly positive outcome. The latter two categories represent different situations in which the adaptive solution fails to resolve the presenting problems for different reasons.

OUTCOME 1: SUCCESSFUL IMPLEMENTATION

If the patient system successfully implements the adaptive solution, the results are usually obvious. The presenting problem gets resolved, and the key patient-system members are satisfied. With the Warrens, Jamie would be successfully employed. For the Schultz family, Mr. Schultz would have learned to support his wife; Mrs. Schultz would have learned to stop her husband from interfering in her conflicts with Lawrence; and the parents would have set and maintained firm, effective, and consistent limits with Lawrence. With the Tanakas, Ted's note would have mollified his father to the extent that the father–son bond could be restored and Mr. Tanaka could support Ted's plans to buy a car, work during the summer, and go to college in the fall. The couple with the sexual problem would have engaged in a program of

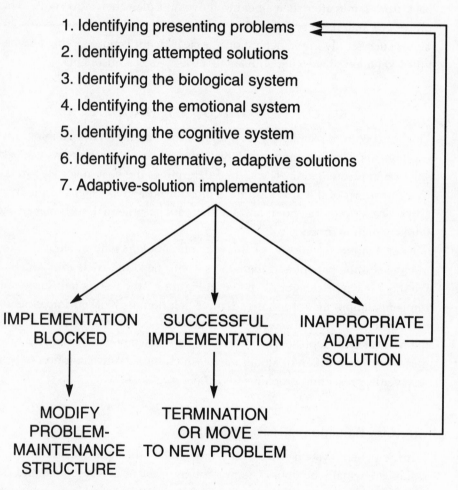

Figure 7.1
The Problem Cycle

ASSESSMENT–INTERVENTION STEPS
AND MAJOR OUTCOMES

1. Identifying presenting problems
2. Identifying attempted solutions
3. Identifying the biological system
4. Identifying the emotional system
5. Identifying the cognitive system
6. Identifying alternative, adaptive solutions
7. Adaptive-solution implementation

IMPLEMENTATION BLOCKED   SUCCESSFUL IMPLEMENTATION   INAPPROPRIATE ADAPTIVE SOLUTION

MODIFY PROBLEM-MAINTENANCE STRUCTURE   TERMINATION OR MOVE TO NEW PROBLEM

marital–sex therapy that resolved their sexual problem and improved their overall sexual relationship.

Decision Making

If the adaptive solution has been implemented successfully and the presenting problem has been resolved to the satisfaction of the key members of the patient system, two therapy options emerge. The first is to begin the process of *terminating* the therapy. Beyond resolution of the presenting problem and the satisfaction of the key patients, the third criterion for deciding to begin terminating is the lack of other presenting problems. The process of terminating has been discussed in Chapter 5.

The second option refocuses the therapy on another presenting problem. This occurs when the pursuit of other presenting problems has been postponed to focus on the most emergent one or when other, nonpresenting problems have become presenting problems.

THERAPIST: Marjorie and Larry, now that the two of you have learned to deal effectively with Lawrence and he's doing much better, what's the next step for us? Where do we go now?

MRS. SCHULTZ: I don't want to stop at this point. I think that we've got some things Larry and I need to sort out in our marriage and since we've gone this far with you, and we both trust you, we should get into those issues and work them out, just like we've done with the problems with Lawrence.

THERAPIST: Larry, what do you want to do at this point?

MR. SCHULTZ: I'm not sure. Maybe enough is enough. Things are a lot better with Lawrence, and they're even better between Marge and me. Maybe we should take a breather and come back if things flare up down the road.

MRS. SCHULTZ: He always wants to do as little as possible when it comes to anything dealing with emotions. That's okay, Larry, dig your head a little deeper in the sand.

MR. SCHULTZ: There she goes getting sarcastic. You obviously haven't learned enough here in therapy to cut that out. Okay, yeah, I think we should continue working on our issues, the issues in our marriage. We should start with why you can't drop your sarcastic bullshit and just say what you mean.

MRS. SCHULTZ: If you didn't have your head so far up your emotional ass that you can't see daylight, maybe I wouldn't have to resort to sarcasm to maintain my sanity with you.

THERAPIST: Hold it. I don't mean to discontinue the festivities you've started, but what I'm taking from your conversation is several things. First, you're both in agreement that we should continue this therapy and focus primarily on your marital issues, now that things with Lawrence are so much better. Second, Marge it seems that you would like Larry to be more emotionally tuned in, and Larry, you'd like Marge to be less sarcastic and critical. We don't have time to get into those issues today. How about we jump into them next session?

MRS. SCHULTZ: Yeah, finally, let's do it. See you next week.

In this excerpt, the therapist primarily facilitates the couple's exploration of their future plans for therapy. Although there is some disagreement between the partners, they resolve it sufficiently on their own to decide to continue therapy with a primary focus on their marital issues. The therapist extracts from their sarcastic exchange specific presenting problems, behaviors that each partner would like to see change in the other. These form the problem focus for the next session as well as the next phase of therapy.

Outcome 2: Inappropriate Adaptive Solution

Two characteristics typify implementation processes that fall into this second category. The first is a competent implementation of the adaptive solution by the key patients. They did what they were supposed to do in the way they were supposed to do it. The second characteristic is that the competent implementation of the adaptive solution was not effective: it did not successfully resolve the presenting problem.

Decision Making

This category views the failure to resolve the presenting problem as deriving primarily from the use of an inappropriate adaptive solution. The therapist and key patients selected the wrong adaptive solution. The feedback clearly suggests that the competently implemented adaptive solution either did nothing or made matters worse.

THERAPIST: How's it going? Is Jamie holding down the job?

MR. WARREN: No. Things took a very strange and upsetting turn.

THERAPIST: Tell me.

MRS. WARREN: Jamie got fired. They fired him on Tuesday. Guess what they fired him for? Yelling obscenities at some customers that were complaining that their clothes weren't properly cleaned. He almost got into a fist fight with one man, and the police were almost called. The owner came out and took over. They sent Jamie home. Then they called Larry and told him they didn't want him back. Apparently, other things had been going on that we weren't aware of.

THERAPIST: Like what?

MR. WARREN: He'd been talking to himself. It upset the other employees. They said he seems strange and very edgy.

THERAPIST: Where is Jamie now?

MRS. WARREN: He's home. He's basically been staying in his room for the last 2 days and doesn't seem to want to see anyone or talk to anyone. At times, I think I hear him talking to himself, but I'm not sure if it's him or his radio.

THERAPIST: How are each of you feeling about this?

MR. WARREN: We're very upset, confused, and worried. We don't know what's going on.

THERAPIST: I also feel worried and concerned. Unfortunately, I think I may know what's going on. Even though your valiant and concerted efforts to help Jamie get a job didn't work in the long run, I think we may have learned something very important about Jamie.

MRS. WARREN: What are you talking about?

THERAPIST: I think that we may have underestimated what's really going on with Jamie. I hesitate to say this, but his behavior may have been a cover-up for what we're seeing in a full-blown form now. And I think that what we're seeing is some kind of mental illness.

MR. WARREN: Do you mean he's mentally ill?

THERAPIST: Perhaps. I'm not sure, but the behavior I've been hearing about since he took the job, both at work and at home, definitely raises the possibility that he's struggling with some kind of mental illness and may well need medication and possibly even hospitalization.

MRS. WARREN: Oh, God. This is what I think I was afraid of. That if we pushed him, something terrible might happen. Now, we've driven him over the edge into insanity.

THERAPIST: I think you may have sensed his underlying fragility that was covered up by his sleeping during the day, allegedly partying at night, and not putting himself in situations that would be demanding or challenging. On the other hand, I don't think you've driven him insane. I'm not sure about what's going on with him, but I suspect that what's emerged would have come out sooner or later. The real pressing issue now is, what's the next step? I've got some ideas.

MRS. WARREN: Like what? He can't stay in his room talking to himself for much longer.

THERAPIST: I agree. I think the first order of business is to get a good psychiatric evaluation for Jamie. He may have to go into a hospital for a while, particularly if he seems to be a potential danger to himself or others. I'm concerned that he started to get aggressive with customers at the cleaners.

The excerpt reflects a number of important issues. First, the therapist takes some responsibility for the failure of the attempted solution with his "underestimated" statement. His use of the word *we* emphasizes the mutual nature of the problem-solving process and his full "joining" with the key patients to solve the presenting problem. The therapist does not blame and blocks Jean's blaming of herself and Bill.

Additionally, the therapist does not define the failure of the adaptive solution to accomplish its desired end as a waste of time, energy, or goodwill. Rather, its failure reveals some important aspects of the problem-maintenance structure that were not apparent previously. The new information about the problem-maintenance structure can now be used to reformulate another, more informed and potentially successful adaptive solution.

As indicated in Figure 7.1, when the adaptive solution falls into this category, the problem-solving process begins anew. In the figure, the arrow from this outcome returns all the way to the first step of the assessment–intervention procedure: identifying the presenting problem (see Chapter 6). The presenting problem may need to be redefined. For instance, with the Warrens, the problem is no longer that Jamie is not getting on with his life and will not get a job or leave home. Now it is that he may have a mental illness and needs to receive the proper treatment so that he can get on with those aspects of his life that can be realized given his potentially diminished capacities.

In regard to the second step—identifying attempted solutions—the adaptive solution that has just been implemented now becomes an attempted solution whose failure needs to be analyzed to design a more effective and informed adaptive solution. The biological, cognitive, and affective systems also need to be reexamined, because the data revealed by the failure of the adaptive solution in fact change the nature of the problem cycle and the problem-maintenance structure. For instance, Bill and Jean Warren now are beginning to think and feel differently about Jamie than they did prior to their confrontation. Instead of viewing him as essentially malingering, they now begin to see him as mentally ill and potentially disabled. Concomitantly, instead of feeling frustration and anger, their primary feelings are sadness, fear, and emerging grief. This new information may lead to a reformulation of the entire problem cycle, generating a different adaptive solution.

OUTCOME 3: BLOCKED IMPLEMENTATION

The third outcome, the most common one, is that the key patients are not able to implement the adaptive solution competently and effectively. They are blocked. Within problem-centered therapy, *a block represents a functional and adaptive deficit within the patient system such that key patients cannot do what they need to do to effectively implement the adaptive solution.*

If the Warrens were blocked, they would not have been able to confront Jamie effectively. When he said "3 weeks" in response to their 2, they might have given in. However, Bill would resent giving in and might lash out verbally at Jamie, depreciating him the way that Jean feared when they planned their confrontation. At that point, Jean might side with Jamie, and the coparental coalition might fall apart. In frustration Bill might withdraw, claiming that he is "washing his hands" of Jamie, who might exploit this coparental collapse by provoking his potential employers into not hiring him.

With the Schultz family, Larry and Marge might fragment like the Warrens, which might lead to an increase in the provocativeness of Lawrence's behavior toward his mother. The couple in sex therapy would fail to engage in their erotic homework tasks. Ted Tanaka, rather than writing to his father, could decide impulsively to call him and try to "talk things out." This might so enrage Mr. Tanaka (because it defined Mr. Tanaka and Ted as peers) that he would harden his already punitive stance. In response, Ted might become more critical of his father, leading to a more extreme rupture in their relationship.

Decision Making

The block that prevents the system from implementing the adaptive solution to the presenting problem is sustained by a unique web of constraints (Breunlin et al., 1992) that constitute the problem-maintenance structure. How the problem-centered therapist explores and ameliorates this structure so that the key patients can competently implement the adaptive solution is the focus of the next chapter.

THE USE OF TASKS IN PROBLEM-CENTERED THERAPY

This chapter has focused primarily on implementing macro adaptive solutions that more or less directly target the presenting problem. The focus on macro solutions should not obscure the central place of *micro adaptive solutions, or therapeutic tasks*. The problem-centered therapist regularly uses in-session and out-of-session tasks throughout therapy. These tasks seldom target the presenting problems per se but the behavioral, biological, cognitive, and emotional activities that lead to or constitute the adaptive solution.

Micro tasks accomplish at least four purposes. First, they keep continual pressure on the patient system to move toward resolving the presenting problems. Second, they provide a series of proximal guidelines as to what constitutes adaptive behavior for the key patients at any particular time.

Micro tasks respond at least in part to the needs of patient-system members to know "what to do now." Third, if the task is accomplished successfully, it moves the system closer to resolving the presenting problem.

Finally, in the case of blocked systems, micro tasks increase the speed with which the problem-maintenance structure is revealed. They force the resistance to the surface rather than waiting for it to emerge. *By expediting revelation of the blocks and possible constraints, tasks increase the cost-effectiveness of the therapy.* The following interventions illustrate within-session micro tasks: asking a passive–aggressive husband to tell his wife what he is angry about right in the session, rather than withdrawing from her and giving her the silent treatment; encouraging an intrusive and controlling mother to allow her husband and teen-age daughter to interact directly around their conflicts without interrupting their interaction; helping a husband who allegedly has no feelings to express his sadness and pain to his wife about the dawning realization that their son may be schizophrenic; and finally, in regard to the alliance, encouraging a timid single mother who is angry at her therapist for letting her down to look directly at the therapist and tell him what she is angry about.

The following illustrate out-of-session, or "homework," tasks: encouraging a conflictual couple to try an intimacy task like nongenital pleasuring (sensate focus); encouraging the same couple to go out alone for an evening together; directing an anxious husband to struggle with his anxiety when his wife is out with her friends rather than calling her on her portable phone; suggesting that a disengaged father and son spend an afternoon together doing something that would be fun for both of them; and recommending that a nonallied couple come to the following session with a list of rules and consequences on which they can agree for their 8-year-old son's obnoxious and antisocial behavior.

In response to the patient system's failure to perform any task, but particularly out-of-session micro tasks, it is seldom if ever appropriate for the therapist to be punitive or to communicate disappointment. The failure to perform out-of-session tasks is almost as valuable to the progress of therapy as their performance. Their nonperformance reveals the block and points to the relevant constraints. The proper attitude on the part of the therapist is curiosity. Combined with empathy, curiosity facilitates identification of the block and exploration of the problem-maintenance structure, the subjects of the next chapter.

CHAPTER 8

Modifying the Problem Cycle—II: Exploring Constraints and Resolving Blocks

WHEN THE PATIENT SYSTEM cannot implement the adaptive solution, it is blocked. Blocks are sustained by a web of constraints that constitute the problem-maintenance structure. The problem-centered principle of application and the assessment–intervention premises specify that the problem-maintenance structure should be explored in a particular sequence that progresses from the immediate to the remote, from the here and now to the historical, and from the interpersonal to the individual. The purpose of this chapter is to describe how the problem-maintenance structure should be worked on to ameliorate most efficiently and effectively the constraints that prevent block resolution and implementation of the adaptive solution.

MODIFYING THE PROBLEM-MAINTENANCE STRUCTURE

Therapy explores the problem-maintenance structure progressively from the top layer toward the bottom, until the patient system can implement the adaptive solution. Once that occurs, exploration of the problem-maintenance structure stops and the therapy either focuses on a different presenting problem or begins the process of termination.

This section addresses work on each level separately. It describes the therapist's role, useful interventions, and the signs that indicate when it is appropriate to shift to the next level. Issues pertaining to the therapeutic alliance on each level and through the transition to the next one are also addressed. The different therapist roles and activities on each level and in the transitions between them are conceptualized with the three content dimensions of the therapeutic alliance discussed in Chapter 3: tasks, goals, and bonds. Finally, the process of "working down" the problem-maintenance structure is illustrated in this chapter by focusing on the two cases that were emphasized in Chapters 1 and 2: the Christmans and the Butlers.

The progression presented below is far cleaner and simpler than usually occurs in therapy. Therapy resembles a war with a series of messy and unpredictable battles against the constraints that block effective problem solving. As in war, the soldiers are usually doing pretty well if they have a rough idea of where they and their allies are, the general location of the enemy, and their overall plan of attack. The rest is improvisation.

CATASTROPHIC EXPECTATIONS

One of the major tools that problem-centered therapists use in modifying constraints is the *catastrophic expectation query*. Derived from gestalt therapy (Perls, 1973), this question asks key patients what they think would happen if they went through a block. It is predicated on the assumption that behind most blocks are frightening expectations about the catastrophic consequences of going through the block. Sometimes these expectations are accurate reflections of what is in fact likely to happen within the patient or the patient system, and sometimes they represent neurotic distortions of potential reactions of self and others.

In work on each level, the catastrophic expectation query offers a direct and effective intervention to clarify the nature of the constraints that prevent resolution of the block. It reveals the concerns and anxieties that link constraints to their blocks and that ultimately prevent patient systems from solving their problems.

MODIFYING ORGANIZATIONAL CONSTRAINTS

Therapy moves to the level of organizational constraints when the key patients have not been able to implement the adaptive solution. They know what they need to do, but they are unable to do it. On this level, the guiding constraint hypothesis asserts that the primary determinants of the problem-solving block pertain to the way in which the patient system organizes itself. The guiding functional hypothesis is that the problems and the patient system's failure to solve them maintain the system's organizational morphostasis.

Goals

Work on this level implements the adaptive solution or explores the constraints that prevent implementation. The primary goal, therefore, is to modify the organizational constraints that either are part of the adaptive solution or prevent its implementation.

With the Christmans, the goal is rebalancing. Specific objectives include greater, if not equal, participation for Joanne in decision making, financial management, and planning; greater access to resources and influence within the marriage; and greater support for her autonomy and self-development. Corollary objectives for Stewart include helping him to accept, if not facilitate, these changes in his marriage; to learn to relinquish some of the responsibilities that leave him overburdened and exhausted; and to explore what he really wants to be doing regarding work, leisure, friends, and home life.

With the Butlers, the primary goal is helping Loretta become a more effective leader. Specific objectives involve helping her to set limits more firmly and consistently, to learn to use rewards effectively, to establish a leadership system among her daughters that involves delegating authority appropriately, and to take care of herself emotionally and physically. Corollary objectives for the girls include helping them to accept their mother's leadership, to take on more responsibility, to learn to resolve their conflicts without violence and destructive triangulation, and generally to strengthen the sibling system.

Tasks

The general task of the therapist is to facilitate organizational change. The active therapist confronts, challenges, and makes recommendations for change. As the leader of the therapy process, the therapist labels maladaptive interaction sequences as such and teaches key patient-system members to identify and modify them. Subsequently, the therapist teaches the patient system to replace those patterns with more adaptive alternatives, modifying the problem cycle and its attendant support cycles.

Many of the techniques of the behavioral orientations shown in the matrix in Figure 2.1 work well on this level. Particularly, the techniques of structural family therapy, such as blocking, enactments, and intensification, are useful. Most therapists working on this level with families use techniques from behavioral approaches to child management that emphasize reinforcement, time out, and negotiated problem solving. Similarly, the techniques of behavioral marital therapy work well with couples on this level. Strategic therapy techniques, particularly paradoxical interventions, if used judiciously, may get systems to do something different.

Although present throughout therapy on all levels, the health and problem-maintenance premises permeate therapist interventions on this level. Everything the therapist communicates to key patients reflects the working premise, "I know you want to and have the resources to change." In this regard, the techniques of solution-focused therapy that emphasize what the system does right are particularly useful. However, the health premise and solution-focused interventions should not blind the therapist to painful realities, such as abuse and addiction, that need to be acknowledged within the patient system. Failure to see such realities may lead key patient-system members to lose confidence in the therapist, but more important, it may prevent the therapist from addressing factors that jeopardize the physical and mental health of system members.

On this level, the therapist needs to identify the contribution of each key system member to the maladaptive interaction sequences. What does each key member do that actively drives or passively permits the maladaptive sequence to unfold? Additionally, the therapist needs to identify what the key members can do differently. In the following example, the Christmans are in the middle of their third session:

JOANNE: Stewart wants to control everything. He wants to know where I'm going at all times and what I'm doing. I feel like he treats . . .

STEWART: Joanne, you know that's nonsense. I don't want to control you. I just like to know where you're going and when you'll be back so we can coordinate our plans and plans for the family. I can't understand why you make such a big deal over these things. You act like an adolescent. Grow up.

JOANNE [silently glaring at Stewart, she turns to the therapist]: He's impossible. He just doesn't understand what I'm talking about. The other night, I was on the phone with a friend and he came in and . . .

STEWART: Now, wait a minute with that story. I needed to make a business call, and I wanted to know who you were talking to and how long you were planning to be on. Tom [the therapist], she's so sensitive to whatever I do. I feel like giving up on the whole thing.

JOANNE: Why don't you give up, not on the marriage, but on your need to control everything? It's not going to work with me anymore, I just . . .

STEWART: Joanne, I *am* thinking of giving up on this marriage. It's become a constant battle, and I'm truthfully getting sick of it.

THERAPIST: I'd like to stop you before you go farther down the "giving up" road. Stewart, did you see what happened each time Joanne tried to talk in the last couple of minutes?

STEWART: Yeah, she starts attacking me with all of this control nonsense. I just won't have it.

THERAPIST: I understand how you feel that you're at the end of your rope with this conflict, but I want to go back to my question, because I don't think you answered it. Did you see what you did each time Joanne tried to talk?

STEWART: Yes, I defended myself. What am I supposed to do, let her go on and on with her diatribe? I'm not a fool.

THERAPIST: I know you're not a fool, and of course you have a right to defend yourself. However, you're still not answering my question. Let me tell you what I saw. Every time she opened her mouth, you cut her off. You did not give her a chance to finish anything she started to say. Joanne, you also participate by letting Stewart cut you off like that. Stewart, what do you think would have happened if you hadn't cut her off?

STEWART: I cut her off because I know what she's going to say, and I don't have to go through the painful process of listening, once again, to her complaints about me.

THERAPIST: I know that's painful for you, but cutting her off and not letting her talk is one of the major things she's complaining about and that keeps getting you into trouble with her. It's like you're even controlling her right to talk, and she lets you get away with it.

JOANNE: What choice do I have? He already thinks I fight him about everything.

THERAPIST: You have the choice of saying, "Stewart, hold on, I'm not finished." You don't have to let him cut you off. You can use the new strength you've discovered in yourself to hold your ground in the conversation.

JOANNE: Okay, Stewart, I want you to shut up and listen until I finish. I'm not going to let you talk over me.

In this vignette, the therapist identifies the maladaptive micro sequence in which Stewart repeatedly cuts Joanne off. Although he does not label it explicitly as maladaptive, it is clear to both Stewart and Joanne that this is not a constructive process. Additionally, the therapist engages in a number of other tasks. He leads the process of the session by focusing on the maladaptive micro sequence and then maintains that focus by not letting Stewart take it in a different direction. By not allowing Stewart to avoid answering his question, the therapist's behavior states that he is "in control" of the process. The therapist also empathizes with Stewart each time before he asks him to identify the micro sequence.

The therapist's identification of Joanne's passive collusion in her silencing process represents a critical intervention. It establishes the therapist as a fair leader of the therapy. He identifies what Stewart does wrong, but he does not stop there. He is not willing to portray Stewart as the villain and Joanne as the victim. Joanne is viewed as a more subtle architect of their process. Both are defined as players with the capacity to alter these micro maladaptive sequences.

Finally, the therapist facilitates alternative, adaptive behavior. He points out and encourages a different, more confrontive set of behaviors for Joanne to use to deal with the problem of Stewart interrupting and controlling. Joanne picks up on the therapist's modeling and even more forcefully confronts Stewart in the session.

Bonds

To work effectively on this level, the key members of the patient system need to trust the therapist. They need to feel that the therapist will not hurt them or allow them to be needlessly hurt by each other. The therapist needs to make the therapy a safe place, without constraining it to the point that painful issues are not explored. After witnessing destructive maladaptive transactions once or twice so that they can be clearly identified, the therapist should stop them before they get launched. The therapist should not be afraid to use personal power and professional authority to stop gratuitously painful transactions.

Beyond trust and a sense of safety, key members of the patient system need to respect the therapist. They need to feel that the therapist is competent, knowledgeable, and able to use skills and knowledge to help them. Most important, they need to respect the therapist's role as the leader of the therapy, with all that implies in regard to fairness and power. This respect is seldom gained only through being a "nice person" or a "good listener." Sometimes with individuals in therapy, feeling accurately and empathically understood leads to respect, but when the direct patient system involves more than one member, respect must inevitably derive from more than feeling understood. *Patients, particularly in family contexts, must feel that the therapist can help them change, not just understand them.* Early in therapy, therefore, the alliance is built, at least in part, by being effective: making something happen.

Two types of interventions play critical roles in creating a sense of therapist efficacy. As mentioned previously, the therapist must block destructive interaction patterns and create a modicum of safety. Second, the therapist must be able to make key patients interact more constructively, at least in session if not outside. This change can be accomplished through the use of direct interaction tasks in session and through homework assignments between sessions.

Key patients must feel that the therapist cares and is committed to helping them change. In this regard, the therapist is not a "neutral" person. The therapist must communicate, through behavior in addition to words, that he or she cares about the key patients and the pain they experience and wants to help them change. The therapist must be their ally for change, for helping them resolve their problems and end their suffering. As an ally, the therapist is an advocate of what is positive and an enemy of what is negative in the patient system.

As described previously, during organizational work early in therapy, the therapist labels and interrupts maladaptive transactions, directs key patients to act more adaptively, and becomes a passionate ally of the part of the patient system that desires change. The risk in this type of activist role is that the therapist becomes a judgmental and possibly even a critical figure. This must not happen. The therapist needs to be forceful, directive, and a strong ally without attacking key patients or criticizing them for not being able to do what they need to do. Lack of compliance at this point is an opportunity for curious exploration rather than punitive criticism.

Leaving the Organizational Level

When organizationally focused interventions do not modify organizational constraints or when they reveal that the primary constraints are not organizational, the therapist begins shifting to the level of biological constraints. This shift should not be done before the therapist's organizational repertoire is exhausted and every effort has been made to bring about change on this level.

MODIFYING BIOLOGICAL CONSTRAINTS

If biological constraints emerge during organizational work that prevent modification of the organizational constraints, they should be pursued early in treatment. If no obvious or potential biological constraints emerge, the therapy bypasses this level and moves to the exploration of experiential constraints.

Goals

The primary goal of work on this level is the modification of the biological constraints that prevent implementation of the adaptive solution. A specific objective is modifying any constraints that link to the organizational constraints that prevent change. If biological constraints emerge, an additional objective is educating key patients about the nature of these constraints and the interventions used to address them.

With the Christmans, no biological constraints emerged in the analysis of the problem cycle. In contrast, with the Butlers, a number of biological constraints became focal. Biological factors in Loretta's depression need to change. Akisha's learning disability needs to be evaluated and addressed therapeutically. Her obesity is also a critical health problem that needs remediation.

Tasks

The therapist's role in exploring biological constraints is active and facilitative. If the therapist is not a physician or biobehavioral expert, *the primary task of work on this level is referring the key patients for the appropriate evaluation and treatment*. With the Butlers, as Loretta's depression emerges as a constraint on her ability to lead her family, the therapist would refer her for a medication evaluation and treatment. The therapist also would refer Akisha for physical–nutritional and learning disability evaluations and intervention.

The referral process is not casual or incidental. It should be taken very seriously by the therapist and not relegated to support staff or the patient's discretion. The therapist should talk with each of the consultants who are being brought in, telling them the primary questions behind the consultation, specifying the goals of the consultation, and making recommendations about the consultation process. For instance, it is appropriate when referring a patient for a medication consultation to recommend to the psychiatrist that appropriate relevant-others (partners, parents, or older children) be included in the consultation. It can also be useful to have the psychiatric consultant join the direct system for a session to answer questions and provide feedback.

The importance of the presence of other key patients during medication consultations cannot be overestimated. When others participate in the consultation, they provide valuable diagnostic information that might not be accurately reported or reported at all by the biologically constrained member. The consultant also functions as a psychoeducator for both the patient and the key members, making sure they understand the nature of the disorder requiring medication; the dosage level, schedule, and potential side effects of the medication; and the desired goals of the psychopharmacological intervention. Including the key members of the patient system as allies in the psychopharmacological treatment process maximizes their support of the intervention and ultimately increases the compliance of the entire patient system in the treatment process.

If the biobehavioral interventions modify the biological constraints sufficiently to permit the organizational changes linked to the implementation of the adaptive solution, the focus of the work moves back to the organizational level, and the option of termination emerges. However, if the biological interventions are not effective, additional biological evaluation and intervention may be indicated. For instance, if Loretta Butler experiences disruptive side effects with the first antidepressant medication she tries, a different antidepressant should be tried. The particular diet and exercise program worked out by a nutritional consultant for Akisha may need to be altered if it is not effective initially.

Just as it was crucial to include other relevant members of the patient system in the initial consultation, it is even more important to include them in the follow-up evaluations. They may notice side effects or progress that the patient fails to observe or report. Additionally, including in the follow-up any key patients who are troubled by or even hostile to the biological intervention frequently neutralizes negative reactions, provides valuable information to the consultant, and maximizes the likelihood of successful intervention.

Bonds

Ideally, the consultant becomes both a beneficiary and a facilitator of the alliance between the therapist and patient systems. Everyone is enlisted as an ally in the process of biobehavioral intervention. This type of broad partnership is particularly important when a complex trial-and-error process is necessary to find the right medication and dosage. The broader and stronger the collective observing ego, the greater the likelihood that the biobehavioral intervention will eventually succeed.

At this point in therapy, the therapist is experienced primarily as a technical expert. The self-object functions of the therapist usually have not yet emerged. If the biobehavioral intervention has been postponed because of patient resistance, however, a strong self-object bond with the therapist may be necessary to get the patient to reconsider the issue at a later time.

When the therapist is a physician or a biobehaviorist, he or she typically is also the biobehavioral expert. With most patient systems, having both of these functions performed by one person is not problematic. With some very complicated systems, however, a specialized biobehavioral intervention may be required that is beyond the scope of most psychosocially oriented therapists. In other cases, having the same person perform both roles may be contraindicated because of the potential negative impact of these dual functions on the alliance. In these situations, it may be necessary to bring in another physician or expert to oversee the biobehavioral evaluation and intervention.

Leaving the Biological Level

When the biological intervention is not sufficiently effective to permit implementation of the adaptive solution, or the key patients (including the identified patient and other key members) do not comply with biobehavioral evaluation or intervention, the therapy moves to the next level, the modification of meaning constraints. However, it is important to remain alert to the possibility of biological constraints emerging later in therapy when the problem cycle is understood more fully and the alliance has grown sufficiently to permit greater patient self-disclosure.

MODIFYING MEANING CONSTRAINTS

If the system has not been able to implement the adaptive solution after biological or organizational work, or both, the therapist shifts to exploring the meaning of the problem, the block or the constraints that have been identified up to this point. In working on this third level, the therapist does not abandon the interest in organizational or biological change but temporarily places it on the shelf. The therapist now primarily explores meaning and builds empathic bridges between key patients.

Goals

The primary goal of intervention on this level is the modification of meaning constraints sufficiently to permit the organizational or biological changes, or both, that will facilitate implementation of the adaptive solution. This goal usually entails expansion of the therapeutic alliance both between the therapist and patient systems and within the patient system itself. With the Christmans, the goal on this level involves modifying Stewart's constraining beliefs about gender roles and married life. With the Butlers, goals include the modification of Loretta's beliefs about the need to assume selflessly all the burdens of the family. Additionally, if meaning constraints blocked her ability to engage adaptively in psychopharmacological intervention, those constraints would be addressed on this level. Similarly, if meaning constraints blocked Akisha's ability to participate in her obesity and educational therapy programs, those constraints would be targeted.

Tasks

There are two primary and interrelated therapist tasks on this level. The first is the *exploration and modification of meaning*. The second is the construction of an *empathic structure* that links the key members of the therapy system in an expanded community of shared meaning. This structure strengthens and expands the bonds aspect of the alliance sufficiently to permit engagement in the tasks that will solve the presenting problem.

Ideally, rather than focusing on the exploration of meaning between the key patients and the therapist, the therapist first facilitates the exploration of meaning between appropriate key patients. This task places key members alternately in the roles of meaning explorer and clarifier with each other, with the therapist as coach. If the key members cannot accomplish this task with and for each other, the therapist takes on the task of exploring and clarifying meaning directly with key members.

With the Christmans, Stewart's sense of Joanne's betrayal of their cultural tradition—her falling from grace—must be explored. Why is it so important to him that Joanne does not challenge him? Why does she need to remain ignorant about their finances and not participate fully in financial decision making? What does it say about him if he permits, or even facilitates, such changes? Can he be a man in his own world if his wife does not adhere to traditional female behavior? Similarly, it is very important for Stewart to understand what the old arrangement meant to Joanne and what the new changes mean.

THERAPIST: Stewart, do you understand what it was like for Joanne when you would not let her see the tax return or know anything about your finances?

STEWART: She didn't like it. But she wouldn't understand it even if I had shown it to her. What was the point?

THERAPIST: So you know she didn't like it. Beyond that, what do you think it was like for her?

STEWART: I'm not sure what you're getting at. What do you mean when you say "what it was like for her"?

THERAPIST: I mean how it made her feel and think about herself, about you. Why don't you ask her now what it was like for her and maybe we'll both learn something.

STEWART [to Joanne]: What was it like for you?

JOANNE: It made me feel worthless. Like a stupid ninny. It also made me feel like you didn't take me seriously. Like I didn't have anything to contribute. The truth is that I was quite depressed in those days. I didn't know it then, but I do now. It got me down to the point where if we didn't have children, I think I might have killed myself.

STEWART: I had no idea you felt that bad.

JOANNE [starting to weep softly]: I did. It was like I didn't exist. It was a nightmare I don't even like to think about. I'm never going back to that. It was death for me.

STEWART: I didn't know how awful it was for you. I don't blame you for not wanting to go back to that.

In this vignette, with Stewart leading the way and the therapist as coach, Stewart and Joanne begin to understand how each of them experienced critical aspects of their own and each other's behavior in the past and how they experience each other now. The creation of such an empathic bridge diminishes polarization. As Stewart understands what the old arrangement meant for Joanne, he softens and moves closer. He enters her world. The meaning of her behavior changes, as does that of his own. In other interactions, as Joanne understands how humiliated and frightened Stewart feels by the changes she is making in her life and her criticism of him, she feels less angry and more willing to negotiate her speed, if not her ultimate destination.

In the eighth session with the Butlers, the therapist begins to explore Akisha's experience of her sister's teasing, as well as the taunts of other teenagers at school.

THERAPIST: Eileen, what do you think it's like for Akisha when you make fun of her and call her names?

EILEEN: I don't know and I don't care. That's her business.

THERAPIST: I don't believe that you don't care. I think you don't like to admit you care about Akisha, but deep down I know you do. What do you think it's like for her?

EILEEN: What's *what* like for her?

THERAPIST: How she feels when you tease her—call her names?

EILEEN [to Akisha]: What's it like for you?

AKISHA: I don't know. It ain't like nothin'.

LORETTA: Akisha, that's not true. You've told me how bad you feel. Like Eileen doesn't even want you for a sister.

THERAPIST: Akisha, tell Eileen about that.

AKISHA: What's to tell? When she calls me a "fat baby," it makes me feel like I'm an ugly piece of shit. Like I have nothing to offer—just an ugly, help-less baby. And when she says that, it makes me want to kill her.

THERAPIST: Eileen, did you know how that hurt Akisha?

EILEEN: I've never paid much attention. When I hear her say what she's said, I guess I made her feel real bad.

LORETTA: And this kind of stuff happens at school. The kids make fun of her and she attacks them. I'm worried that some day she'll pull a knife or a gun and really hurt somebody.

AKISHA: Yeah, those kids at school always run their mouths about me. They've always got something nasty to say.

THERAPIST: Is it worse when Eileen teases you or the kids at school?

AKISHA: The kids at school. They really make me feel like killing somebody.

THERAPIST: Anybody know why it's worse for Akisha at school?

EILEEN: Because she's alone. There's nobody for her to talk to, like at home. If I get on her, there's Betty and Mom. At school, there's no one to look out for her.

THERAPIST: Akisha, is Eileen right?

AKISHA: Yeah. I'm all alone there. And those kids really don't like me. If I was dying, they'd just walk over me. Even when Eileen gets on me, I know deep down she cares. She's just mad or needs somebody to pick on.

EILEEN: She's right. I don't know why I get on her so.

THERAPIST: Well, maybe we can figure that out.

Beyond continuing to build on the strengths in this family ("I don't believe you don't care"), the therapist in this vignette helps Eileen to understand Akisha's experience of Eileen's teasing as well as Akisha's pain at school. Now that Eileen understands how painful it is for Akisha to be teased, she will be less likely to do it. The empathic bridge makes it harder for Eileen to avoid seeing her sister as a sensitive and hurt young woman. Her empathic understanding of her sister has expanded greatly.

In work on this level, it is critical to appreciate the role of emotion. As can be seen in these vignettes, the exploration of meaning in large part involves emo-tional meaning: how people feel. The revelation of emotional experience in a safe and empathic context usually deepens community and diminishes polar-ization. As people empathically enter each other's world, conflicts diminish and collaboration increases. The construction of an empathic bridge between two or more people is invariably accompanied by a felt shift, a softening. When such a shift does not occur, the bridge is usually not strong enough to diminish the affective polarization that underlies organizational polarization.

In some systems, the key patients cannot explore their meaning con-straints with each other directly because they are so alienated, narcissisti-cally impaired, or experientially incompetent. In such systems, rather than coaching, the therapist directly explores, clarifies, and changes meaning. Empathic reflections that accurately clarify the thoughts and feelings of the key patients constitute the primary tool of the therapist in this regard. The therapist also actively reframes events and behaviors in the problem cycle. For example, if Stewart and Joanne had not been able to expand their empathic framework, the therapist might have more actively redefined Joanne's new behavior as a flight from death as opposed to an attempt to undermine or dethrone Stewart.

Bonds

In working on meaning, the therapist gets closer to the key patients. When the therapist facilitates the creation of an empathic structure, he or she becomes a member of that emerging community of meaning. The therapist is touched and transformed along with the key members of the patient system.

In working on this level, the bond to the therapist takes two forms. In the first, the therapist functions as a facilitator of meaning, coaching the key members to explore and understand each other more deeply. In this role, the therapist is somewhat behind the scenes. Rather than passing the tissues to a weeping wife, the therapist gives the tissue box to the husband.

When the key members cannot function empathically for each other because their anger is too great, they are too limited narcissistically, or they are experientially incompetent, the therapist becomes more central. In this second form, the bond to the therapist is more direct and intense. The key members feel understood and even empathically defended by the therapist, even if they cannot effectively and accurately understand each other.

This second form of the bond heralds the formal launching of the mirror-ing transference aspect of the bond. The therapist functioned to some extent in this regard during the early sessions in defining and understanding the presenting problems. Now, however, the therapist functions explicitly like a mirror, positively and accurately reflecting the meanings the key members attribute to themselves, each other, and the problem cycle. In feeling seen, heard, and understood by the therapist, the key members feel closer to the therapist, who now starts to be perceived more fully as a potentially sooth-ing self object. In mirroring the unique experience of the key patients, the therapist not only strengthens the alliance with them, but also simultane-ously strengthens the self structures of the key patients. This strengthening makes the narcissistically impaired key patients more able to engage in the empathic and organizational tasks they were unable to perform.

In behavioral terms, the empathically reflective therapist also functions as a model for empathically constrained patients. This is particularly important for experientially incompetent patients, who may be able to empathize but do not know how. The therapist shows them how and then challenges and coaches them to do it with each other. In this regard, the therapist also explicitly nurtures the development of an idealizing and twinship transference. Presenting him- or herself as a model, the therapist is saying, "I have the skills; watch me and imitate me." The therapist is the idealized expert communicator. Additionally, the therapist gives away his or her skills as a teacher, and in so doing makes the key patients become like him or her. Both of these components of the emerging bond not only strengthen the alliance, but also strengthen the selves of the key patients.

Leaving the Level of Meaning

When the key patients are not able to permit the construction of an empathic structure that diminishes the powers of their organizational and biological constraints, or when the construction of that structure does not shift meaning sufficiently to permit adaptive problem solving, the therapy needs to shift to the next level and address the transgenerational constraints from the families of origin of the key patients. Of course, therapists should not relinquish the exploration of contemporary meaning before exhausting the empathy building and meaning transforming interventions in their repertoire. Additionally, in shifting to lower levels, the therapist does not abandon meaning but expands it through the exploration of historical constraints. In fact, meaning is the bridge that links the historical metaframeworks to the biological and organizational constraints.

MODIFYING TRANSGENERATIONAL AND FAMILY-OF-ORIGIN CONSTRAINTS

In moving to the transgenerational level, the therapist's focus becomes increasingly historical. The exploration of transgenerational and family-of-origin constraints usually is begun in the prior stage, in that many of the meanings that patients attribute to themselves, each other, and critical components of the problem-solving process derive from their families of origin. However, in contrast to exploring family of origin at the meaning level, the work at this level directly addresses the family of origin.

As mentioned previously, the family of origin does not refer only to blood relations. Fictive kin constitute important and sometimes the only living members of some patients' families of origin. They are members of the patient's family of origin by virtue of their past or present meaning to the patient and their role in his or her life.

Work on this level requires three primary therapist roles. As a *system analyst*, the therapist helps the patients see the constraining patterns linked to the family of origin. As a *coach*, the therapist helps key patients change their interaction patterns with their families of origin outside of therapy. Finally, the therapist is a *direct facilitator* of change between key patients and appropriate members of their families of origin in guest sessions.

Goals

The primary goal of this work is the modification of transgenerational patterns of meaning and behavior that interfere with the patient system's ability to solve the presenting problem. A second, related goal is the direct modification of the interaction patterns between key patients and appropriate members of their families of origin that block adaptive problem solving. These interaction patterns may or may not be part of the larger transgenerational patterns targeted in the first goal.

Tasks

Initially, work on this level involves a thorough analysis of the families of origin of key adult patients. The purpose of this analysis is not just understanding, empathic bridge building, and meaning transformation; it is also appropriate action. This action ranges from helping key patients change their interactions with their families of origin outside of therapy, to inviting key family-of-origin members into the direct system for guest therapy sessions. As the therapy moves along this continuum, the therapist's role shifts increasingly from analyst and coach to facilitator of direct interaction.

The key task in this analytic component *shifts* the therapeutic process *from the here-and-now focus of the preceding levels to the histories of the families of the blocked patients.* The new focus is not on early histories of key patients in their families of origin but on the histories of their families over at least the last three generations. The therapist searches with particular interest for the invisible loyalties and psychosocial debts (Boszormenyi-Nagy & Spark, 1973) that tie key patients to their families of origin in ways that constrain adaptive problem solving.

In making this shift, the therapist must create a *sense of curiosity* with the key patients about their families of origin. This sense of curiosity makes the key patients' experience of their families of origin ego dystonic: something that is at least one step removed from being a "given." A genogram (McGoldrick &

Gerson, 1985, 1988) can be a useful tool to initiate this process by visually identifying family members, key events, the general quality of dyadic and triadic relationships, and broad transgenerational patterns.

Genograms are not the only method for accessing this information. A third and perhaps even more important task identifies *constraining assumptions* and patterns of behavior linked to the family of origin. In the following dialogue, the therapist begins to explore Loretta Butler's family of origin.

THERAPIST: Loretta, how did you come to learn that you've got to be and do everything for everybody?

LORETTA: Ever since I was little, that's the message I got. It was be like Grandma and not like my mother. Mother was not only weak, but bad. Grandma was all good, taking care of everybody and never complaining.

THERAPIST: So you got the message, it's a choice between being Mom or Grandma—those are the alternatives.

LORETTA: Exactly. There's not much middle ground.

THERAPIST: The lack of middle ground is killing you. You've got to find a place and identity for yourself what fits for you, not your grandmother or your mother.

LORETTA: How? I tell myself I can't do everything, but then I naturally slide into taking everything on and then not being able to cope.

THERAPIST: So what if you got better at saying *no* as your first reaction when someone asks you for something?

LORETTA: Everybody would be shocked. My aunt and my sisters wouldn't believe it.

THERAPIST: How do you think they'd react if they knew you were coming here to find help for your family and yourself?

LORETTA: They'd be disappointed. I shouldn't be washing my dirty laundry in public. Family business is private.

THERAPIST: I wonder if that's how they'd react? Maybe they know you're human and need help. Maybe they know Grandma's become a myth no one can live up to. Also, maybe Grandma wasn't so great. Look at all your mother's troubles.

Beyond creating a sense of curiosity about Loretta's family of origin, the therapist in this vignette highlights and begins to challenge some of the constraining assumptions that Loretta experiences as deriving from her family. The therapist also lays the groundwork for the next stage of intervention: action.

A critical methodological component in challenging constraining assumptions and moving toward action is the exploration of the *catastrophic expectations* behind the constraining assumption. The "what if" and "how do you think they'd react if" interventions elicit and provide a framework for testing these expectations. Typically, transgenerational catastrophic expectations constitute some of the most frightening that patients articulate in the course of therapy.

Once the therapist has identified constraining assumptions linked to the family of origin, the therapy moves toward out-of-therapy modification of these assumptions and behavior patterns: homework. With Loretta, this involves encouraging her to talk with her aunt and her siblings about the constraining assumptions. Do they feel disappointed by her getting therapy for herself and her children? Would they be disappointed if they found out she was considering taking an antidepressant medication? Finally, the critical questions become, What if they did disapprove or feel disappointed in Loretta? Is Loretta sufficiently differentiated from her family of origin to tolerate their potential negative reactions?

With the Christmans, the therapist challenges the unholy alliance between Stewart, his mother, and his sister. Why are they involved now that he and Joanne are having trouble? Joanne has never been hostile or inappropriate with them; what has prevented them from forming a better relationship with her? Would they rather have him for themselves than have him create a happy and healthy marriage with Joanne? Has their following of the family values in regard to women helped them have happy and fulfilling lives?

If Stewart can permit himself to explore these questions in therapy with Joanne, he may be able to begin to explore them outside of therapy with his mother and sister. In fact, their therapist recommended that Stewart do some homework talking with his mother and sister separately about their lives and their sense of themselves as women. The purpose of this "assignment" was to help him think through his own thoughts and values in regard to gender roles, his gendered legacy from his family of origin, and ultimately how he now feels and thinks about Joanne and his relationship with her.

Consistent with the work of Murray Bowen (1978), a major objective of this homework phase of transgenerational/family-of-origin work is greater differentiation of the selves of the key patients from their families of origin. Ideally, this differentiation allows them to differ from the central members of their family of origin without cutting off the relationship. Within problem-centered therapy, differentiation is not a goal unto itself but an objective along the path of modifying transgenerational constraints.

Another helpful tool in this homework–action phase is the use of family rituals designed to resolve unfinished family-of-origin issues (Imber-Black &

Roberts, 1992). For instance, Loretta Butler's family of origin never adequately grieved for her mother. There was such a strong sense of shame and failure attached to her mother's death for the family of origin, and in particular for her grandmother, that when Loretta's mother died, it was like hearing news about a distant relative. Loretta did not attend the funeral and was not even sure where her mother was buried.

The therapist recommended that Loretta find out where her mother was buried. Through her youngest aunt, Loretta learned that her mother was buried in a cemetery outside Joliet, Illinois. With the therapist's support, Loretta decided to have a memorial service for her mother at the gravesite with the members of her family of origin who would participate. Two of Loretta's aunts, an uncle, and her siblings joined Loretta and her daughters at the service, which was planned and conducted by Loretta and her siblings.

When out-of-therapy work does not modify the constraints on this level, the therapy shifts to the last and most extreme variant of family-of-origin work: guest sessions with selected members of key patients' families of origin. For instance, if her aunts and uncle and, even more crucially, her siblings had refused to participate in the memorial service, Loretta might have invited all or some of them to participate in guest sessions.

Chapter 5 articulated the theory and process of guest sessions. Building on that presentation, engaging the patient system in an initiative to conduct a set of guest sessions with a key patient's family of origin can have three possible outcomes. First, it can produce constructive change in the interaction between the key patients and the invited members of the family of origin. Second, invited members can come to the sessions but not participate in a constructive manner. Third, invited members may refuse to attend. With a carefully planned and executed initiative, each outcome can be therapeutic for the patient system.

Stewart Christman invited his mother and sister to three guest sessions. Because of the still unresolved relational issues between Stewart and Joanne, with the help of the therapist, Stewart and Joanne agreed that Joanne would not participate in the first guest session. Much to Stewart's surprise, his mother and sister refused to come in to therapy even with Stewart alone. His catastrophic expectation was that the guest sessions might kill his mother, but he never suspected she would refuse to come in the first place.

Their refusal stunned Stewart. He realized that his mother and sister were not sufficiently committed to him to endure the anxiety of guest sessions. Joanne's willingness to engage in therapy and her efforts to change their relationship stood out in contrast to his mother and sister's refusal. His mother and sister were willing to engage so long as he played by their rules.

When he differentiated, they were unwilling to stay involved. In them, he saw his own brittle rigidity and capacity for conditional involvement. As a result of this "failed" initiative, Stewart grew closer to Joanne and more tolerant of her efforts to differentiate within their relationship. The failure to engage his sister and mother was probably more therapeutic for him and his wife than the sessions would have been if they had taken place.

Similarly, the sessions can be therapeutic if key members of the family of origin attend but fail to change. If Stewart's sister and mother had come in, Stewart would have attempted to talk with them about his experience of them in regard to Joanne and himself. He also would have tried to learn more about their experience of him and Joanne. The beginnings of an empathic structure may have emerged that could have facilitated constructive interaction among all four of them.

If Stewart had not been able to get anywhere with his sister and mother, however, he would still have had the opportunity to change his own behavior with them. *Helping patients take a differentiated stand without cutting off from their families of origin is the most important task on this level.* The psychological maturation that derives from that process permits patients to see what is really important to them, who they are, and what they want to do in regard to the constraints that have blocked their behavior in the past.

As a result of the family-of-origin initiative, Joanne became increasingly empathic and sympathetic toward Stewart. When she saw him going forth to do battle with his sister and mother, she felt more allied and proud of his courage. When he failed to engage them, she sympathized with his pain and anger. Stewart's experience of her compassion and empathy made him feel closer to her. If guest sessions had occurred with his mother and sister, her role as a witness probably would have produced similar results in their relationship. Most significantly, the initiative resulted in Stewart reinvesting emotionally in Joanne; getting a sense of his own legacy of rigidity and contingent involvement; and clarifying his own values and thoughts about Joanne's desire for growth and differentiation within the context of their marriage.

Beyond facilitating differentiation in the face of refusal to attend or change, *an additional task of family-of-origin sessions is constructing a transgenerational empathic structure for constructive change.* Of course, this outcome depends on whether the guests come in and constructively engage. If Loretta had invited her siblings into therapy, it would have been ideal if they came to understand Loretta's and their own unresolved grief in relationship to their mother and its impact on Loretta's ability to be the mother and person she would like to and needs to be. This understanding would have provided the empathic structure for a communal grieving process that could free Loretta to take the reins of leadership with her daughters.

Similarly, if Stewart's mother and sister had joined him and Joanne, ideally they would have come to understand Joanne and the meaning of her desire to share power and participate more fully in decision making. This experience would have required Adele and Sally to reflect on their own identities as women and to share with Stewart and Joanne their fears about Joanne's changes and their impact on Stewart. Additionally, they might have shared their concerns about the impact of Joanne's changes on their sense of themselves as women. Ideally, such communication would diminish the polarization between Joanne and her in-laws, making them more real and human to each other. The establishment of genuine fondness and relatedness between Joanne and her in-laws would be the ideal outcome.

This section has emphasized differentiating without cutting off from family of origin as the ideal. Under a relatively rare set of conditions, however, a cutoff may be warranted as a last resort. The first condition that warrants a cutoff occurs when key family-of-origin members act destructively to key patients after repeated in- and out-of-therapy attempts to change their behavior. The second condition occurs when the key patients cannot develop sufficient immunity to the destructive behavior of family-of-origin members. The combination of insufficient immunity and destructive behavior warrants at least reducing the exposure of key patients to, if not cutting off altogether from, destructive family-of-origin members.

Bonds

As the therapist's role progresses from out-of-therapy coaching to direct facilitation in guest sessions, an increasingly strong bond is required. That bond necessitates strong self-object transferences. Key patients need to feel supported and comforted by the mirroring aspects of the transference. Through mirroring they feel linked to the therapist and able to tolerate the anxiety of engaging the family of origin. Through idealizing, the key patients need to feel that the therapist knows how and is able to help them to say and do what they need to with their guests. Finally, through twinning, the patients need to feel that they can do what the therapist, in preparation sessions, has shown them can be done. By copying the therapist, the patients learn the new behaviors to change or differentiate within their family of origin.

During the guest sessions, patients need to feel linked to the therapist, who has helped them prepare for the sessions and is there for them if they falter. The hovering and supportive therapist encourages them to do what they need to do. Similarly, if the family-of-origin members refuse to engage or are destructive in the sessions, the bond with the therapist provides the support and solace to help the patients let go and grieve the loss of hope.

Finally, it is appropriate to consider the bond between the guests and the therapist in family-of-origin sessions. Technically, the members of the family of origin in guest sessions are not patients of the therapist: they have not contracted with the therapist. They are guests of the key patients. Although the therapist must be committed to the welfare and sensitivity of all of the members of the patient system, the therapist's primary commitment has to be to the key patients of the direct system. That is the primary bond.

Nevertheless, the therapist should be as supportive and empathic as possible with the guests without jeopardizing the alliance with the key patients. Some degree of empathic mirroring of the guests is essential. Additionally, the guests may request a session alone with the therapist prior to or during the episode of guest sessions. With the approval of the key patients, such sessions can be helpful in establishing a preliminary alliance with the guests that helps them engage constructively in the guest sessions. Such sessions prior to the guest sessions also let the therapist directly assess the guests and provide an opportunity to clarify and focus the guests' expectations about the sessions.

In concluding, it is appropriate to clarify another variant of family-of-origin work. That variant, also discussed in Chapter 5, involves situations in which patients who are parents invite their adult children and their spouses for guest sessions. A thorough exploration of this variant is beyond the scope of this chapter, but suffice it to say that the concepts, strategies, and tactics for work on this level articulated previously can be applied equally well to guest sessions with adult children.

Leaving the Family-of-Origin Level

When family-of-origin/transgenerational work fails to permit the patient system to implement the adaptive solution to the presenting problem, the therapy begins to shift toward the psychodynamic legacy of the family of origin. Frequently, family-of-origin work reveals that the patients are not struggling so much with the parents and siblings of today as with the internalized parents and siblings that have become part of their inner object world. Unfortunately, it is usually difficult to see the role of the internal objects without first clarifying the role of the external objects (key members of the family of origin).

The second criterion for shifting to the level of object relations is that relatively brief exploration of the family-of-origin/transgenerational level has failed to reveal any obvious or likely constraints. This is typically apparent when the key members of the family of origin actively support implementation of the adaptive solution and have strong positive alliances with the therapy system.

MODIFYING OBJECT RELATIONS

On this level, therapy explicitly addresses the psychological objects that compose the psyche of the key patients and the ways in which their internal operation and interpersonal deployment constrain adaptive problem solving. Typically, the object relations of the key patients have already been addressed in work on prior levels; however, work on this level is more concentrated, sustained, and explicitly focused on object relations. Object relations is a primary rather than a secondary focus. Additionally, the therapist tends to be less directive, emphasizing exploration and interpretation.

Goals

Work on this level changes the object relations of the patients sufficiently to permit them to implement the adaptive solution to the presenting problem. A primary objective of this work is helping patients develop insight into their object relations. This insight develops the collective observing ego and provides a cognitive framework for remanaging and redeploying the object relations. The most critical remanagement objective is the reowning of or taking responsibility for denied and projected parts of the psyche.

Tasks

The first task on this level is to *identify the objects and their operations that block the system* from implementing the adaptive solution. This therapist behavior is typically referred to as interpretation and makes unconscious entities and operations conscious. On a subtask level, the therapist helps the key patients become aware of their inner worlds and the parts of those worlds that block problem solving. As with family-of-origin work, the therapist creates a sense of curiosity within the patient system about key patient's inner worlds.

Despite work on prior levels, Stewart Christman was still unable to accept Joanne's desire for increased participation in their decision making and for greater autonomy within their relationship. He continued to experience her as unrelentingly angry and challenging. He began to get a glimpse of his rigidity and contingent commitment in the confrontation with his sister and mother, but he had yet to face and acknowledge fully the parts of himself that might be stimuli to Joanne's anger and sense of constraint within the marriage.

On this level, the therapist's first task is to help Stewart become aware of the parts of himself that he has repressed, denied, and projected onto others. In particular, Stewart needs to become more aware of his own anger, controlling rigidity, and fears about relinquishing control. Useful techniques in this process are *confrontation, dream interpretation,* and the *interpretation of underlying, unconscious conflicts.*

Clearly, proper timing is essential in the use of all of these techniques. Patients need to be ready to "see" these parts before the therapist confronts the patient with them or interprets their existence. Frequently, the introduction of dream analysis into the therapy prepares patients to face unconscious parts of themselves. As they began work on this level, the therapist asked Stewart and Joanne about dreams. Stewart responded that he seldom if ever dreamed, whereas Joanne reported dreaming frequently. Despite his protestations, three sessions later Stewart reported the following dream:

STEWART: I am about to get into bed with Joanne, when I notice that there is an extra door in the wall of our bedroom. I turn off the light, and as I'm getting into bed, the door begins to open. I get into bed and think of hiding under the covers but feel too frightened to even move. Joanne doesn't seem to notice that an intruder is coming into our room. As the door opens wider, I see a tall man with curly hair. He feels menacing. I finally can move and I jump up, run to the window, open it, and yell for help. The problem is, I can't scream. Nothing comes out. Then I wake up.

THERAPIST: Sounds pretty frightening, a nightmare.

STEWART: Yes, definitely. If this is what dreaming is like, I'd rather skip it.

THERAPIST: Is it okay if we work on this dream a little?

STEWART: Sure, shoot.

THERAPIST: Tell me more about the intruder.

STEWART: He was big and like I said he had curly hair. He was mostly shadow, so I couldn't see him very clearly.

THERAPIST: What race? What hair color? Was he wearing a suit or was he casually dressed?

STEWART: As a matter of fact, he was wearing what looked like a leather jacket, motorcycle gang style. He was white I think, with dark hair.

THERAPIST: About how tall was he and what did he weigh?

STEWART: Maybe around 6 feet, 180 or 190 pounds.

JOANNE [chuckling]: It sounds a lot like you, Tom [the therapist]—hair, height, and weight, although we've never seen your motorcycle jacket.

THERAPIST [jokingly]: I'll bring it in next session. Stewart, tell me about motorcycle gangs. What are those guys like?

STEWART: They're angry, hostile, got chips on their shoulders, and are looking for a fight with anybody who challenges them.

THERAPIST: Could you imagine for a second that you were one of those guys. What would you say? What would you say to Stewart and Joanne, over there in bed?

STEWART: I'd say, "Watch out, I'm gonna rape your wife, take your money, and maybe even kill you. I'm a mean son of a bitch, and you better not fuck with me."

THERAPIST: Well, you got right into the part. I'd be scared of that character myself. I can see why you were scared and calling for help. Is there some part of you that has a chip on his shoulder and is pissed off about something?

STEWART: I don't know that I've really ever felt that way. Sometimes I get irritated, but I don't think I ever get to the point where I could be dangerous.

THERAPIST: You mean like the intruder in the dream?

STEWART: Yeah. He's a destructive person. I've never been and never will be like that.

THERAPIST: I agree with that, but I wonder if there isn't a part of you that you're starting to get more in touch with, particularly as you let yourself get closer to Joanne, that is pretty angry and maybe has a chip on his shoulder. I was struck particularly by your reaction to your mother and sister's refusal to come in for therapy with you and Joanne. You were pissed off.

STEWART: Yeah, I was pretty mad. They never come through when I need them to. My dad never could deal with them either.

THERAPIST: How do you feel about the fact that they've never really come through for you when you wanted something from them that they weren't fully in agreement with?

STEWART: I wouldn't call it a chip on my shoulder, but I resented it in the past and I resent it now.

JOANNE: Stewart, why is it so hard for you to say you're angry? It's okay to be pissed off. You don't always have to be so cool.

THERAPIST: When you got angry as a kid, how did they respond to it?

STEWART: Quickly and harshly. If I swore, they'd wash my mouth out with soap. If I resisted, she'd get the strap and hit me. Arguing was not permitted.

Therapist: How did that make you feel?

Stewart: I dreaded it so much that I hardly ever did it. I learned to go along with the program. But I guess maybe underneath I did resent it.

Therapist: And where did that resentment go?

Stewart: I don't know. I guess I tried to bury it.

Therapist: It's starting to resurrect itself. It's coming out of the closet, and even though it's scary, we've got an opportunity to get to know it, and maybe it won't be so scary.

In this vignette, the therapist accomplishes a number of tasks. He reads the dream as a sign and uses it as an opportunity to increase Stewart's readiness to consider exploring this part of himself. Additionally, he defines the part as angry, resentful, and with a chip on its shoulder. Going further, he even asks Stewart to identify with and talk for the part, a beginning step in ownership. The therapist also links the part to the recent experiences with Stewart's family of origin and then helps Stewart locate its formation in his early experiences in his family. Finally, the therapist communicates to Stewart that he, Joanne, and the therapist are allied (saying "we've got an opportunity . . . ") in the quest to integrate this part and that he is confident it can be done. He inspires hope.

The second major task in working on this level is *changing the way in which the key patients experience and manage their objects* so that they do not interfere with their ability to solve the presenting problem. Clearly, these changes grow out of the identification and understanding tasks mentioned previously. The guiding principle of this work is the concept of *taking responsibility*. Ideally, each key patient takes responsibility for his or her own parts and the thoughts and feelings that compose them.

To help patients take responsibility for their internal processes, the therapist needs two interrelated strategies. The first *blocks the inappropriate interpersonal deployment of internal objects*. The second *helps the patients own their own parts*. On a tactical level, the therapist interrupts maladaptive projective and transference processes and heightens patients' knowledge and experience of their projected objects. With Stewart Christman, the therapist stops Stewart from attributing (projecting) his own angry feelings to Joanne and attempts to heighten his own experience of his anger and resentment.

With overadequate–underadequate dyads, the therapist stops the overadequate member from projecting his or her underadequate part onto the member in the underadequate role and blocks the underadequate member's efforts to project his or her overadequate part onto the member in the overadequate role. This means that the overadequate member faces the prospect of reowning his or her projected experiences of low self-esteem, insecurity, and incompetence, and the underadequate member faces reowning his or her experiences of strength, competence, and adequacy.

With the Butlers, work on this level involves helping Eileen reown her neediness and sense of deprivation, rather than projecting them onto Akisha, and getting her to act them out. Concomitantly, Akisha needs to reown her strength, maturity, and confidence rather than projecting them onto her sisters. This is done by helping patients experience, ideally in the here and now, their disowned parts.

THERAPIST: Eileen, what's it like for you when you see your mom down, dragging in after work and looking beat?

EILEEN: I feel bad. Particularly because she has to deal with that fat baby over there and her whining and crying.

THERAPIST: Eileen, don't attack Akisha, at least for a little while. Akisha, don't defend yourself. Eileen is just trying to pick a fight with you and get you upset. Don't fall for it.

AKISHA: I know she's just trying to make trouble. I'm cool.

THERAPIST: Eileen, back to my question. How do you feel when you see your mom down?

EILEEN: It makes me down too. But not for long. I try to stay up and get Mama up if I can.

THERAPIST: What are some of the things you think about and feel when you let yourself feel down for a little while?

EILEEN: I don't know. Maybe I wonder if it's worth it. If there's any point to it.

THERAPIST: You mean life?

EILEEN: Yeah.

THERAPIST: So you really feel pretty down at those times. Is there anyone that you share those feelings with?

EILEEN: No, I keep them to myself. I don't want to bother anyone with that stuff.

THERAPIST: You keep it all inside. That's a lot to keep to yourself. I bet sometimes that makes you feel kind of lonely. Like there's nobody there for you.

EILEEN: Yeah [starting to cry softly].

THERAPIST: Loretta, what's it like for you to hear and see Eileen feeling like this?

LORETTA: It breaks my heart. Eileen, you can talk to me, Honey. I didn't know you got so down. (She moves her chair closer to Eileen and places her hand on Eileen's arm.)

THERAPIST: Akisha, did you know how lonely and down Eileen feels sometimes?

AKISHA: No, because she's always getting on me.

THERAPIST: How is it for you to see her like this?

AKISHA: It makes me sad too. Eileen, I'm sorry you feel so bad. If you weren't such a bitch to me, maybe you could even talk to me. I'm not so bad to talk to, you know.

In this vignette, the therapist interrupts Eileen's attempt to initiate a problem sequence with Akisha. More specifically, she blocks Eileen's efforts to continue the projective identification process with her little sister. The therapist then focuses on the needy, despairing, and lonely part of Eileen, heightening her experience with reflections of feeling and a communication-sharing query. After Eileen experiences and communicates that part, the therapist helps Loretta comfort Eileen right in the session. Most significantly, in regard to the collective projection process and the overadequate–underadequate dynamic, as Eileen reowns the pained and needy part of herself, Akisha is freed up to act more maturely and competently. She invites Eileen to turn to her for comfort.

Bonds

Work on this level is seldom as easy as portrayed in the vignettes presented above. If the primary constraints derive from this level of the problem-maintenance structure, they are not likely to yield to quick and simple intervention. The crucial variable that facilitates this work is the therapeutic alliance and, in particular, the bonds component. Without a strong bond to the therapist, work on powerful object constraints cannot be effective. In this work, the therapist frequently reflects back to patients aspects of themselves that they would rather not know about. In this sense, the therapist does not always reflect positive aspects of the patients to themselves. Work on this level in particular requires a strong mirroring transference, predicated on the key patient's experience of the *therapist as an accurately empathic self object*. The therapist must not falsely reassure and must see and talk about what exists within the inner worlds of the key patients that interferes with their solving their problems. That requires courage, tenacity, and ingenuity on the part of the therapist. Additionally, the therapist needs to communicate a sense of respect for the emerging object, even while recommending that it be managed differently.

In addition to the accurate empathic function, the therapist on this level either facilitates comfort and soothing, as with Loretta and Eileen, or when the patients cannot perform that function, directly comforts and supports. The therapist's warmth and compassion play critical roles, as does the patient's capacity to absorb them. The work and time spent traversing prior levels create the relational context in which that warmth and compassion can be genuinely expressed and received.

Leaving the Level of Object Relations

Therapy shifts from explicitly focusing on object relations when such work does not lead to sufficient change in the object relations of the key patients. Making this determination is never easy; however, a major clue is unrelenting defensiveness. When no matter what the therapist does, patients continue to act in ways that prevent reorganization of their collective object relations, a shift is appropriate.

MODIFYING SELF CONSTRAINTS

Deficiencies in the self structures of the key patients and in the narcissistic transferences between them constitute the profoundest constraints. The fragility of the self system and its constituent self structures, the key patients' narcissistic vulnerabilities, underlie the psychological defensiveness and rigidity that prevent modification of the object relations.

Goals

There are two primary and interrelated goals on this level. The first is to *strengthen the self system of the key patients* sufficiently to permit them to implement the adaptive solution to the presenting problem. This entails decreasing their narcissistic vulnerability, increasing the cohesiveness and resilience of their selves, and helping them function more adaptively as self objects for each other. This first goal attends to the adaptive quality of the network of narcissistic transferences within the patient system.

The second goal is to *strengthen the individual self structures of key patients*. Although it is related to the first, this goal is primarily concerned with the individual self structures of the key patients, to some extent regardless of the degree to which the patients support each other. The first goal, the strengthening of the network, is the ideal. The second is frequently what must be settled for. The first cannot happen without the second, whereas the second can occur somewhat independently of the network.

For instance, if Stewart Christman cannot take on more appropriate self-object functions for Joanne, at some point she might decide to leave him. This outcome would probably occur if the narcissistic network between them did not get stronger, but Joanne got stronger. In this scenario, it is conceivable that Stewart could also become stronger, without the couple learning to function more adaptively as self objects for each other. This outcome could result in a less wrenching divorce process.

The relationships between the key patients constitute the primary vehicle for strengthening the self system between them. The primary vehicle for strengthening the individual self structures of the patients is the relationship with the therapist; the second is their relationships with each other. These relationships, and particularly the alliance bonds within them, are the principal foci of work on this level.

Tasks

Work on self constraints involves two primary tasks. The first *facilitates the development of healthier narcissistic transferences between the key vulnerable patients*. The second *facilitates the development of the self structures of the key vulnerable patients*. The first task targets the relationships between the key patients, whereas the second targets the relationship between the therapist and the key patients.

Work on this level does not have the same type of explicit focus as work on the other levels. The bonds component of the alliance, the primary focus of this work, at times can become the explicit focus of the therapy, but it usually occurs and develops implicitly, as a by-product of the interaction within and between the patient and therapist systems. The self system and individual self structures of key patients constitute a focus on every level of the problem-maintenance structure throughout therapy.

The self level can be thought of as a tall, pyramidal structure that juts up into the problem-maintenance structure. This means that the self structures of the key patients and the narcissistic transferences between them and the therapist become increasingly focal as therapy progresses down the problem-maintenance structure. It also means that self constraints contribute more to the problem cycle as the problem-maintenance structure gets deeper.

Even at the bottom, the base of the pyramid does not fill all the space. Even when the therapy moves to the lowest, self level, the relationship between the therapist and key patients never becomes as singular a focus of the therapy as the content of the other levels. However, it becomes a primary focus for the therapist, who on this level attends continually, but tacitly, to the bonds aspect of the alliance. This tacit quality derives from the way in which self psychology postulates that the self grows. The three necessary and sufficient mechanisms for the development and strengthening of the self are optimal frustration, empathic responsiveness, and transmuting internalization.

Optimal frustration links to Winnicott's (1965) notion of the good enough mother and the problem-centered concept of the good enough therapist. The frustration component asserts that the therapist naturally and inevitably fails to gratify aspects of the patients' narcissistic transferences. The optimal component means the frustration should not traumatize the patients but should fit their growing capacity for frustration and disappointment.

With optimal frustration, the failure needs to occur in small doses, on a fairly regular basis over the course of therapy. These failures should not be planned; they occur naturally within the course of any therapeutic relationship. In Chapter 3, these failures were discussed as tears in the therapeutic alliance.

In their tenth month of therapy, Stewart and Joanne Christman were beginning to break through their block about joint decision making. Joanne was taking more responsibility for their financial management and planning, and Stewart was supporting her initiative. However, Joanne forgot to pay a bill for some plumbing work on their house, and the plumber called Stewart's office inquiring about the payment. Stewart blew up at Joanne that night and called Tom, their therapist, for a special session the next day.

Over the phone, Tom was reluctant to schedule a special session concerning what he considered to be a relatively trivial incident. Stewart was upset with Tom's casual and unresponsive attitude but did not communicate that at the time to Tom. When he got off the phone, however, he ranted to Joanne saying that not only was she incompetent, but Tom was as well. In the next session, Tom brought up the incident.

THERAPIST: Stewart and Joanne, I'm interested in how each of you felt about the incident that occurred this week and our brief phone conversation.

JOANNE: Stewart was pretty upset with you and me. He felt both of us were telling him, "Hey, what's the big deal? So she forgot to send a check within a couple of weeks of receiving the bill."

THERAPIST: Stewart, is that how you felt, particularly about what I was saying over the phone?

STEWART: Yes. I felt you just didn't get it. We had an agreement; she was supposed to handle this kind of stuff, and she screwed up. She didn't stick to the agreement and then, to add insult to injury, she wouldn't even own up. She acted like I was overreacting.

THERAPIST: And you also felt I thought you were overreacting?

STEWART: Yes. The plumbing bill is not the issue. What you and Joanne both don't seem to get is that she did not stick to her part of the deal. That's what is upsetting me.

THERAPIST: Joanne, what are your thoughts about what Stewart is saying? Can you understand what got him so upset?

JOANNE: Kind of, but it still seems like an overreaction. The plumbing company expects to be paid immediately, whereas most companies expect payment within 30 days. I'm sorry, but I didn't know that. Next time I'll pay them right away or call them if there's going to be any delay.

STEWART: Well, finally she said she's sorry and she didn't know what she should have known. It's right on their bill: "Payment due upon receipt." But I appreciate you saying you know what you did wrong and you won't do it again.

THERAPIST: Good. It feels like the two of you have reached some degree of resolution about this. Are you comfortable with where things stand now, Joanne?

JOANNE: Pretty much. It's hard for me to realize how important this is to Stewart, but I'm getting the picture.

THERAPIST: Stewart, what about you and me? You felt that I was brushing you off and not taking your upset seriously.

STEWART: Yeah. I was calling for help. I didn't want things to get out of hand with us, and I thought you might help.

THERAPIST: And you sure didn't feel that I was helping you.

STEWART: Well, maybe just talking calmed me down a bit. At least getting it off my chest and having you know.

THERAPIST: Even if you felt I didn't really understand?

STEWART: Yes. You listened even if you didn't understand.

THERAPIST: Well, I'm sorry that I wasn't able to understand what was happening for you at that moment. I think I was preoccupied with stuff that was happening at home when you called, and in retrospect, I don't think I was fully there. Maybe I should have said I would call you back when I could have had more time and space to listen.

STEWART: Listen, that's okay. No one's perfect. Not even me.

This vignette illustrates a number of important tasks. As discussed in Chapter 3, the injurious therapist needs to respond to the narcissistically injured patient with *empathic responsiveness*. This involves several steps. The first step is for the therapist to understand how the injured patient felt in response to his or her failure to gratify the patient's transferential needs. In the session, both the therapist and Joanne try to understand Stewart's reaction to their roles in what happened, without evaluating it.

In the second and third steps, the injurious party takes responsibility for his or her action in the injury process and apologizes. In the vignette, Joanne acknowledges her lack of knowledge about the plumbing bill and apologizes for her mistake. In addition to apologizing, Tom says that he was not fully present in the phone conversation and that maybe he should have handled the call differently. Finally, as illustrated, there needs to be some commitment to change—to avoid repeating the same mistake.

Another important process in this vignette is the way in which Tom first addresses the injury process between Stewart and Joanne before moving on to what happened between Stewart and him. Work on this level first attempts to repair and strengthen the self-object functions of the key patients for each other. If necessary and appropriate, it then moves on to the self-object functions of the therapist for the key patients.

The last major task in self work is facilitating *transmuting internalization*. This is the process whereby the self object's function gets internalized, and the self develops a greater capacity to perform that self-object function for itself. Within self psychology, the developmental goal is not the autonomous self, but the cohesive, vigorous, and resilient self that still needs and effectively uses self objects but also has the capacity to function with some degree of independence from the vicissitudes of the self objects. It is as if the healthy self has its own backup generator in case there is a power failure on the main line. The growth of the self structure through transmuting internalization makes the self more resilient and independent.

Stewart's response at the end of the vignette reflects some degree of self growth. He lets go of his sense of injury and is even able to joke at the end about how he is not perfect. Typically, the process of transmuting internalization is not observable. Only its outcome is visible: a more resilient, less easily injured self. The therapist can facilitate this process, however, by not being too quick to come to the aid of an injured patient or to get another patient to do so. It is best to give injured patients some space to work on restoring their own narcissistic equilibrium before rushing in to repair the damage. Second, it is useful to give the system some time to respond before the therapist jumps in. When patients cannot rebalance themselves, and when other key patients cannot rebalance them, only then should the therapist become a direct player.

Silent Self Work: The Therapist as Penelope

Another process illustrated in the vignette is how the content of work on this level usually derives from another, more superficial level. In this case, the content derived primarily from the organizational level: financial management. It could just as easily derive from any other level.

Once the therapist moves to the level of self work, he or she primarily attends to relationships between the key patients and their relationships with the therapist. The content of the interaction is no longer as relevant in its own right. It now becomes a vehicle to work self issues through optimal frustration, empathic responsiveness, and transmuting internalization.

What distinguishes work on this level, therefore, is not the content of the process, but what the therapist primarily attends to: the relationships between and within the therapy system in regard to the growth of the self system and individual self structures. It is as if the therapist has temporarily given up hope of change on the higher levels of the problem-maintenance structure and is working on the self system and self structures of the key patients, waiting for them to get strong enough to permit adaptive problem solving on those higher levels.

This perspective is particularly critical for *borderline patient systems*, which put therapists in a unique sort of double bind. These patient systems desperately need things to change; they are in great distress. Because of the extreme fragility and vulnerability of their self system and self structures, however, they cannot tolerate the changes once they start to occur. Additionally, the more borderline the system, the less the therapist can label the lack of readiness to change without jeopardizing the alliance.

The therapist has to appear to be working on change on higher levels of the problem-maintenance structure, while at the same time actively impeding or slowing down the change process to avoid scaring the patient system away from therapy. And this work must be done silently, without informing the patient system of the basic doing and undoing dynamic. It is like Penelope in the *Odyssey*, covertly undoing at night the weaving she did during the day, never finishing the shroud she is making for Odysseus until he finally comes home. In the clinical situation, the emergence of the strengthened self is the equivalent of Odysseus' return. The therapist, like Penelope, patiently bides time until change is possible. The more disturbed and vulnerable the system, the longer the wait. With certain systems, it may take years before the self system and structures get strong enough to permit change to occur.

Shifting to an Individual Context

The bonds aspect of work on this level has already been addressed. What has not been addressed in this chapter is the issue of when work on self constraints should be done individually, as opposed to conjointly. This subject has been touched on both in Chapter 3 in the discussion of progressive bonding and in Chapter 5 in the context of defining the direct system. The presumption throughout this chapter has been that most if not all of the work is being done conjointly, in the presence of the appropriate key patients.

With some systems, conjoint work does not result in sufficient change to permit adaptive problem solving. With these systems, the work on the self eventually must be done in an individual context. In this context, the primary vehicle for the growth of the self is the relationship between the individual patient and the therapist.

There are two types of systems that require individual work. The first is the conflictual system in which the other key patients cannot contain themselves or be contained by the therapist sufficiently to maintain a minimal degree of safety and trust. With these systems, the individual key members do not and probably should not open themselves up in the presence of destructive key members. To do so would be to expose themselves to an unnecessary and destructive narcissistic retraumatization. Individual work is necessary and appropriate until the key patients become strong enough to tolerate the potential destructiveness of the others, or until the others are no longer so potentially destructive.

The second type of patient system in which individual work is necessary is the system in which key patients cannot open themselves up sufficiently in the presence of the other patients to do the self work they need to do. This second type of system differs from the first in that the other patients are not destructive to the key patient. Typically, the patient in need of individual work in this system has not invested sufficiently in the relationship with the therapist for the therapist to become a powerful enough self object that his or her normal failures optimally frustrate the patient. Seeing such patients individually, usually more than once or twice a week, intensifies the bond sufficiently that they begin to care about the therapist's responsiveness, and the possibility of self growth emerges.

The narcissistic requirements of such patients is such that they cannot do the work they need to do on a self level without an intensive, individual relationship with the therapist. It is close to impossible to identify these patients and patient systems early in therapy. The best diagnostic clue with them, therefore, is their failure to change in conjoint work on more superficial levels of the problem-maintenance structure. This process diagnosis reveals the need for an intensive, individual work context.

The issue of whether or not the therapist who has been doing the conjoint work should become the individual therapist has already been discussed in Chapter 3. Suffice it to say at this point that the primary criterion in that decision is the extent to which the patient system and the other key patients currently need the therapist and are likely to need him or her in the future as a conjoint therapist. If they do or are likely to in the near future, another therapist should be sought for the individual work.

CONCLUSION AND SUMMARY

This presentation of the process of working on the problem-maintenance structure depicts the process as being simpler, more linear, and neater than it is in actual practice. There usually is considerable sliding back and forth and up and down the structure as work progresses. For instance, object relations issues may be addressed early on in therapy with systems in which object constraints are obvious. Even though they are addressed, however, they are not likely to constitute primary foci of change. In other words, the degree and nature of the focus, not the simple fact of focusing, define the primary level on which the therapy system works at any particular time.

Additionally, there invariably are systems for which it becomes clear to the therapist that there are no significant constraints on a particular level. This is perhaps most obvious with systems in which there appear to be no biological constraints that block problem solving. That can also be the case, however, with other levels such as organization, family of origin, and so on. In other words, failure to change on a level is not the only criterion for shifting to the next lower level. Lack of evidence of significant constraints constitutes the second criterion for shifting.

THE PROBLEM-MAINTENANCE STRUCTURE AS A HEURISTIC DEVICE

Going back to the underlying assumption of interactive constructivism, the concept of the problem-maintenance structure presented in this chapter is just a concept. Yes, there is a problem-maintenance structure, or set of factors that prevent the patient system from solving its problems, but what that structure looks like will never be known. This chapter has presented a model of that ultimately unknowable structure that is designed to help therapists and patients work as efficiently, comprehensively, cost-effectively, and honestly as possible.

Epilogue

AUTHENTICITY, RESPONSIBILITY, AND CREATIVITY: TOWARD THE LIFE CYCLE PRACTICE OF PROBLEM-CENTERED THERAPY

THE PROBLEM-CENTERED MODEL represents a framework for the cost-effective integration of the prevailing forms of psychotherapy. The model integrates so many distinct forms of therapy, each with its own complexities and nuances, that it would be unreasonable to expect any therapist to become an expert in all of these approaches, much less integrate them. Problem-centered therapy is not a rigid prescription for the conduct of psychotherapy. Beyond its function as a model, problem-centered therapy also represents a framework for therapist growth, creative innovation, effective collaboration, and life cycle practice.

AUTHENTICITY AND RESPONSIBILITY

The problem-centered model offers a road map of psychotherapy. It delineates the major metaframeworks on the map and identifies the orientations and contexts that constitute the major roads that run through them. Additionally, it suggests preferred routes and guidelines for traveling in the simplest, most direct and cost-effective way. Ultimately, however, each particular psychotherapist or traveler must find his or her own preferred and particular routes and modes of traveling. In a mature practitioner those routes and travel modes will specifically reflect that therapist's unique self. They will be authentic in that they express and bring to bear on the therapeutic process the "true self" of the therapist. That true self imparts a specificity to a therapist's work that is as unique as that therapist's fingerprint.

Each problem-centered therapist must find his or her own way to be a behavioral family therapist, an experiential couple therapist, or an individual psychodynamic therapist. Additionally, each problem-centered therapist must find his or her own way to move from one of these forms of therapy to the others. The problem-centered therapist manifests authenticity in two ways: by finding his or her preferred way of addressing the constraints within the metaframeworks, and by applying this personalized technology to each case in a unique way.

Psychotherapeutic authenticity means practicing psychotherapy in such a way that it is congruent with a therapist's personality, temperament, and personal values. Personal and professional honesty undergird authenticity. Authenticity exists at every level of psychotherapeutic development. It also deepens and becomes more powerful with experience. A beginning therapist must be honest and personally authentic. However, it is unrealistic and inappropriate to expect a beginning or an intermediate-level problem-centered therapist to be comfortable enough with each of the major orientations and contexts that they will be well integrated with and reflective of his or her values, temperament, and personality. Some degree of discomfort and poor fit are expected and appropriate as that therapist learns new theories, techniques, and styles of relating to patient systems. But that therapist's practice can still be authentic if he or she is honest about his or her level of training and expertise, knowledge, and even to some extent his or her degree of discomfort with new techniques and styles.

The authentic practice of a mature and highly experienced problem-centered therapist will have a very different feel. That therapist will have found ways to work within and between the metaframeworks that fit—that are consistent with his or her personality, values, and temperament. For instance, in the behavioral domain, a mature therapist whose inclinations are more quantitative and logical might use more conventional social learning techniques that ask patients to count and/or rate behaviors on standard or idiosyncratic (invented for the particular case) scales. Another mature therapist with more charismatic/intuitive inclinations might use more confrontative and directive interventions. His or her style may be "hotter" and more intense than the "cooler," more reflective quantitative/logical therapist. Addressing meaning, the charismatic/intuitive therapist would be more likely to focus on emotional constraints, whereas the quantitative/logical therapist would probably attend more to cognitive constraints.

Psychotherapeutic authenticity, however, is not sufficient. For responsible practice, therapeutic authenticity must be constrained by the realities of the patient system, the health delivery context, and problem-centered therapy itself. In regard to the patient system, the primary factor that constrains therapeutic authenticity is the problem-maintenance structure. Even though the charismatic/intuitive therapist may prefer to target affective constraints when working experientially, the problem-maintenance structure of a particular patient system may be loaded with cognitive constraints. To be a responsible and authentic problem-centered therapist with that system, the charismatic/intuitive therapist must be able to work with cognitive constraints. That cognitive work may have a more affective flavor, but it will still be cognitive work because that is what the problem-maintenance structure of that system requires.

The primary health care delivery constraint is the extent to which a case must be treated within the context of managed care. A therapist who prefers to work without time limits must constrain that preference when working with a case that can be seen only for a certain number of sessions. That does not mean that the therapist will have to like it or pretend to like it. Authentic practice may mean not hiding this preference. However, it should not be shared in such a way as to undermine a responsible care manager or the realities of the patient system's health care context.

Lastly, the problem-centered model constrains authenticity. A more reflective, introspective, and intellectual therapist might prefer to work primarily psychodynamically on object relations constraints. A more pragmatic and action-oriented therapist might prefer to work behaviorally on here-and-now behavioral and cognitive constraints. What these therapists prefer and want to do is not enough for the responsible practice of psychotherapy. If the primary constraints in a patient system are behavioral, the psychodynamically inclined therapist must address them or he or she is not practicing responsible and responsive psychotherapy. Similarly, if the primary constraints with another system are on the object relations and self levels, the behaviorally inclined therapist must address them or he or she is not practicing responsibly. The responsible problem-centered trainee cannot say, "I don't want to learn that kind of work," and the responsible problem-centered therapist cannot say, "I don't do that kind of work." The authentic and responsible problem-centered trainee and therapist learn to and do "that kind of work"—whatever it is. As authentic therapists, they will do that kind of work in their own way, but they will do it.

Of course, responsible authentic practice has its limits. Within the context of problem-centered therapy, as stated earlier, there is probably no therapist who can or will be expert in every orientation and context and in the transitions between them. When a therapist realizes that he or she does not have the skills to help a particular patient system because of that system's problem-maintenance structure, that therapist enlarges the therapist system by either bringing in additional therapists with the necessary skills to consult or referring the appropriate key patients to those therapists.

Bringing in consultants or referring patients typically reflects and usually heightens psychotherapeutic authenticity. The therapist is being honest with the key patients about his or her limitations as a therapist or possibly even as a person. For instance, a therapist who is going through a divorce might find it too painful and incapacitating to work with a couple going through a similar divorce. A referral to another therapist might be the most appropriate, authentic, and responsible way to proceed. Similarly, a therapist who was severely abused as a child and who is now in intensive individual therapy working on the memories and feelings associated with the abuse may find it impossible to work with a patient system that needs to address early abuse. A carefully conducted referral would be appropriate. The extent to which the therapist would disclose the real reasons for the referral depends on their potential impact on the key patient's ability to engage in therapy now and in the future.

Authenticity lends power, natural authority, and leadership to the practice of psychotherapy. Authenticity undergirds the bond component of the alliance, making therapy a genuine and unique encounter that at its deepest moments touches and strengthens the selves of the therapist and the key patients. Ultimately, what we have to offer clients on the most fundamental level is ourselves. The problem-centered therapist should be a model of what he or she is trying to teach clients, and basically that is a stance toward problems and problem solving. Patients should leave therapy as stronger problem solvers. They should feel empowered in their ability to struggle with and overcome or come to terms with what they could not have handled before. The problem-centered therapist gives them his or her skills, talent, and knowledge.

This is not an argument for gratuitous or promiscuous therapist self-disclosure. Patients look to who we are as much as what we do. They need to see that the therapist does have some answers and does not have others, that the therapist struggles in all of his or her perfection and imperfection to help them learn to solve their problems, that the therapist teaches patients a process of living and problem solving.

Ultimately, there are no answers. Reality can never be known in any definitive sense. Nevertheless, on a provisional and local level, certain types of information that we call answers can lead to very effective courses of action. Fundamentally, though, therapy is not about answers. What we teach is a method—a stance. We give our clients tools for their journey. We empower them as travelers. And whether we chose to or not, we show them ourselves as travelers every step of the way.

THERAPIST GROWTH, CREATIVITY, AND IMPROVISATION

Beyond being a framework for the authentic and responsible conduct of psychotherapy, problem-centered therapy is a framework for therapist growth, therapeutic improvisation, and creativity. In regard to therapist growth, every problem-centered therapist will confront his or her own limitations, particularly lack of knowledge and skills in regard to certain metaframeworks, orientations, and contexts. Regardless of his or her level of development, problem-centered practice will continually challenge a therapist to learn more about the constraints in a particular metaframework and the techniques and orientations for modifying them. In this regard, the problem-centered model helps to identify areas of new learning and provides a framework for integrating that new learning into an existing practice structure.

As a framework for creativity and improvisation, problem-centered therapy lays out broad strategies and clinical options that partially define the context in which therapy occurs. Against that framework, at any particular moment in treatment, the therapist creates a unique integration of theory and practice. The problem-centered model is intended to facilitate that creativity by contextualizing it with a flexible but defined structure.

A LIFE CYCLE THERAPY AND LIFE CYCLE THERAPIST

Not only a model for the creative and disciplined development of the therapist over the professional life cycle, problem-centered therapy is also a model for the conduct of therapy over the life cycle of patient systems. Patients who have had a successful and constructive experience in problem-centered therapy are likely to return to therapy when they find themselves blocked in their efforts to solve critical problems. This return to therapy is natural and appropriate. In this regard, the problem-centered therapist functions like a family doctor, to whom patients return with various problems over the course of their lives.

This vision of problem-centered therapy assumes that most people will have multiple episodes of therapy over the course of their lives. It implies that there is not necessarily going to be one big therapy that solves people's problems and immunizes them forever against problem-solving failures and impasses. Each episode of therapy will be focused around particular problems that people have not been able to solve on their own.

This vision is consistent with many of the cost-controlling and cost-effectiveness concerns of managed care. Problem-centered therapy attempts to make each episode of care as brief, inexpensive, and direct as possible. Each episode is defined by a particular problem, whose resolution will signal the conclusion of that episode. The therapist's familiarity with the key players in the system over their life cycle theoretically maximizes the likelihood that each subsequent encounter will be more informed, knowledgeable, and efficient than the previous one. The efficiency of subsequent encounters with the same therapist is particularly enhanced by the key patients' alliance with the therapist and the therapist system. Deeper constraints within the problem-maintenance structure can be addressed more rapidly by virtue of the preexisting alliance.

CONCLUSION

Problem-centered therapy provides a framework for the authentic and responsible conduct of psychotherapy. It offers therapists a structure for life-long growth and learning, as well as creative innovation. Lastly, it holds out a model for providing patient systems with problem-centered episodes of care over the life cycle.

References

Ahrons, C. R. (1994). *The good divorce: Keeping your family together when your marriage comes apart*. New York: HarperCollins.

Alexander, J., & Parsons, B. V. (1982). *Functional family therapy*. Monterey, CA: Brooks/Cole.

American Psychiatric Association (1994). *Diagnostic and statistical manual of mental disorders* (4th ed.). Washington, DC: American Psychiatric Association.

Anderson, H., & Goolishian, H. A. (1988). Human systems as linguistic systems: Preliminary and evolving ideas about the implications for clinical theory. *Family Process, 27,* 371–391.

Bandura, A. (1977). *Social learning theory*. Englewood Cliffs, NJ: Prentice-Hall.

Barlow, D. H. (1988). *Anxiety and its disorders: The nature and treatment of anxiety and panic*. New York: Guilford Press.

Barton, C., & Alexander, J. F. (1981). Functional family therapy. In A. Gurman & D. Kniskern (Eds.), *Handbook of family therapy* (pp. 403–443). New York: Brunner/Mazel.

Bateson, G. (1972). *Steps to an ecology of mind*. New York: Ballantine Books.

Baucom, D. H., & Epstein, N. (1990). *Cognitive-behavioral marital therapy*. New York: Brunner/Mazel.

Beck, A. T. (1989). *Love is never enough: How couples can overcome misunderstandings, resolve conflicts, and solve relationship problems through cognitive therapy*. New York: HarperCollins.

Beck, A. T., Rush, A. J., Shaw, B. F., & Emery, G. (1979). *Cognitive therapy of depression*. New York: Guilford Press.

Bellack, A. S., & Hersen, M. (1977). *Behavior modification: An introductory textbook*. Baltimore: Williams & Wilkins.

Bergin, A. (1971). The evaluation of therapeutic outcomes. In A. Bergin & S. Garfield (Eds.), *Handbook of psychotherapy and behavior change: An empirical analysis*. New York: Wiley.

Bordin, E. S. (1979). The generalizability of the psychoanalytic concept of the working alliance. *Psychotherapy: Theory, Research, and Practice, 16,* 252–260.

Bordin, E. S. (1980). *New developments in psychotherapy research*. Presidential address presented at the Annual Conference of the Society for Psychotherapy Research, Asilomar, CA.

Boszormenyi-Nagy, I. (1965). Intensive family therapy as process. In I. Boszormenyi-Nagy & J. Framo (Eds.), *Intensive family therapy: Theoretical and practical perspectives*. New York: Harper & Row.

Boszormenyi-Nagy, I., & Spark, G. M. (1973). *Invisible loyalties*. New York: Harper & Row.

Boszormenyi-Nagy, I., & Ulrich, D. N. (1981). Contextual family therapy. In A. Gurman and D. Kniskern (Eds.), *Handbook of family therapy* (pp. 159–186). New York: Brunner/Mazel.

Bowen, M. (1978). *Family therapy in clinical practice*. Northvale, NJ: Jason Aronson.

Breunlin, D., & Schwartz, R. (1986). Sequences: Toward a common denominator of family therapy. *Family Process, 25,* 67–88.

Breunlin, D., Schwartz, R., & B. Mac Kune-Karrer (1992). *Metaframeworks: Transcending the models of family therapy*. San Francisco: Jossey-Bass.

Buber, M. (1958). *I and thou* (2nd ed.). New York: Scribner.

Buckley, W. (1968). *Modern systems research for the behavioral scientist*. Chicago: Aldine.

Catherall, D. R. (1992). Working with projective identification in couples. *Family Process, 31,* 355–368.

Chamberlain, P., & Rosicky, J. G. (in press). The effectiveness of family therapy in the treatment of adolescents with conduct disorders and delinquency. *Journal of Marital and Family Therapy*.

Cleghorn, J. B. (1987). Formulations of self and family systems. *Family Process, 26,* 185–202.

de Shazer, S. (1988). *Clues: Investigating solutions in brief therapy*. New York: Norton.

Dicara, L. V., Barber, T. X., Kamiya, J., Miller, N., Shapiro, D., & Stoyva, J. (Eds.). (1975). *Biofeedback and self control*. Chicago: Aldine.

Dollard, J., & Miller, N. E. (1950). *Personality and psychotherapy*. New York: McGraw-Hill.

Ekman, P., & Friesen, W. V. (1975). *Unmasking the face*. Englewood Cliffs, NJ: Prentice-Hall.

Ellis, A. (1974). *Humanistic psychotherapy: The rational-emotive approach*. New York: McGraw-Hill.

Epstein, N. B., & Bishop, D. S. (1981). Problem-centered systems therapy of the family. In A. Gurman & D. Kniskern (Eds.), *Handbook of family therapy*. New York: Brunner/Mazel.

Fairbairn, W. R. D. (1952). *Psychoanalytic studies of the personality*. London: Tavistock.

Falicov, C. (1988). Learning to think culturally. In H. Liddle, D. Breunlin, & R. Schwartz (Eds.), *Handbook of family therapy training and supervision* (pp. 335–357). New York: Guilford Press.

Falloon, I. R. H., Boyd, J. L., McGill, C. W., Williamson, M., Razani, J., Moss, H. B., Gilderman, A. M., & Simpson, G. M. (1985). Family management in the prevention of morbidity of schizophrenia: Clinical outcome of a two-year longitudinal study. *Archives of General Psychiatry, 42*, 887–986.

Feldman, L. B. (1976). Strategies and techniques of family therapy. *American Journal of Psychotherapy, 30*, 14–28.

Feldman, L. B. (1985). Integrative multi-level therapy: A comprehensive interpersonal and intrapsychic approach. *Journal of Marital and Family Therapy, 11*, 357–372.

Feldman, L. B. (1992). *Integrating individual and family therapy*. New York: Brunner/Mazel.

Feldman, L. B., & Pinsof, W. (1982). Problem maintenance in family systems: An integrative model. *Journal of Marital and Family Therapy, 8*, 295–308.

Fishman, H. C. (1993). *Intensive structural family therapy: Treating families in their social context*. New York: Basic Books.

Framo, J. L. (1992). *Family of origin therapy: An intergenerational approach*. New York: Brunner/Mazel.

Freud, A. (1966). *The ego and the mechanisms of defense* (Rev. ed.). New York: International Universities Press.

Freud, S. (1912). *The dynamics of transference* (Standard Edition, Vol. 12). London: Hogarth Press.

Gill, M. M. (1982). Analysis of transference: Vol. 1. Theory and technique. *Psychological Issues Monograph 53*. New York: International Universities Press.

Gitlin, M. (1990). *The psychotherapist's guide to psychopharmacology*. New York: Free Press.

Goldstein, M. J., & Miklowitz, D. J. (1994). Family intervention for persons with bipolar disorder. In A. B. Hatfield (Ed.), *Family intervention in mental illness* (pp. 23–35). San Francisco: Jossey-Bass.

Goldstein, M. J., & Miklowitz, D. J. (in press). The effectiveness of psychoeducational family therapy in the treatment of schizophrenic disorders. *Journal of Marital and Family Therapy.*

Goodrich, T. J., Rampage, C., Ellman, B., & Halstead, K. (1988). *Feminist family therapy: A casebook.* New York: Norton.

Goolishian, H. A., & Anderson, H. (1987). Language systems and therapy: An evolving idea. *Psychotherapy, 24,* 529–538.

Goolishian, H. A., & Anderson, H. (1992). Strategy and intervention versus nonintervention: A matter of theory? *Journal of Marital and Family Therapy, 18,* 5–15.

Gottman, J. M. (1993). Studying emotion in social interaction. In M. Lewis & J. Haviland (Eds.), *Handbook of emotions.* New York: Guilford Press.

Gottman, J. M., & Krokoff, L. J. (1989). Marital interaction and satisfaction: A longitudinal view. *Journal of Consulting and Clinical Psychology, 57,* 47–52.

Greenberg, J., & Mitchell, S. (1983). *Object relations in psychoanalytic theory.* Cambridge, MA: Harvard University Press.

Greenberg, L. S. (1993). Emotion and change processes in psychotherapy. In M. Lewis & J. Haviland (Eds.), *Handbook of emotions.* New York: Guilford Press.

Greenberg, L. S., & Johnson, S. (1988). *Emotionally focused therapy for couples.* New York: Guilford Press.

Greenberg, L. S., & Pinsof, W. M. (1986). Process research: Current trends and future perspectives. In L. Greenberg & W. Pinsof (Eds.), *The psychotherapeutic process: A research handbook.* New York: Guilford Press.

Greenberg, L. S., & Safran, J. (1987). *Emotion in psychotherapy.* New York: Guilford Press.

Guerney, B. (1977). *Relationship enhancement.* San Francisco: Jossey-Bass.

Guntrip, H. (1969). *Schizoid phenomena, object relations and the self.* New York: International Universities Press.

Gurman, A. (1981). Integrative marital therapy: Toward the development of an interpersonal approach. In S. Budman (Ed.), *Forms of brief therapy.* New York: Guilford Press.

Hahlweg, K., & Jacobson, N. S. (Eds.). (1984). *Marital interaction: Analysis and modification.* New York: Guilford Press.

Hahlweg, K., Revenstorf, D., & Schindler, L. (1984). Effects of behavioral marital therapy on couples' communication and problem solving. *Journal of Consulting and Clinical Psychology, 52,* 553–566.

Haley, J. (1976). *Problem solving therapy*. San Francisco: Jossey-Bass.

Hoffman, L. (1971). Deviation-amplifying processes in natural groups. In J. Haley (Ed.), *Changing families: A family therapy reader*. New York: Grune & Stratton.

Hogarty, G. E., Anderson, C. M., Reiss, D. J., Kornblith, S. J., Greenwald, D. P., Ulrich, R. F., & Carter, M. (1991). Family psychoeducation, social skills training, and maintenance chemotherapy in the aftercare of schizophrenia. *Archives of General Psychiatry, 48,* 340–347.

Hooley, J. M., Orley, J., & Teasdale, J. D. (1986). Levels of expressed emotion and relapse in depressed patients. *British Journal of Psychiatry, 148,* 642–647.

Horvath, A. O., & Greenberg, L. S. (1994). *The working alliance: Theory, research and practice*. New York: Wiley.

Imber-Black, E., & Roberts, J. (1992). *Rituals for our times: Celebrating healing and changing our lives and relationships*. New York: HarperCollins.

Izard, C. E. (1977). *Human emotions*. New York: Plenum Press.

Izard, C. E. (1993). Organizational and motivational functions of discrete emotions. In M. Lewis & J. Haviland (Eds.), *Handbook of emotions*. New York: Guilford Press.

Jacobson, N. S., & Holtzworth-Monroe, A. (1986). Marital therapy: A social-learning cognitive perspective. In N. S. Jacobson & A. S. Gurman (Eds.), *Clinical handbook of marital therapy* (pp. 29–70). New York: Guilford Press.

Jacobson, N. S., & Margolin, G. (1979). *Marital therapy: Strategies based on social learning and behavior exchange principles*. New York: Guilford Press.

Johnson, S., & Greenberg, L. S. (1994). Emotion in intimate relationships: Theory and implications for therapy. In S. Johnson & L. Greenberg (Eds.), *The heart of the matter: Perspectives on emotion in marital therapy* (pp. 3–27). New York: Brunner/Mazel.

Kaplan, H. S. (1974). *The new sex therapy: Active treatment of sexual dysfunctions*. New York: Brunner/Mazel.

Kempler, W. E. (1971). Experiential family therapy. In J. Haley (Ed.), *Changing families: A family therapy reader* (pp. 133–145). New York: Grune & Stratton.

Kerr, M. E. (1981). Family systems theory and therapy. In A. Gurman and D. Kniskern (Eds.), *Handbook of family therapy*. New York: Brunner/Mazel.

Kiser, D. J., Piercy, F. P., & Lipchik, E. (1993). The integration of emotion in solution-focused therapy. *Journal of Marital and Family Therapy, 19,* 233–242.

Kohut, H. (1971). *The analysis of the self*. New York: International Universities Press.

Kohut, H. (1977). *The restoration of the self.* New York: International Universities Press.

Kohut, H. (1984). *How does analysis cure?* Chicago: University of Chicago Press.

Kramer, J. R. (1985). *Family interfaces: Transgenerational patterns.* New York: Brunner/Mazel.

Kramer, P. D. (1993). *Listening to Prozac.* New York: Penguin Books.

Lawson, G. W., & Cooperrider, C. A. (1988). *Clinical psychopharmacology: A practical reference for nonmedical psychotherapists.* Rockville, MD: Aspen.

Lovaas, O. I., Koegel, R. L., Simmons, J. Q., & Long, J. S. (1973). Some generalizations and follow-up measures on autistic children in behavior therapy. *Journal of Applied Behavior Analysis, 6,* 131–166.

Lovaas, O. I., & Simmons, J. Q. (1969). Manipulation of self-destruction in three retarded children. *Journal of Applied Behavior Analysis, 2,* 143–157.

McGoldrick, M., & Gerson, R. (1985). *Genograms in family assessment.* New York: Norton.

McGoldrick, M., & Gerson, R. (1988). Genograms and the family life cycle. In B. Carter & M. McGoldrick (Eds.), *The changing family life cycle: A framework for family therapy* (2nd ed.). New York: Gardner Press.

Masters, W. H., & Johnson, V. E. (1970). *Human sexual inadequacy.* Boston: Little, Brown.

Meichenbaum, D. H. (1977). *Cognitive behavior modification.* New York: Plenum Press.

Minuchin, S. (1974). *Families and family therapy.* Cambridge, MA: Harvard University Press.

O'Hanlon, W. H., & Weiner-Davis, M. (1989). *In search of solutions: A new direction of psychotherapy.* New York: Norton.

Palazzoli, M. S., Boscolo, L., Cecchin, G., & Prata, G. (1978). *Paradox and counterparadox: A new model in the therapy of the family in schizophrenic transaction.* New York: Jason Aronson.

Patterson, G. R. (1976). The aggressive child: Victim and architect of a coercive system. In E. Mash, L. Hamerlynck, & L. Handy (Eds.), *Behavior modification and families* (pp. 267–316). New York: Brunner/Mazel.

Patterson, J. E., & Magulac, M. (1994). The family therapist's guide to psychopharmacology: A graduate level course. *Journal of Marital and Family Therapy, 20,* 151–173.

Perls, F. S. (1973). *The gestalt approach and eye witness to therapy.* Palo Alto: Science & Behavior Books.

Pinsof, W. (1983). Integrative problem centered therapy: Toward the synthesis of family and individual psychotherapies. *Journal of Marital and Family Therapy, 9,* 19–35.

Pinsof, W. (1988). The therapist–client relationship in family and marital therapy: A systems perspective. *Journal of Integrative and Eclectic Psychotherapy, 7,* 303–313.

Pinsof, W. (1989). A conceptual framework and methodological criteria for family therapy process research. *Journal of Consulting and Clinical Psychology, 57,* 53–60.

Pinsof, W. (1992a). Toward a scientific paradigm for family psychology: The integrative process systems perspective. *Journal of Family Psychology, 5,* 432–447.

Pinsof, W. (1992b). Commentary: Culture and psychotherapy integration. *Family Process, 31,* 116–118.

Pinsof, W. (1994a). An overview of integrative problem centered therapy. *Journal of Family Therapy, 16,* 103–120.

Pinsof, W. (1994b). An integrative systems perspective on the therapeutic alliance: Theoretical, clinical and research implications. In A. Horvath & L. Greenberg (Eds.), *The working alliance: Theory, research and practice.* New York: Wiley.

Pinsof, W., & Catherall, D. (1986). The integrative psychotherapy alliance: Family, couple and individual therapy scales. *Journal of Marital and Family Therapy, 12,* 137–153.

Reiss, D. (1971). Varieties of consensual experience: I. A theory for relating family interaction to individual thinking. *Family Process, 10,* 1–27.

Rogers, C. R. (1951). *Client-centered therapy: Its current practice, implications and theory.* Boston: Houghton Mifflin.

Ruesch, J. (1973). *Therapeutic communication.* New York: Norton.

Satir, V. M., & Baldwin, M. E. (1983). *Satir: Step by step.* Palo Alto: Science & Behavior Books.

Scharff, D. E., & Scharff, J. S. (1987). *Object relations family therapy.* Northvale, NJ: Jason Aronson.

Schwartz, R. C. (1995). *Internal family systems therapy.* New York: Guilford Press.

Slipp, S. (1988). *The technique and practice of object relations family therapy.* Northvale, NJ: Aronson.

Sluzki, C. E. (1975). The coalitional process in initiating family therapy. *Family Process, 14,* 67–78.

Smith, M. L., Glass, G. V., & Miller, T. I. (1980). *The benefits of psychotherapy.* Baltimore: Johns Hopkins University Press.

Snyder, D. K., Wills, R. M., & Grady-Fletcher, A. (1991). Long-term effectiveness of behavioral versus insight oriented marital therapy: A 4-year follow-up study. *Journal of Consulting and Clinical Psychology, 59,* 138–141.

Solomon, M. (1992). *Narcissism and intimacy: Love and marriage in an age of confusion.* New York: Norton.

Stanton, M. D. (1981). Strategic approaches to family therapy. In A. Gurman & D. Kniskern (Eds.), *Handbook of family therapy* (pp. 361–402). New York: Brunner/Mazel.

Summers, F. (1994). *Object relations theories and psychopathology: A comprehensive text.* Hillsdale, NJ: Analytic Press.

Tannen, D. (1994). *Gender and discourse.* New York: Oxford University Press.

Tomm, K. (1987). Interventive interviewing: Part 2. Reflexive questioning as a means to enable self-healing. *Family Process, 26,* 167–184.

Tomm, K. (1988). Interventive interviewing: Part 3. Intending to ask circular, strategic or reflexive questions? *Family Process, 27,* 1–18.

von Bertalanffy, L. (1968). *General systems theory: Foundations, development, applications.* New York: Braziller.

von Glasersfeld, E. (1984). An introduction to radical constructivism. In P. Watzlawick (Ed.), *The invented reality: How do we know what we believe we know? Contributions to constructivism.* New York: Norton.

Wachtel, P. L. (1977). *Psychoanalysis and behavior therapy.* New York: Basic Books.

Wachtel, P. L., & Wachtel, E. F. (1986). *Family dynamics in individual psychotherapy: A guide to clinical strategies.* New York: Guilford Press.

Watzlawick, P., Jackson, D., & Beavin, J. (1967). *Pragmatics of human communication.* New York: Norton.

Watzlawick, P., Weakland, J. H., & Fisch, R. (1974). *Change: Principles of problem formation and problem resolution.* New York: Norton.

White, M., & Epston, D. (1990). *Narrative means to therapeutic ends.* New York: Norton.

Winnicott, D. (1965). *The maturational processes and the facilitating environment.* New York: International Universities Press.

Wolf, E. S. (1988). *Treating the self: Elements of clinical self psychology.* New York: Guilford Press.

Wong, B. (1991). *Learning about learning disabilities.* San Diego, CA: Academic Press.

Index